CW00552013

The Day Book, 1840—1869 of The Rev. William Law

CONTENTS

		Page
MAP		iv
PREFACE		v
BIOGRAPHY - Rev.William Law		vii

SECTION 1 - Births or Baptisms

(a) Alphabetical list of entries of births or
     baptisms by child's SURNAME 1

(b) Index of Mothers by maiden name, with
     (SURNAME) of issue for reference to 1(a) ... 57

(c) Index of Fathers of illegitimate issue with
     (SURNAME) of issue for reference to 1(a) ... 64

SECTION 2 - Marriages

(a) Alphabetical list of Marriages by Male
     SURNAME with all given marriage information ... 65

(b) Index of Brides by SURNAME with Husband's
     name for reference to 2(a) ... 76

SECTION 3 - Deaths or Burials

     Alphabetical list of Deaths or Burials by
     deceased's SURNAME. Married females entered
     by both SURNAME and (OTHER NAME) ... 81

SECTION 4 - Miscellany

     Historical Events ... 95

     Boats Lost ... 99

     Poor Money ... 100

     Elders ... 101

THE QUOAD SACRA PARISH

OF

PORTLETHEN

(erected 1856)

WITHIN THE CIVIL PARISH OF

BANCHORY DEVENICK

PREFACE

The records from which this book is compiled are in private
safe-keeping and are not available to be consulted.

The Aberdeen and North East Scotland Family History Society
wish to extend their thanks to the owner for allowing this
valuable piece of history to be made available and produced
in this format.

The records consist of the "Day Book" or diary of the Rev.
William Law, covering the years of his Ministry at Portlethen
from 30th July 1840 to 28th February 1869.
There are also copies of parts of three Registers of Births,
Deaths and Marriages covering the period July 1856 - Dec 1869.

For this publication, all have been combined as one record.

Both the Day Book and the Registers are in correct date order,
but in this transcription, each entry is recorded in full and
listed alphabetically throughout the first three sections.

The fourth section which is mainly events, is in the original
date order.

Abbreviations used in the Record are assumed to be as follows

     w.f. white fisher   f.h. farm hand
     s.f. salmon fisher   lab. labourer
     f.s. farm servant   O.   old (Portlethen)

Abbreviations used by the authors-

     b.   born   d. died
     bap. baptised   bur. buried
     mar. married

PORTLETHEN MAP

The map on the opposite page is reproduced from the O.S. map
No.45 (outline edition) 1 inch = 1 mile scale with additional
information from Robertson 1822 and Roy 1750 maps and various
written sources

Rev. William Law

William Law, born 1797, son of Arthur Law, farmer, Kincardine O'Neil :
educated at Marischal College, Aberdeen, M.A. (1816) and became
Schoolmaster at Maryculter. Appointed Missionary at Portlethen 1827 but
continued his duties at Maryculter, riding over to Portlethen each Sunday
on a pony, which had been presented to him.
Formally ordained Minister of Portlethen 30 July 1840. Demitted office of
Schooolmaster at Maryculter and he and his family removed to the Manse of
Portlethen in September 1840.

Married Isabella Mathewson 17 February 1824.

Issue - Agnes M. Law - b. 21 February 1836 Maryculter
                    m. George Lamb, accountant, Aberdeen
            Sarah Christina Bower Law - b. 19 January 1838 Maryculter
                        m. Jas. Stewart M.A., Banchory Ternan
            William Law - b. 29 March 1840 Maryculter
                    d. 19 July 1864 India

After nearly 30 years of service and on account of his age and failing
health he was obliged to apply for an assistant and successor.
He died suddenly of apoplexy on 11 January 1870 in the 73rd year of his
age.

The Following Entries From Mr. Law's personal Day Book are of events
concerning his own family.

9th September 1840 -   Removed from Maryculter to Manse of Portlethen

5th March 1844 -   At Lairney, at my brother James's marriage

30th September 1851 -   Tuesday, at Mrs. Smith's (aunt) funeral,
                          Wellington Place, Aberdeen

17th February 1855 -   Mrs. Law died here this morning at 5 O'clock
                          having been unable to swallow even a drop of
                          water for the preceding 15 days, and for two -
                          months before only liquids -from disease of
                          throat. 'Her latter end was peace'. Mrs Law was
                          born at Skene Square, Aberdeen, 30 September,
                          1798 (age 57 accordingly). She died on the
                          morning of her Marriage Day (31 years before)
                          She was a kind and affectionate Wife and Mother
                          lived respected and died lamented by her
                          sorrowing husband, son and two daughters as
                          well as others

21st February 1855 -   Buried Mrs. Law in the New Churchyard of
                          Maryculter in the grave of her Mother and five
                          of her family. Deep snow, additional horses being
                          required for the Hearse - many present

5th December 1855 –	My daughter Agnes M. Law, went to Mrs Marshsll in Garliestown, Wigtonshire as a governess – Parish of Sorby
31st October 1858 –	My daughter, Sarah Christina Bower Law, was proclaimed with James Stewart, Banchory Ternan
8th May 1862 –	This day, my son William Law left at 4.15 p.m. per Railway for London, on his way to India as an Overseer to the London Assam Tea Company for four years. (age 22 years)
18th September 1864 –	I have this day received intimation of the death of my son William Law who died of appoplexy at Nazarah, Upper Assam, Calcutta, India on the 19th July last after three hours illness – He lived respected and died regretted by all who knew him in that quarter, during his residence of two years and four months

Headstone in Maryculter Churchyard

Erected by Sarah Stewart in memory of her beloved parents, the Rev. William Law, for 25 years schoolmaster in this parish and for 30 years Minister at Portlethen who died at Manse of Portlethen on 11th January 1870 age 73 yrs. Also Isobella Mathewson or Law who died at Manse of Portlethen on 17th Feb. 1855 aged 57 years. Also her brother William who died in Assam, India on 10th July 1864 aged 24 years.

SECTION 1(a)

Alphabetical list of entries of birth / baptisms by child's SURNAME

ABERCROMBY	Andrew : Andrew Abercromby in E.Cookston and Isobel Baxter a son b.12 Jul. bap.6 Aug. 1843
ADAM	Mary Baird : John Adam in Drumoak and Is.McKenzie in Findon a dau. b.27 Apr. bap.25 Nov. 1848
ADAMS	John : Mary Adams,Hill of Findon an ill. son b.6 Sep. 1866 bap.4 Mar. 1867
AITKEN	Betsey : Andrew Aitken,Nellfield,Aberdeen and wife Ann Nicol,Rumleygowan a dau. b.10 ult.bap.25 Sep.1864
AITKEN	Mary Ann : Andrew Aitken and wife Ann Nicol,Aberdeen a dau. bap. at Rumleygowan,by cert.28 Apr.1866
ALEXANDER	Ann : Jas.Alexander,Midmar and Margt.Low,Hill of Findon an ill.dau. b.Synod's Lands 12 Jul.bap.19 Nov.1855
ALEXANDER	Ann : John Alexander,Mill of Findon and his wife Margt.Hay a dau. b.8 ult. bap.6 Mar.1859
ALEXANDER	Elizabeth : John Alexander,Mill of Findon and his wife Margt.Hay a dau.b.6 Sep.bap.20 Oct.1855
ALEXANDER	George : John Alexander,Mill of Findon and wife Margt.Hay a son b.22 Oct.bap.1 Nov.1853
ALEXANDER	Isabella :John Alexander,Mill of Findon and wife Margt.Hay a dau. b.30 Aug.bap.21 Sep.1851
ALEXANDER	Jane : Jo.Alexander and wife Margt.Hay in Hillside a dau. b.10 Nov.bap.18 Dec.1847
ALEXANDER	Jessie : James Alexander and Jane Hutcheon,Mains of Hillside a dau. b.21 Jun.bap.17 Jul.1842
ALEXANDER	John : John Aexander,Mill of Findon and wife Margt.Hay a son b.9 ult.bap.18 Oct.1849
ALEXANDER	Robert : John Alexander,Mill of Findon and wife Margt.Hay a son b.7 ult.bap.21 Feb.1857
ALLAN	Alexander : Jas.Allan and Margt.Sinclair in E.Cookston a son b.7 ult.bap.23 Nov.1845 (Mother Sponsor)
ALLAN	Alexander : Wm.Allan,Brechin and Eliza.Chalmers,Burnthillock an ill.son b.29 Oct.bap.30 Dec.1855
ALLAN	Andrew : Jo.Allan,labourer,Findon and wife Jane Wood a son b.30 ult.bap.9 Feb.1861
ALLAN	George : John Allan,Findon and wife Jane Wood a son b.28 Sep.bap.30 Oct.1855
ALLAN	James : James Allan and Margt.Smith his wife,E.Cookston a son b.17 Mar.bap.19 Mar.1847
ALLAN	James : Jas.Allan E.Cookston and wife Margt.Smith a son B.30 ult.bap.9 Aug.1848-mother sponsor
ALLAN	Jane : bap.dau.to John Allan and Jane Gordon,Roadside,Cairmrobin b.25 Apr.bap.5 May 1841
ALLAN	Jane : Jo.Allan wife Jane Wood in Findon a dau.b.19 ult.bap.1 Mar.1851
ALLAN	Jessie Smith : James Allan,E.Cookston and wife Margt.Smith a dau.b.14 Mar.bap.30 Apr.1854
ALLAN	John : John Allan and wife Jane Wood,Findon a son b.26 Aug.bap.10 Sep.1853
ALLAN	John Smith : Jas.Allan E.Cookston and wife Margt.Smith a son b.13 ult.bap.28 Apr.1844
ALLAN	Margaret Davidson : bap.a dau.to James Allan and Margaret Smith,E.Cookston 11 Jan.1841,John Smith sponsor
ALLAN	Martha : John Allan s.f.Findon and wife Jane Wood a dau.b.5 ult.bap.17 Jul.1858
ALLAN	William : bap.a son to James Allan,Cookston and Jane Masson,Portlethen (ill.),9 Aug.1840,her father sponsor
ALLAN	William : Jas.Allan and Margt.Smith,E.Cookston a son b.7 ult.bap.23 Jan.1851
ANDERSON	(----) : bap.a dau.to Wm.Anderson 15 Young St.Aberdeen 19 Nov.1859

ANDERSON	Ameliah : Wm.Anderson 170½ Gallowgate and wife Sarah Thomson,Findon a dau.b.24 ult.bap.13 Nov.1857
ANDERSON	Ann : James Anderson and wife Ann Walker a dau.b.15 ult.bap.31 Oct.1848
ANDERSON	Christian : Geo.Anderson,near Cairnrobin and wife Eliz.Hutcheon a dau.b.2 Nov.bap.22 Nov.1842
ANDERSON	David Collard : David Anderson Jr. & Margt.Collard,Findon an ill.son b.22 ult.bap.21 Sep.1856
ANDERSON	Elizabeth : Jas.Anderson and wife Ann Walker a dau.b.14 Oct.at E.Cookston bap.25 Oct.1851
ANDERSON	George Reid : D.Anderson and Jane Anderson in Findon an ill. son b.20 ult.bap.23 Jun.1849
ANDERSON	James : bap.a son to Andrew Anderson and Ann Robb in Cairnrobin b.11 May bap.24 May 1841
ANDERSON	Jane : Geo.Anderson and wife Eliza.Hutcheon,Cairnrobin a dau.b.15 ult.bap.31 Jan.1846
ANDERSON	Jane : Jas.Anderson,Fiddestown and Eliza.Leiper an ill.dau.b.2 Aug.bap.5 Oct.1862
ANDERSON	Rachel Thomson : Wm.Anderson and Sarah Thomson, Findon an ill.dau.b.1 May bap.21 Sep.1856
ANDERSON	William : Wm.Anderson and Ann Milne,Hillside an ill.son b.16 Jan.bap.3 Mar.1853 Wm.Milne sen.sponsor
ANDERSON	William : Wm.Anderson and wife Sarah Thomson,17 Bank St.,Ferryhill,Abdn.son b.22 Feb.bap.23 Jun.1868(Manse)
ANGUS	Andrew : Geo.Angus,Hillhead of Portlethen and wife Margt.Tosh a son b.25 Sep.bap.28 Oct.1849
ANGUS	George : Geo.Angus,Hillside of Portlethen and wife Margt.Tosh a son b.6 ult.bap.30 Mar.1845
ANGUS	Henry : bap.a son to Geo.Angus and Margt.Tosh in Portlethen Nov.1840
ANGUS	Joseph : Geo.Angus,Portlethen and wife Margt.Tosh a son b.30 May bap.18 Jul.1847
ANGUS	William : Geo.Angus,Hillhead of Portlethen and wife Margt.Tosh a son b.29 Nov.bap.11 Dec.1842
ARCHIBALD	Mary Jane : Wm.Archibald,P.O.Hillside and wife Jane Henry a dau.b.19 ult.in Dee Village,bap.22 Nov.1862
ASHER	Alexander : Alexr.Asher,Bothy Bridge and wife Jane Duncan a son b.4 ult.bap.10 May 1857
ASHER	James : Al.Asher and wife Jane Duncan,Bothybridge a son b.27 Nov.bap.9 Dec.1854
ASHER	Jessie : Alex.Asher and wife Jane Duncan a dau.b.11 ult.bap.16 Nov.1859 at Bothy Bridge
ASHER	John : Al.Asher,Bothybridge and wife Jane Duncan a son b.17 ult.bap.7 May 1862
BAIN	Christian Moir : James Bain,lab.Downies,wife Is.Taylor a dau.b.11 ult.bap.20 Oct.1859
BALNEVIS	Ameliah : bap.a dau.to Geo.Balnevis and Isobel Hutcheon in Redmyre 14 Nov.1840
BALNEVIS	David : Geo.Balnevis,Redmyre and Isobel Hutcheon a son b.8 May bap.24 Jun.1843
BANGE	William : Wm.Bange,Foveran and Eliza.McCleran,Hill of Portlethen a son b.9 Sep.1855,bap.28 Jan.1856
BARRON	James Blair : Jas.Barron,Abdn.and Eliza.Blair,Cairnrobin an ill.son b.22 Aug.bap.8 Dec.1862
BAXTER	Isobel : bap.a dau.to Geo.Baxter and Jane Adam in Hill of Findon 23 Aug.1840
BEATON	William Shewan : Peter Beaton,wright,Hillside and Christian Moir,Aberdeen,ill.son,b.26 May bap.16 Jul.1846
BEATTIE	George : Wm.Beattie,Langhillock and wife Jane Petrie a son b.2 Aug.bap.19 Sep.1853
BEATTIE	James : William Beattie(s.f.to Jas.Hutcheon)and wife Jane Petrie a son b.30 Sep.1855 at Revly, Cammochmore bap.at Revly,Fetteresso 6 Dec.1855

BEATTIE	Jessie : Wm.Beattie W.Cookston and wife Jane Petrie a dau.b.2 May ult.bap.3 Aug.1858
BEATTIE	Mary : Wm.Beattie nr.Cassieport and wife Jane Petrie a dau.b.17 Nov.ult.bap.28 Jan.1861
BEGG	Margt.Helen : James Begg,blacksmith and Mary Ann Rust his wife a dau.b.at E.Cookston 12 May bap.23 May 1869
BIRD	Rachel Balneves : Geo.Bird,Logie Buchan and Eliza.Robbie,Redmyre an ill.son b.26 Sep.1853 bap.7 Feb.1854
BLACK	John : Francis Black,Hillside and Isabel McKenzie,Hill of Findon,ill.son b.23 ult.bap.28 Feb.1846 Grandfather being sponsor.
BLACKHALL	Lilly Ann : Wm.Blackhall,Old Machar and wife Lilly Robertson a dau.b.31 ult.bap.at Cairnrobin 24 Feb.1866
BLAIR	Bell : bap.a dau. to James Blair and Elizabeth Reid in Cassieport b.15 Aug.bap.22 Aug.1841
BLAIR	Elspet : Elizabeth Blair,Cairnrobin an ill.dau.b.19 Jul.bap.28 Sep.1859
BLAIR	Elspet Kirton : Jas.Blair,Synod's Lands and wife Eliz.Reid a dau.b.20 Jan.bap.16 Mar.1855
BLAIR	James : Jas.Blair and wife Eliz.Reid,Badentoy a son b.29 Mar.1852 bap.2 Apr.1852
BLAIR	Margaret : James Blair,Cassieport and wife Elizabeth Reid a dau.b.30 ult.bap.15 Oct.1844
BLAIR	Mary : Jas.Blair W,Cookston and wife Eliz.Reid a dau.b.12 ult.bap.20 Mar.1847
BLAIR	Robert Reid : Jas.Blair W.Cookston and wife Eliz.Reid a son b.21 Jan.bap.26 Feb.1850
BOOTH	Child : bap.28 Dec.1867
BOOTH	Agnes : David Booth,Belhelvie and Jane Kane,Hillside an ill.dau.b.31 May ult.bap.14 Aug.1859
BRAND	Child : bap.18 Feb.1843 at Cove Parish of Nigg
BRIDGEFORD	David : Christian Bridgeford,Hill of Portlethen and Geo.Balnevis,Newhills an ill.son, b.7 May 1861 bap.12 May 1862
BRIDGEFORD	Mary : bap.a dau.to Robert Bridgeford and Christian Baird in Hill of Portlethen b.20 Jul.bap.3 Aug.1841
BRIDGEFORD	Williamina : bap.a dau.to Christian dau.of R.Bridgeford,Hill of Portlethen(parties F.Church) 25 Nov.1854 father said to be Andrew Thomson,Fetteresso
BROCKIE	Ann : Wm.Brockie,Muirton of Barras and Margt.Hunter,Hill of Findon an ill.dau.b.30 ult.bap.12 Oct.1861
BROWN	Elizabeth : Robert Brown,Hill of Portlethen and wife Eliz.Leiper a dau.b.30 ult.bap.5 Jul.1845
BROWN	Elspet Massie : ill.dau.of Eliz.Brown,servant b.at 13 Downies on 1 Jul.bap.30 Jul.1869
BROWN	Jane : Robert Brown and wife Elspet Leiper in Moss Side a dau.b.10 ult.bap.20 Nov.1847
BROWN	Margaret : P.Brown,Downies and wife Elspet Leiper a dau.b.26 Sep.bap.3 Nov.1849
BROWN	Mary Ann : dau.of the late John Brown b.at Cairngrassie,Fetteresso 4 Jul.1848 bap.2 Jun.1867 at Manse
BRUCE	Alexander : Jas.Bruce,Hill of Findon and wife Jane Smith a son b.8 Sep.ult.bap.at Manse 22 Nov.1868
BUCHAN	Margt.Eliz. : Jas.Buchan,Newmachar and Mary Coutts,Hill of Portlethen an ill.dau.b.9 Apr.bap.26 May 1866
BURCHELL	John : John Burchell,plate layer,Abdn.Railway,Portlethen and wife Eliza.Hunter a son b.8 Jan.bap.14 May 1851
BURNETT	Alex.Harper : Jo.Burnett and wife Jane Shepherd a son b.15 Nov.bap.at Hillside of Findon 18 Dec.1851
BURNETT	Isobel : John Burnett,Synod's Land and wife Jane Shepherd a dau.b.29 Aug.bap.10 Nov.1843

BURNETT   Jane : John Burnett and wife Jane Shepherd,Hillside a dau.b.28 Dec.1853 bap.13 Jan.1854(died)
BURNETT   Margaret : John Burnett,Hillside and wife Jane Shepherd a dau.b.18 ult.bap.17 Apr.1849

CAIE   Elizabeth : Alex.Caie,Mains of Findon and wife Isobel Davidson a dau.b.6 Oct.bap.15 Oct.1842
CAMERON   Jane : Peter Cameron,tailor,Hillside and wife Jane Littlejohn a dau.b.20 Dec.1855 bap.23 Jan.1856
CAMERON   Jonathan Wright : Richard Cameron and wife Christian Wright a son b.23 Sep.bap.20 Dec.1854
CAMPBELL   Son : Alex.Campbell,servt.Mains of Portlethen,wife Helen Brownie a son b.16 Mar.bap.11 Apr.1869
CAMPBELL   Catherine : Al.Campbell,Barclayhill,wife Eliza.Jamieson a dau.b.12 ult.bap.2 Jul.1863-Manse
CAMPBELL   Elizabeth : Alex.Campbell,cattleman,Mains of Portlethen,wife Helen Brownie a dau.b.8 Dec.1867 bap.4 Jan.1868
CAMPBELL   Isabella Ann : Al.Campbell,Barclayhill and wife Eliz.Jamieson a dau.b.22 ult.bap.20 Apr.1861
CAMPBELL   James : Al.Campbell,Barclayhill and wife Eliza.Jamieson a son b.14 ult.bap.5 Aug.1865
CAMPBELL   James Stewart : Robert Campbell,Newmills and Jane McCrobbie,Hill of Turnemidle an ill.son b.19 Jun.ult.bap.5 Sep.1859
CAMPBELL   Mary Ann : John Campbell,Rail.lab.Inverness and wife Mary Monro a dau.b.11 Jul.bap.20 Oct.1849
CAMPBELL   Rachel : Alex.Campbell and wife Eliz.Jamieson a dau.b.3 Apr.bap.31 May 1857
CAMPBELL   William : Al.Campbell,Hill of Findon and wife ---- Jamieson a son b.30 ult.bap.26 Dec.1858
CARNEGGIE   ---- : William Carneggie,Doghillock and wife Mary Stewart 27.Sep.1857
CARRNEGGIE   Dau. : Bap.a dau.to A.Carrneggie,Sketraw for Mr.Thomson of Fetteresso 12.Feb.1844
CARNEGGIE   Mary : Had a dau.b.24 Jul.bap.29 Sep.1857
CARR   Alexander : Alex.Carr,Mains of Findon and wife Is.Davidson a son b.25 ult.bap.5 Sep.1844
CARR   Ann : John Carr and wife Ann Patterson in E.Cookston a dau.b.31 May bap.14 Jun.1851
CARR   Ann : Al.Carr,Mains of Findon and wife Is.Davidson a dau.b.26 Oct.bap.7 Nov.1853
CARR   George : Al.Carr,Mains of Findon and wife Is.Davidson a son b.28 ult.bap.19 Aug.1858
CARR   Helen : Al.Carr,Mains of Findon and wife Is.Davidson a dau.b.12 ult.bap.23 May 1846
CARR   Isabella : Al.Carr,Mains of Findon,wife Isobel Davidson a dau.b.28 ult.bap.16 Mar.1850
CARR   James : Bap.a son to Alex.Carr and Isobel Davidson in Mains of Findon b.14 Mar.bap.4 Apr.1841
CARR   John : John Carr and wife Ann Patterson,Cookston a son b.23 Sep.bap.16 Oct.1858
CARR   Joseph : Al.Carr,Mains of Findon,wife Is.Davidson a son b.13 May bap.21 Jun.1856
CARR   Mary : Jo.Carr and Ann Patterson,Cookston a dau.b.1 Aug.bap.30 Sep.1854
CARR   Robert : Alex.Carr,Mains of Findon and wife Isobel Davidson a son b.24 Sep.bap.11 Oct.1851
CARR   William : Al.Carr and wife Is.Davidson,Mains of Findon a son b.20 ult.bap.12 Apr.1848
CHALMERS   Agnes : David Chalmers,shoemaker,Hillside and wife Jane Donald a dau.b.5 Jan.bap.24 Feb.1856
CHALMERS   Daniel : D.Chalmers,Hillside and wife Jane Donald a son b.25 Dec.last bap.29 Jan.1860

CHALMERS	David : David Chalmers and wife Jane Donald,Hillside a son b.9 ult.bap.1 Nov.1857
CHALMERS	Elizabeth : John Chalmers and wife Ann Robertson,Bourtreybush a dau.b.1 Dec.1854 bap.4 Jan.1855
CHALMERS	Elspet : John Chalmers and wife Ann Robertson,S.Lodge,Kingcausie a dau.b.5 ult.bap.13 Jun.1858
CHALMERS	George : D.Chalmers,shoemaker,Hillside and wife Jane Donald a son b.13 Sep.bap.30 Oct.1864
CHALMERS	Helen : Jo.Chalmers and Ann Robertson,Bourtreybush a dau.b.30 ult.bap.10 Jan.1851
CHALMERS	Jane : John Chalmers and wife Ann Robertson,Bourtreybush a dau.b.12 Oct.bap.16 Nov.1852
CHALMERS	Jane : David Chalmers and wife Jane Donald,Hillside a dau.b.31 Mar.bap.25 May 1867
CHALMERS	Jessie : D.Chalmers,Hillside and wife Janat Donald a dau.b.26 Apr.ult.bap.17 May 1862
CHALMERS	Jessie : John Chalmers and wife Ann Robertson a dau.b.29 ult.bap.5 Sep.1863 at Bourtreybush
CHALMERS	Mary Ann : John Chalmers,Brunthillock and wife Ann Robertson an ill.dau.b.29 ult.bap.2 Aug.1848
CHALMERS	William : D.Chalmers,Hillside and wife Eliz.Anderson a son b.16 Jun.bap.25 Jul.1868 at Manse
CHISOM	Alexander : Bap.an ill.son to John Chisom and Mary Edward(since dead)in Elsick,Fetteresso 15 Mar.1841
CHISHOLM	William : Wm.Chisholm,lab.,Findon and Isobella Howie,there an ill.son b.21 Jun.bap.2 Sep.1850
CHRISTIE	Andrew : John Christie,boatbuilder,Cannochmore, wife Ann Strachan,a son b.25 Sep.bap.26 Nov.1864,Bourtrybush
CHRISTIE	Ann : Dau.of Andrew Christie,crofter,Hill of Portlethen and Mary Ann Troup his wife,b.8 Jul.bap.10 Aug.1869
CHRISTIE	Christina : Wm.Christie and wife Agnes Beattie a dau.b.20 ult.bap.at Cairngrassie 12 Jun.1864
CHRISTIE	Eliz. : Andrew Christie,Hill of Portlethen and wife Eliz.Troup a dau.b.2 ult.bap.19 Nov.1850
CHRISTIE	James : Andrew Christie,Backhill of Portlethen and wife Mary Ann Troup a son b.24 Oct.last bap.28 Nov.1860
CHRISTIE	Jane : Andw.Christie,Backhill of Portlethen, wife Mary Ann Troup a dau.b.30 ult.bap.16 May 1862
CHRISTIE	Jemmima : Dau.of John Christie,boatbuilder,Cannochmore,Cookney and wife Ann Strachan b.26 May bap.7 Jul.1869
CHRISTIE	Jessie : Wm.Christie,Ag.lab.,wife Agnes Beattie resid.at Cairngrassie a dau.b.17 Sep.bap.24 Nov.1867(Manse)
CHRISTIE	Margaret : Andrew Christie and wife Mary A.Troup,Backhill of Portlethen a dau.b.23 Mar.bap.29 Apr.1853
CHRISTIE	Mary : Andrew Christie and Mary Ann Troup his wife,Hill of Portlethen and wife Mary Ann Troup a dau.b.17 ult.bap.17 Jun.1848
CHRISTIE	Susan : Andrew Christie,Hill of Portlethen and wife Mary Ann Troup a dau.b.9 ult.bap.5 Aug.1865
CLERIHEW	Alexander Charles : son of Rev.Clerihew bap.at Cookney 3 Jan.1852
COCKIE	Rebecca : Al.Cockie,coachman Kingcaussie a dau.bap.12.Mar.1867
COOK	Elizabeth : Wm.Cook,Findon and wife Bratrice Hay a dau.b.5 Jan.bap.3 Feb.1854
COOK	William : Wm.Cook,Rumleygowan and wife Beatrice Hay a son b.19 Oct.bap.30 Nov.1850
COOPER	Jane : Jas.Cooper,E.Cookston and Ann Kan,Hillside of Portlethen an ill.dau.b.13 Dec.bap.19 Jan.1864
COPLAND	Barbara : Geo.Copland and wife C.Smith,Hill of Portlethen a dau.b.12 ult.bap.30 May 1848
COPLAND	Christ. Smith : Margaret Copland,Hill of Portlethen an ill.dau.b.1 Jan.ult.bap.6 May 1866
COPLAND	Margaret : Mary Copland,Moss-side of Portlethen an ill.dau.b.12 Dec.1863 bap.14 Feb.1864
COSSAR	Alexander : Francis Cossar and Ann Fraser,Hill of Portlethen an ill.son b.19 Jul.bap.19 Aug.1865
COSSAR	Isabella : Francis Cossar,Bridge of Dee and wife Jane Ann Fraser a dau.b.25 Apr.bap.22 May 1867

COUTTS	Child : Bap.in Nigg 21 Mar.1843
COUTTS	Charlotte Fiddes : Wm.Coutts,Hillside and wife Elspet Gregory a dau.b.28 ult.bap.8 Feb.1847
COUTTS	David Smith : Jas.Coutts,Hill of Portlethen and wife Eliz.Brown a son b.26 ult.bap.16 Dec.1848
COUTTS	Elizabeth : David Coutts and Ann Gordon,Cairngrassie an ill.dau.b.21 Jan.bap.28 Feb.1862
COUTTS	Geo.Duncan : Wm.Coutts,Hill of Findon,wife Elspet Gregory a son b.15 May bap.10 Jul.1849
COUTTS	Helen : Jas.Coutts and Eliz.Bruce,Hill of Portlethen a dau.b.19 ult.bap.13 Dec.1845
COUTTS	James : James Coutts,Hill of Portlethen,wife Eliz.Bruce a son b.27 ult.bap.1 Oct.1843
COUTTS	James : Thomas Coutts,wife Isabella Christie,Hill of Portlethen a son b.21 ult.bap.12 Jan.1862
COUTTS	James : Mary Coutts,Hill of Portlethen an ill.son b.8 Aug.bap.19 Oct.1862
COUTTS	Margaret : David Coutts and Margaret Yeats,E.Cookston an ill.dau.b.29 ult.bap.25 Nov.1865 mother dead
COUTTS	William : Thos.Coutts and wife Is.Christie,Glashfarquhar a son b.27 Dec.1863 bap.21 Feb.1864
CRABB	David : John Crabb,F.serv. Backhill of Portlethen,wife Ann Burnett a son b. 22 ult.bap.9 Oct.1868 at Manse
CRABB	Margaret : Jo.Crabb,Backhill of Portlethen and wife Ann Burnett a dau.b.11 ult.bap.5 May 1866
CRAGGIE	Ann : Wm.Craggie,Hill of Portlethen and wife Mary Stewart a dau.b.29 ult.bap.24 Sep.1859
CRAGGIE	Lewis : Wm.Craggie and wife Margt.Stewart a son b.30 Mar.bap.at Bourtreybush 9 Apr.1855
CRAIG	Son : Jos.Craig,w.f.Portlethen and wife Christ.Allan a son b.10 Jan.bap.26 Feb.1855
CRAIG	Agnes : Bap.a dau.to Jos.Craig and Martha McDonald,w.f.Burnbanks,Parish of Nigg b.17 Nov.bap.14 Dec.1842
CRAIG	Agnes : Widow John Craig,Portlethen a dau.b.11 ult.bap.19 Jun.1847
CRAIG	Agnes : Dau.of John Craig,w.f.37 Portlethen and wife (----)Wood b.2 Sep.bap.5 Sep.1869
CRAIG	Alexander : Al.Craig,w.f.Portlethen,wife Margaret Wood a son b.2 Nov.bap.7 Nov.1842
CRAIG	Alexander : Jo.Craig,w.f.Portlethen,wife Margt.Forbes a son b.17 ult.bap.5 Jul.1845
CRAIG	Alexander : Al.Craig,w.f.Portlethen and wife Lilly Wood a son b.and bap.15 Jul.1846
CRAIG	Alexander : Jas.Craig and wife Elspet Craig,17 Portlethen a son b.3 Jun.bap.19 Jul.1851
CRAIG	Alexander : Joseph Craig w.f.12 Portlethen and wife Ann Leiper a son b.26 ult.bap.18 Apr.1857
CRAIG	Alexander : Jas.Craig w.f.34 Portlethen and wife Jane Leiper a son b.31 ult.bap.21 Jan.1860
CRAIG	Alexander : Joseph Craig w.f.44 Portlethen and wife Lilly Craig a son b.18 May bap.17 Jun.1868
CRAIG	Alex.Brown : John Craig w.f.and wife Barbara Moir,55 Portlethen a son b.7 Mar.bap.27 Mar.1852
CRAIG	Andrew : Andrew Craig w.f.42 Portlethen and Helen Craig an ill.son b.22 Sep.bap.4 Nov.1853
CRAIG	Andrew : William Craig w.f.10 Portlethen and wife Helen Craig a son b.17 ult.bap.4 Apr.1857
CRAIG	Andrew : Andrew Craig w.f.33 Portlethen and Elspet Craig,38 there,an ill.son b.2 ult.bap.26 Sept.1857
CRAIG	Andrew : James Craig w.f.45 Portlethen and wife Jane Craig a son b.31 Aug.bap.2 Oct.1857
CRAIG	Andrew : James Craig w.f.58 Portlethen and wife Christian Allan a son b.12 ult.bap.25 Oct.1857
CRAIG	Andrew : Jas.Craig w.f.Portlethen and wife Jane Leiper a son b.21 ult.bap.3 Oct.1863
CRAIG	Ann : See Mary and Ann twins

CRAIG	Ann :	John Craig w.f.Portlethen and wife Margt.Flatt a dau.b.28 ult.bap.24 Dec.1846
CRAIG	Ann :	Geo.Craig w.f.Portlethen and wife Eliz.Craig a dau.b.15 ult.bap.19 Feb.1848
CRAIG	Ann :	Jos.Craig w.f.26 Portlethen and Ann Leiper an ill.dau.b.12 Sep.bap.6 Nov.1852
CRAIG	Ann :	Jas.and Elspet Craig w.f.17 Portlethen a dau.b.20 Jan.bap.18 Feb.1854
CRAIG	Ann :	Geo.Craig w.f.6 Portlethen and wife Margt.Allan a dau.b.and bap.23 May 1855
CRAIG	Ann :	John Craig w.f.55 Portlethen and wife Barbara Moir a dau.b.5 Jun.bap.14 Jul.1855
CRAIG	Ann :	John Craig Elder Portlethen and wife Elspet Main a dau.b.29 ult.bap.4 Jul.1857
CRAIG	Ann :	John Craig Elder Portlethen and wife (----)Craig a dau.b.28 ult.bap.9 Apr.1859
CRAIG	Ann :	James Craig w.f.58 Portlethen and wife Christina Allan a dau.b.21 ult.bap.5 Jul.1860
CRAIG	Ann :	Jas.Craig w.f.34 Portlethen and wife Jane Leiper a dau.b.8 ult.bap.22 Apr.1861
CRAIG	Ann :	Joseph Craig w.f.12 Portlethen and wife Ann Leiper a dau.b.20 ult.bap.4 May 1861
CRAIG	Ann :	Joseph Craig w.f.14 Portlethen and wife Ann Leiper a dau.b.18 ult.bap.24 Aug.1861
CRAIG	Ann :	Jas.Craig w.f.8 Portlethen and wife Jessy Craig a dau.b.5 ult.bap.9 Mar.1862
CRAIG	Ann :	Jos.Craig w.f.14 Portlethen and wife Ann Leiper a dau.b.19 ult.bap.25 Aug.1867
CRAIG	Ann :	Ill.dau.of Isabella Leiper and Joseph Craig b.at Village of Findon b.21 Nov.
		bap.12 Dec.1869 - Jas.Leiper 19 Findon sponsor -
CRAIG	Bell :	Jos.Craig w.f.Portlethen and wife Helen Coull a dau.b.8 bap.10 Jul.1843
CRAIG	Betsy :	James Craig w.f.Portlethen and wife Margt.Craig a dau.b.14 ult.bap.29 Jan.1859
CRAIG	Christian :	John Craig w.f.6 Portlethen and wife Margt.Allan a dau.b.4 Oct.bap.6 Nov.1852
CRAIG	Elizabeth :	Geo.Craig w.f.64 Portlethen and wife Eliz.Burnett a dau.b.30 Apr.bap.30 May 1863
CRAIG	Elizabeth :	John Craig 64 Portlethen and wife Eliz.Burnett a dau.b.12 bap.14 Feb.1846
CRAIG	Elspet :	Jas.Craig w.f.8 Portlethen and wife Jessy Craig a dau.b.18 ult.bap.20 Jul.1856
CRAIG	Elspet :	Wm.Craig w.f.and Helen Craig his wife in Portlethen a dau.b.and bap.10 Mar.1856
CRAIG	Elspet :	John Craig,Portlethen and wife Elspet Main a dau.b.19 ult.bap.26 Jan.1847
CRAIG	Elspet :	Geo.Craig w.f.9 Portlethen and wife Margt.Craig a dau.b.30 ult.bap.6 Feb.1847
CRAIG	Elspet :	Geo.Craig w.f.62 Portlethen and wife Ann Allan a dau.b.29 Jul.bap.7 Aug.1852
CRAIG	Elspet :	Geo.Craig w.f.6 Portlethen and wife Margt.Allan a dau.b.24 ult.bap.7 Jul.1859
CRAIG	George :	John Craig w.f.Portlethen and Elspet Craig a son b.12 Jan.bap.14 Jan.1861
CRAIG	George :	Geo.Craig w.f.Portlethen,wife Agnes Wood a son b.3 Oct.bap.8 Oct.1842
CRAIG	George :	Geo.Craig w.f.Portlethen and wife Eliza.Craig a son b.12 Sep.bap.15 Sep.1841(mother dead)
CRAIG	George :	Jas.Craig w.f.and wife Is.Wood in Portlethen a son b.15 inst.bap.19 Aug.1843
CRAIG	George :	Geo.Craig w.f.Portlethen and Ann Wood,Findon an ill.son b.16 Jul.bap.26 Aug.1854
CRAIG	George :	Jas.Craig w.f.34 Portlethen and wife Jane Leiper a son b.31 ult.bap.9 Jan.1847

CRAIG	George	: Geo.Craig w.f.9 Portlethen and wife Margt.Craig a son b.4 Feb.bap.10 Feb.1855
CRAIG	George	: Geo.Craig w.f.55 Portlethen and Margt.Craig 3 there an ill.son b.30 Mar.bap.1 May 1858
CRAIG	George	: James Craig w.f.Portlethen and wife Jessie Craig a son b.22 ult.bap.27 Mar.1859
CRAIG	George	: Wm.Craig w.f.and wife Eliza.Craig 4 Portlethen a son b.21 ult.bap.24 Mar.1862
CRAIG	George	: Joseph Craig w.f.14 Portlethen and wife Ann Leiper a son b.14 ult.bap.21 Mar.1863
CRAIG	George	: John Craig,elder Portlethen and wife Elspet Main a son b.14 ult.bap.17 Nov.1864
CRAIG	George	: Wm.Craig w.f.8 Portlethen and wife Eliz.Craig a son b.12 ult.bap.17 Nov.1867
CRAIG	George	: Andrew Craig w.f.Portlethen and wife Elspet Craig a son b.28 ult.bap.9 Oct.1868(Manse)
CRAIG	Georgina	: Geo.Craig w.f.6 Portlethen and wife Margt.Allan a dau.b.18 ult.bap.4 Jun.1858
CRAIG	Helen	: Geo.Craig w.f.5 Portlethen and wife Eliza.Craig a dau.b.6 ult.bap.16.Nov.1850
CRAIG	Helen	: Geo.Craig w.f.62 Portlethen and wife Ann Allan a dau.b.4 Oct.bap.27 Dec.1851
CRAIG	Helen	: Jo.Craig w.f.43 Portlethen and wife Margt.Flatt a dau.b.4 Aug.bap.30 Sep.1853
CRAIG	Helen	: James Craig w.f.54 Portlethen and wife Jane Craig a dau.b.24 ult.bap.29 Jun.1861
CRAIG	Helen	: Andrew Craig w.f.16 Portlethen and wife Helen Craig a dau.b.22 ult.bap.27 May 1862
CRAIG	Helen	: Alex.Craig w.f.3 Portlethen,Christina Masson an ill.dau.b.15 ult.bap.8 Nov.1868(Manse)
CRAIG	Isabella	: Alex.Craig w.f.3 Portlethen and wife Margt.Craig a dau.b.14 ult.bap.24 Oct.1857
CRAIG	Isabella	: Joseph Craig 14 Portlethen and wife Ann Leiper a dau.b.3 ult.bap.14 Jan.1860
CRAIG	Isabella	and Jane : Geo.Craig w.f.9 Portlethen and wife Margaret Craig twin daus.b.21 ult.bap.23 Mar.1860
CRAIG	Isobel	: Bap.a dau.to Joseph Craig w.f.Portlethen and Isobel Wood b.13 bap.20 Dec.1841
CRAIG	Isobel	: James Craig w.f.Portlethen and Lilly Craig a dau.b.1 Sep.bap.7 Sep.1841
CRAIG	Isobel	: Jas.Craig w.f.Portlethen and wife Lilly Craig a dau.b.10 Mar.bap.15 Apr.1843
CRAIG	Isobel	: Wm.Craig w.f.Portlethen and Isobel Wood an ill.dau.b.4 Mar.bap.15 Apr.1843
CRAIG	Isobel	: John Craig w.f.Portlethen and wife Elspet Main a dau.b.16 bap.21 Sep.1844
CRAIG	Isobel	: Jas.Craig w.f.Portlethen and wife Elspet Main a dau.b.31 ult.bap.29 Jan.1848
CRAIG	Isobel	: John Craig w.f.Portlethen and wife Margt.Flatt a dau.b.5 ult.bap.26 Feb.1849
CRAIG	James	: Bap.a son to James Craig w.f.and Elspet Craig in Portlethen b.11 Jun.bap.19 Jun.1841
CRAIG	James	: Bap.a son to John Craig w.f.Portlethen and Barbara Moir b.17 bap.22 Dec.1841
CRAIG	James	: Bap.a son to Widow Craig,Cove Parish of Nigg b.2 Dec.bap.14 Dec.1842
CRAIG	James	: Jas.Craig w.f.Portlethen and wife Helen Coull a son b.18 ult.bap.16 Aug.1845
CRAIG	James	: Jas.Craig w.f.34 Portlethen and wife Jane Leiper a son b.9 Nov.bap.25 Dec.1852
CRAIG	James	: Jas.Craig w.f.Portlethen and wife Margt.Craig a son b.15 Jan.bap.24 Feb.1855
CRAIG	James	: John Craig w.f.43 Portlethen and wife Margt.Flatt(twins 1 dead)b.18 Mar.bap.26 Apr.1856
CRAIG	James	: Andrew Craig w.f.42 Portlethen and wife Helen Craig a son b.13 Apr.bap.24 May 1856
CRAIG	James	: James Craig w.f.8 Portlethen and wife Jessie Craig a son b.11 May bap.14 Jun.1856

CRAIG	James :	Jas.Craig w.f.45 Portlethen and wife Margt.Craig a son b.24 ult.bap.28 Mar.1861
CRAIG	James :	John Craig w.f.64 Portlethen and wife Eliza.Burnett a son b.1 ult.bap.31 Mar.1861
CRAIG	James :	Wm.Craig 4 Portlethen and wife Eliz.Craig a son b.22 inst.bap.29 Jul.1863 at 4 there
CRAIG	James :	Geo.Craig w.f.15 Findon and Margt.Leiper there an ill.son b.17 ult.bap.29 Aug.1867
CRAIG	Jane :	see Isabella and Jane, twins
CRAIG	Jane :	Bap.a dau.to Geo.Craig w.f.and Elspet Craig in Portlethen 23 Jan.1841
CRAIG	Jane :	James Craig w.f.Portlethen and wife Lilly Craig a dau.b.2 ult.bap.20 Sep.1845
CRAIG	Jane :	Jas.Craig w.f.8 Portlethen and wife Jessie Craig a dau.b.7 Oct.bap.10 Nov.1853
CRAIG	Jane :	James Craig w.f.Portlethen and Margt.Craig a dau.b.25 ult.bap.3 Jan.1857
CRAIG	Jane :	Joseph Craig w.f.47 Portlethen and wife Jane Christie a dau.b.18 ult.bap.27 Nov.1858
CRAIG	Jane :	Jo.Craig w.f.64 Portlethen and wife Eliza Burnett a dau.b.26 ult.bap.19 Apr.1859
CRAIG	Jane :	Joseph Craig w.f.Portlethen and wife Ann Leiper a dau.b.22 ult.bap.23 Jul.1865
CRAIG	Jane Gordon :	Jas.Craig w.f.35 Portlethen and wife Jane Leiper a dau.b.22 Oct.bap.21 Nov.1857
CRAIG	Jemima :	Jas.Craig w.f.54 Portlethen and wife Jane Craig a dau.b.15 Aug.bap.30 Sep.1853
CRAIG	Jessie :	Jo.Craig w.f.Portlethen and wife Elspet Main a dau.b.16 ult.bap.29 Sep.1849
CRAIG	Jessie :	James Craig w.f.8 Portlethen and wife Jessie Craig a dau.b.5 Sep.bap.9 Oct.1852
CRAIG	Jessie :	Geo.and Eliza.Craig w.f.5 Portlethen a dau.b.10 Apr.bap.17 May 1856
CRAIG	Jessie :	Jas.Craig w.f.8 Portlethen and wife Jessie Craig a dau.b.1 ult.bap.17 Nov.1867(Manse)
CRAIG	John :	John Craig w.f.Portlethen and wife Margt.Flatt a son b.and bap.16 Jun.1844
CRAIG	John :	Jo.Craig w.f.Portlethen and wife Barbara Moir a son b.9 bap.15 Mar.1845
CRAIG	John :	Jas.Craig w.f.Portlethen,wife Elspet Craig,son b.,Stonehaven 3 bap.10 May 1845 by Rev.Silver Dunottar
CRAIG	John :	Wm.Craig w.f.Portlethen and wife Helen Craig a son b.2 ult.bap.13 Jan.1849
CRAIG	John :	Jo.Craig w.f.Portlethen and wife Barbara Moir a son b.23 ult.bap.8 Sep.1849
CRAIG	John :	Jas.Craig w.f.Portlethen and wife Jane Leiper a son b.20 ult.bap.5 Oct.1850
CRAIG	John :	Jo.Craig w.f.7,Portlethen and wife Elspet Main a son b.10 Apr.bap.22 May 1852
CRAIG	John :	John Craig w.f.64 Portlethen and wife Eliza.Burnett a son b.16 Nov.bap.28 Dec.1852
CRAIG	John :	Geo. Craig w.f.9 Portlethen and wife Margaret Craig a son b.13 ult.bap.19 Sep.1857
CRAIG	John :	Andrew Craig w.f.Portlethen and wife Helen Craig a son b.30 ult.bap.27 Nov.1858
CRAIG	John :	Jo.Craig w.f.Portlethen and wife Margaret Craig a son b.9 ult.bap.17 Mar.1860
CRAIG	John :	Geo.Craig w.f.5 Portlethen and wife Eliza.Craig a son b.4 ult.bap.9 Dec.1860
CRAIG	John :	Jas.Craig w.f. 33 Portlethen and wife Christn.Allan a son b.27 ult. bap.30 Nov.1867 at the Manse
CRAIG	John :	Son of Joseph Craig w.f. 14 Portlethen and wife Ann Craig b.19 Aug.bap.29 Aug.1869
CRAIG	John Hay :	Alex.Craig w.f.3 Portlethen and wife Margaret Wood a son b.5 Jan.bap.4 Feb.1852
CRAIG	John Trail :	Jas.Craig w.f.Portlethen and wife Margaret Forbes a son b.20 Nov. bap.27 Nov.1842

CRAIG	John Wood : John Craig w.f. 37 Portlethen and wife Jessy Wood a son b.7 ult.bap. 11 Aug.1867
CRAIG	Joseph : Bap. a son to John Craig w.f. and Agnes Wood in Portlethen b.24 Mar.bap.3 Apr.1841
CRAIG	Joseph : Al.Craig w.f.Portlethen and wife Margaret Wood a son b.2 ult.bap.16 Aug.1845
CRAIG	Joseph : Jo.Craig w.f.43 Portlethen and wife Margaret Flatt a son b.26 May bap.2 Aug.1851
CRAIG	Joseph : Wm.Craig w.f.10 Portlethen and wife Helen Craig a son b.and bap.22 Feb.1853
CRAIG	Joseph : Jo.Craig w.f.64 Portlethen and wife Eliz.Burnett a son b.11 Oct.bap.20 Nov.1853
CRAIG	Joseph : James Craig w.f.54 Portlethen and wife Jane Craig a son b.8 May bap.21 Jun.1856
CRAIG	Joseph : Joseph Craig w.f.14 Portlethen and wife Ann Leiper a son b.15 ult.bap.3 Jul.1858
CRAIG	Joseph : Joseph Craig w.f.47 Portlethen and wife Jane Christie a son b.14 ult.bap.8 Sep.1861
CRAIG	Joseph : Geo.Craig w.f.and Ann Allan his wife,Portlethen a son b.4 ult.bap.30 Nov.1861
CRAIG	Joseph : Geo.Craig w.f.46 Portlethen and wife Ann Allan a son b.15 Dec.bap.21 Dec.1867 at Manse
CRAIG	Joseph : James Craig and wife Jane Leiper a son b.2 Jan.bap.3 Jan.1869 at 34 Portlethen
CRAIG	Lilly : Andrew Craig w.f.Portlethen and Elspet Craig there,an ill. dau.b.24 Mar.bap.7 Jun.1859
CRAIG	Margaret : Bap. an ill. dau.to Alex.Craig and Margaret Wood in England 244 Jan.1841
CRAIG	Margaret : Jo.Craig w.f.Portlethen and wife Agnes Wood a dau.b.5 bap.12 Oct.1844
CRAIG	Margaret : Widow Al.Craig or Lilly Wood in Portlethen a dau.b.3 ult.bap.12 Oct.1848
CRAIG	Margaret : Geo.Craig w.f.Portlethen and wife Janat Craig a dau.b.26 ult.bap.4 Apr.1849
CRAIG	Margaret : Jas.Craig w.f.8 Portlethen and wife Jessie Craig a dau. b.and bap.27 Apr.1850
CRAIG	Margaret : Geo.Craig w.f.9 Portlethen and wife Margaret Craig a dau.b.9 ult.bap.4 May 1850
CRAIG	Margaret : Jo.Craig w.f.64 Portlethen and wife Eliza Burnett a dau.b.10 ult.bap.30 Nov.1850
CRAIG	Margaret : Geo.Craig w.f.and Ann Allan 65 Portlethen a dau.b.8 Aug.bap.30 Sep.1854
CRAIG	Margaret : Geo.Craig w.f.39 Portlethen and Ann Wood,Findon an ill.dau.b.4 ult.bap.27 Jun.1857
CRAIG	Mragaret : Jas.Craig w.f.55 Portlethen and Ann Wood 45 Portlethen an ill.dau.b.27 Dec.1861 bap.3 Feb.1862
CRAIG	Margaret : Jo.Craig w.f.29 Portlethen and wife Mragaret Craig a dau.b.26 ult.bap.30 Dec.1862
CRAIG	Margaret : Jas.Craig w.f.58 Portlethen and wife Christina Allan a dau.b.23 ult.bap.30 May 1863 at the Manse
CRAIG	Margaret : John Craig w.f.29 Portlethen and widow Lilly Wood there an ill.dau.b.18 Jul.bap.4 Jul.1868 at the Manse
CRAIG	Margaret : George Craig w.f.38 Portlethen and wife Ann Main a dau.b.27 Feb.bap.7 Mar.1869
CRAIG	Margaret Main : Geo.Craig w.f.Portlethen and wife Margt.Leiper a dau.b.29 bap.31 Dec.1844
CRAIG	Mary : Bap.a dau.to Joseph Craig w.f.Portlethen and Margaret Craig b.and bap.23 Jul.1841
CRAIG	Mary : Al.Craig w.f.and wife Margt.Wood a dau.b.31 ult.bap.18 Nov.1848
CRAIG	Mary : Wm.Craig w.f.and wife Helen Craig 10 Portlethen a dau.b.4 ult.bap.5 Apr.1851
CRAIG	Mary : Al.Craig w.f.Portlethen and widow Lilly Wood there an ill.dau.b.18 Jul.bap.29 Aug.1858
CRAIG	Mary : Geo.Craig w.f.62 Portlethen and wife Ann Allan a dau.b.8 ult.bap.1 Jun.1864
CRAIG	Mary & Ann twins : John Craig w.f.Portlethen and Margt.Flatt there had 2 children b.4 Aug.bap.13 Aug.1842

CRAIG	Mary Christie : Isabella Craig,Portlethen an ill.dau.b.20 Dec.1868 bap.21 Feb.1869
CRAIG	Mary Forbes : Jas.Craig w.f.Portlethen and wife Margt.Forbes a dau.b.8 ult.bap.16 Jul.1848
CRAIG	Robert : Wm.Craig w.f.10 Portlethen and wife Helen Craig a son b.21 ult.bap.14 May 1859
CRAIG	William : Bap.a son to John Craig and Mary Low,Hill of Findon 22 Sep.1840
CRAIG	William : Jas.Craig w.f.Portlethen and wife Lilly Craig a son b.19 ult.bap.20 Nov.1847
CRAIG	William : John Craig w.f.Portlethen and wife Barbara Moir a son b.1 ult.bap.10 Apr.1847
CRAIG	William : Jas.Craig w.f.Portlethen and wife Elspet Craig a son b.4 ult.bap.17 Mar.1849
CRAIG	William : Geo.Craig w.f.Portlethen and wife Ann Allan there an ill.son b.9 Jan.bap.4 May 1850
CRAIG	William : Wm.Craig w.f.24 Portlethen and wife Jane Allan,Cove an ill.son b.1 Apr.1852 bap.15 May 1852
CRAIG	William : Geo.Craig w.f.6 Portlethen and wife Eliz.Craig a son b.23 Sep.bap.26 Oct.1853 by Rev.Dewar
CRAIG	William : Al.Craig w.f.3 Portlethen and wife Margt.Wood a son b.3 Jun.bap.22 Jul.1854
CRAIG	William : Wm.Craig w.f. Portlethen and wife Is.Craig a son b.4 Jan.bap.24 Feb.1855
CRAIG	William : John Craig w.f.7 Portlethen and wife Elspet Main a son b.8 Jan.bap.24 Feb.1855
CRAIG	William : Wm.Craig w.f.Portlethen and Eliza.Craig there an ill.son b.31 ult.bap.4 Sep.1859
CRAIG	William : Jo.Craig w.f.29 Portlethen and wife Margt.Craig a son b.14 ult.bap.18 Feb.1865
CRAIG	William : James Craig w.f.34 Portlethen and wife Jane Leiper a son b.17 ult.bap.19 Feb.1866
CRAIG	Wm. Law : James Craig w.f.Portlethen and wife Margaret Craig a son b.8 Nov.bap.19 Nov.1842
CROMBIE	George : Jo.Crombie,Badentoy and wife Helen Kane a son b.5 ult.bap.3 Nov.1849
CROMBIE	John : Jo.Crombie and wife Helen Kane a son b.in Dundee 7 Jan.1847 bap.by Rev.Loggan there-3 Nov.1849
CRUICKSHANK	James : John Cruickshank,parish of Logie Buchan and Elizabeth Scorgie,Mill of Portlethen an ill.son b.3 Aug.bap.13 Oct.1850
CRUICKSHANK	Jane Leonard : Jo.Cruickshank and wife Is.Yeats,8 John St.Abdn. a dau.b.Mar.bap.7 Apr.1865
CUSHNIE	Helen : Bap.a dau.to James Cushnie and Margt.Mason in Whitebruntland 19 Oct.1840
DALE	James : Robert Dale,rail.Guard,wife Margt.Carneggie,residing College St.Abdn.a son b.11 ult.bap.17 Jan.1851
DALE	Pat.Wm.Scott Carneggie : Robert Dale,A.R.guard,Wellington Rd.Abdn.and wife Margt.Carneggie a son b.31 Aug.bap.17 Sep.1855
DALE	Rob.Patterson Doig : Robert Dale,rail guard,Abdn. and wife Margt.Carneggie,Ferryhill,Abdn.a son b.20 Jan.bap.9 Feb.1853
DANIEL	Hanna Gordon : Cumming Daniel,Longside and Ann Anderson,Badentoy an ill.dau.b.20 Oct 1854 bap.23 Jan.1855 (uncle sponsor)
DEMPSTER	Geo.: Geo.Dempster and wife Mary Copland,Hill of Portlethen a son b.14 May bap.4 Aug.1866
DEMPSTER	Mary : Geo.Dempster and wife Mary Copland,Hill of Portlethen a dau.b.19 May bap.at the Manse 2 Aug.1868

DONALD	Alex.	: Wm.Donald,Hill of Findon and wife Eliz.Howie a son b.29 ult.bap.14 Jun.1845
DONALD	Ann	: Wm.Donald and wife Eliz.Donald,nr.Badentoy a dau.b.18 Jun.bap.15 Jul.1854
DONALD	Ann	: Jas.Donald and wife Ann Leiper, E.Cookston a dau. b. 9 Feb.bap.at the Manse 15 Mar.1868
DONALD	David	: David Donald,Glashfarquhar and wife Ann Barclay a son b.30 ult.bap.17 Oct.1857
DONALD	Elspet	: Wm.Donald,Badentoy and wife Eliz.Howie a dau.b.10 Jul.bap.23 Aug.1851
DONALD	Geo.	: Wm.Donald and wife Eliz.Howie,Badentoy a son b.7 ult.bap.4 Oct.1848
DONALD	Isabella	: Jas.Donald,lab.,E.Cookston and wife Ann Leiper a dau.b.21 bap..29 Jul.1866
DONALD	Jas.	: Wm.Donald,Hill of Findon and wife Eliz.Howie a son b.31 Aug.bap.4 Oct.1842
DONALD	Jas.	: Jessie Donald,Glashfarquhar an ill.son b.23 Aug.1860 bap.23 Jan.1861
DONALD	Margt.	: Duncan Donald and wife Christian Fenton a dau.b.24 ult.bap.at Cairnrobin 23 Jul.1864
DONALD	Wm.	: Duncan Donald and wife Christian Fenton a son b.10 Dec.ult.bap.at Cairnrobin 10 Jan.1866
DONALDSON	Alex.	: Smith Donaldson,Nigg and Mary Hunter,Hill of Findon an ill.son b.13 ult.bap.3 Nov.1862
DONALDSON	Barbara	: David Donaldson,E.Cookston and wife Eliza.Park a dau.b.27 Jul.ult.bap.29 Aug.1861
DONALDSON	Eliz.	: David Donaldson,Roadside of Cookston and wife Eliz.Park a dau.b.5 Jul.ult.bap.28 Aug.1864
DONALDSON	Helen	: David Donaldson,mason,Cookston and wife Eliz.Park a dau.b.30 Dec.1868 bap.2 May 1869
DONALDSON	Margt.Ann	: David Donaldson,E.Cookston and wife Eliz.Park a dau.b.2 Nov.ult.bap.16 Dec.1866
DOUGLASS	Robt.Alex.	: David Douglass and wife Margt.Welsh,Burnthillock a son b.12 May ult.bap.17 Jun.1866
DOW	Margt.	: Peter Dow and Eliz.Wood in Findon an ill.dau.b.1 May bap.6 Jun.1848
DUFF	Agnes	: Dau.of Al.Duff,coal merchant,3 Afflick St.Abdn. bap.9 Feb.1855
DUNBAR	Agnes	: Jas.Dunbar,E.Cookston and wife Helen Davidson a dau.b.13 Nov.bap.11 Dec.1852
DUNBAR	Andrew	: Jas.Dunbar,E.Cookston and wife Helen Davidson a son b.3 ult.bap.21 Jan.1844
DUNBAR	Ann Guthrie	: Jas.Dunbar and wife Mary Keith,100 Union St.Abdn. a dau.b.there 15 Dec.1857 bap.6 Feb.1858
DUNBAR	Margt.	: Bap.a dau.to Jas.Dunbar and Mary Keith,Union St.Abdn. 9 Oct.1859
DUNBAR	Mary	: Jas.Dunbar and wife Helen Davidson a dau.b.13 ult.bap.1 Feb.1851
DUNBAR	Robert Walker	: Jas.Dunbar and wife Helen Davidson a son b.at E.Cookston 15 ult.bap.30 Dec.1848
DUNBAR	William	: Jas.Dunbar,E.Cookston and wife Helen Davidson a son b.6 ult.bap.1 Dec.1846
DUNCAN	Alexander	: Son of David Duncan,farmer and wife Mary Forbes b.at Hillside 20 Aug.1869 bap.26 Sep..1869
DUNCAN	Andrew George	: David Duncan and wife Mary Forbes,Hillside a son b.29 Jan.bap.5 Mar.1865
DUNCAN	Ann	: R.Duncan,Braeside of Findon and wife Ann Cumming a dau.b.30 ult.bap.30 Nov.1850
DUNCAN	David	: David Duncan,Hillside and wife Mary Forbes a son b.24 ult.bap.13 Mar.1859
DUNCAN	George	: David Duncan,Old Machar and wife Mary Forbes a son b.15 May 1855 bap.17 Jun.1855
DUNCAN	Isabel Collie	: Jas.Duncan,Hillside and wife Mary Forbes an ill.dau.b.4 Feb.ult. bap.at Hillside 25 May 1865—Grandmother sponsor
DUNCAN	James	: David Duncan,Hillside and wife Mary Forbes a son b.5 ult.bap.10 May 1857

DUNCAN	Jessie : David Duncan and Mary Forbes,Hillside an ill.dau.b.9 Aug.1853 bap.24 Sep.1853
DUNCAN	John Forbes : David Duncan,Hillside and wife Mary Forbes a son b.5 ult.bap.16 Jun.1867
DUNCAN	Mary : David Duncan,Hillside and wife Mary Forbes a dau.b.4 ult.bap.26 May 1863 by Rev.Dr.Paul
DUNCAN	Robert : Robert Duncan (Free Church) Fiddestown and wife Ann Cumming a son b. 23 Apr. bap.26 May 1849
DUNCAN	William : D,Duncan, Hillside and wife Mary Forbes a son b.22 ult.bap 21 Apr.1861
DURNO	Agnes : Al.Durno and Agnes Masson, Langhillock an ill.dau. b.31 ult.bap.14 Jan 1865
DURWARD	Christina : John Durward, Mains of Portlethen and wife Eliza.Robb a dau.b.3 ult.bap.23 Jun 1863 at Manse
DUTHIE	David Smith : Wm.Duthie, England and wife Susan Tavendale a son b. 11 Sep. ult.bap.30 Oct.1864
DUTHIE	James : Ann Taylor, Hillside and Jas.Duthie, Glasgow, an ill. son b. 13 May ult. bap 2 Aug. 1859
DUTHIE	Jane : John Duthie,merchant,Portlethen and Margaret Main, Hillhead of Portlethen,an ill. dau.b.27 Oct.1853 bap.18 Mar.1854 (girl's father sponsor)
DUTHIE	Robert : Wm.Duthie, Precentor,and wife Susan Tavendale a son b.29 May ult.bap 30 Jun.1867
EDWARDS	James : John Miller Edwards and Christian Rose his wife, Brunthillock, a son bap.26 Nov.1859
ESSELMONT	John : Wm.Esselmont, Fraserburgh and Clementina McDonald, Bothy Bridge an ill. son b.14 Nov. bap.9.May 1868
EWAN	George Swanson : R.Ewan and wife Ann Swanson, Badentoy a son b.23 ult. bap.4 Nov.1850
EWEN	James : John Ewen, Cairmrobin and wife Christian Strachan a son b.18 Jun.bap.10 Jul.1852
EWEN	Jane Swanson : Jo.Ewen and wife Jane Swanson,a dau.b.22 May in W.Cookston bap.13 Jun.1854
EWEN	Jemmima Cumming : Robert Ewen, labourer, Badentoy and wife Ann Swanson a dau. b.14 ult. bap.2 Sep.1856
EWEN	John : Widow John Ewen, Hill of Charleston a son b.29 Jun bap.15 Jul.1854
EWEN	John Simpson : Robert Ewen and Ann Swanson,Moss-side of Portlethen a son b.11 Aug. ult.bap.3 Nov.1859
EWEN	Martha Johnston : Robert Ewen, Hill of Portlethen and wife Ann Swanson a son b. 8 Mar. ult. bap.13 Apr.1861
EWEN	Wm.Cumming : Robert Ewen, Hill of Portlethenand wife Ann Swanson a son b. 20 Oct. bap.20 Nov.1852
FARQUHAR	Elizabeth Blackhall : Jas. Farquhar and wife Mary Lawson, Portlethen a dau. b.31 Dec.1851 bap. 1 Jan.1852
FARQUHAR	George : Jas.Farquhar and wife Mary Lawson,Hill of Portlethen a son b.19 May 1855 bap.21 Jul.1855
FARQUHAR	James : Jas.Farquhar,Hill of Portlethen and wife Mary Lawson a son b.18 May last bap.16 Jul.1845
FARQUHAR	John : Jas.Farquhar and wife Mary Lawson a son bap.14 May 1847 in Aberdeen
FARQUHAR	Mary : Jas.Farquhar and wife Mary Lawson a dau.b.18 Jul.1853 bap.29 Aug.1853
FARQUHAR	Robert Lawson : Jas.Farquhar and Mary Lawson,Hill of Portlethen a son b.14 ult.bap.1 Mar.1850
FARRIER	Jane : David Farrier,Hill of Findon and wife Jane Lesslie a dau.b.23 ult.bap.28 Jun.1845
FERGUSON	Jess : John Ferguson,writer,Aberdeen and Margt.Chisholm,E.Cookston an ill.dau.b.20 ult.bap.6 Jan.1849

FERGUSON Wm. : Wm.Ferguson,rail.lab.,Portlethen(from Ireland) and Eliz.Craig,Portlethen a son b.10 Jul.bap.3 Nov.1849

FERRIER Ann : David Ferrier and wife Jane Lesslie a dau.b.6 ult.bap.24 May 1850

FERRIER Helen : D.Ferrier,Hill of Findon and wife Jane Lesslie a dau.b.2 Feb.bap.5 Mar.1843

FERRIER Isobel Lesslie : David Ferrier and wife Jane Lesslie,Findon a dau.b.22 ult.bap.25 Oct.1847

FERRIER James : David Ferrier and wife Jane Lesslie,Synod's Lands a son b.7 Nov.bap.18 Dec.1852

FINDLAY Ann : D.Findlay and wife Eliz.Henderson,E.Cookston a dau.b.24 ult.bap.10 Aug.1849

FINDLAY Ann : Wm.Findlay,Bishopston and wife Ann Milne a dau.b.26 ult.bap.15 Jun.1862

FINDLAY Charles : Wm.Findlay,Bishopston and wife Helen Milne a son b.24 ult.bap.7 May 1867

FINDLAY David Sinclair : Wm.Findlay,Bishopston and wife Helen Reid Milne a son b.24 Aug.bap.19 Oct.1858

FINDLAY Elizabeth : Bap.a dau.to David Findlay,shoemaker,Hillside and Elizabeth Henderson b.8 Jul.bap.18 Jul.1841

FINDLAY Elspet : Findlay,farmer,Bishopston and wife Helen Milne a dau.b.6 Jan.bap.1 Mar.1869

FINDLAY George : Wm.Findlay, Bishopston and wife Helen Milne a son b.12 ult. bap.18 Jun.1860

FINDLAY Helen : Wm.Findlay, Bishopston and wife Helen Rae Milne a dau.b.31 Jul. bap.15 Sep.1863

FINDLAY James : D.Findlay, Hillside and wife Eliza.Henderson a son b.14 bap.25 Feb.1844

FINDLAY James : Wm.Findlay and wife Helen Milne, Bishopston a son b.20 Jan.bap.15 Mar.1865

FINDLAY Mary : Jo.Findlay and wife Mary Lamb, Cassieport a dau. b.13 Jun.bap.21 Aug.1864

FINDLAY William : Wm.Findlay, Nigg and wife Eliza.Howie,Findon a son b.5 May bap.10 Jul.1859

FINNIE Alexander : Al.Finnie and wife Margt.Mackie, Cookston a son b.25 Dec.bap.2 Feb.1868 at the Manse

FORBES Alexander : Robert Forbes, Dunnottar and Isobel Taylor, Balquhain an ill. son b.3 Oct.1851 bap.7 Nov.1851

FORBES David McDonald : son of Charles Forbes,engineman and wife Helen Wright,at 4 Wellington Rd.Abdn. b.24 Aug bap.14 Nov.1869

FORBES Helen : Chas.Forbes and wife Helen Wright a dau. b.4 Aug. bap.1 Sep.1862 at Hillside

FORBES James : Charles Forbes,Railway surfaceman,Nigg and wife Helen Wright a son b.1 Dec.1863 bap.17 Apr.1864

FORBES Jessie Banks : Chas.Forbes and wife Helen Wright,Synod's Lands a dau.b.9 Dec.1867 bap.21 Mar.1868 at Manse

FORBES John : Charles Forbes and wife Helen Wright a son b.17 May ult.bap. at Hillside near Moss-side 11 Nov.1858

FORBES Jonathan : Charles Forbes, Hillside and wife Helen Wright a son b.23 ult. bap.20 Oct.1860

FOWLER Christina : Thomson Fowler, Charleston and wife Christina Harper a dau. b.16 Mar. ult. bap.20 Apr.1861

FRASER Alexander : Wm.Fraser and Ann Shepherd in Hill of Findon a son b.18 ult.bap.9 Jun.1849

FRASER David : Robert Fraser and wife Ann Adam,Hill of Portlethen a son b.27 Oct.ult.bap.10 Dec.1859

FRASER George : Bap.a (dau.)to Al.Fraser and Margt.Johnston,Portlethen 4 Oct.1840

FRASER Isabella : Wm.Fraser and Ann Shepherd, Hill of Portlethen a dau.b.17 Aug. bap.6 Sep.1851

FRASER Janat Donald : and,

FRASER Jane Ann : Al.Fraser, Drainpark and wife Margaret Johnston, twin daus. b.24 Jul.bap.25 Jul.1843

FRASER Jane : Wm.Fraser and wife Ann Shepherd in Hill of Portlethen a dau.b.6 ult. bap.22 Jan.1848

FRASER   Robert : Wm.Fraser, Hill of Portlethen and wife Ann Shepherd a son b.4 bap.10 Feb.1844

FRASER   Sarah Law : Wm.Fraser and wife Ann Shepherd a dau. b.3 Feb.bap.20 Mar 1853

FRASER   William : Wm.Fraser, Hill of Portlethen and wife Ann Shepherd a son b.9 ult.bap.25 Oct.1845

FRASER   William Davidson : Wm.Fraser,Kinellar and Mary Davidson,Mains of Findon an ill.son b.14 Mar.bap.16 Jul.1855

GALL   William : Wm.Gall,police officer,Burnside and wife Eliz.Thomson a son b.18 Jan.ult.bap.18 Feb.1859

GEDDES/KANE   Henry : Henry Geddes and Elspet Kane, E.Cookston an ill.son b.17 Dec.1861 bap.2 Mar.1862

GIBB   Alexander Taylor : John Gibb, Hill of Portlethen and wife Margaret Taylor a son b.29 ult. bap.30 Jan.1860

GIBB   Ann : John Gibb, Hill of Portlethen and wife Margt.Taylor a dau. b.3 Jan.ult. bap.6 Mar.1858

GIBB   Jas.Brown : Jas. Brown,Foveran, and Hutcheon Gibb, Hillside an ill. son b.5 Mar.ult. bap.26 Apr.1862

GIBB   Wm. : John Gibb, lab.,Hill of Portlethen and wife Margt.Taylor a son b.1 Jan.bap.28 Feb.1855

GILLENDERS   John : A.Gillenders, Craigentath,Maryculter,a son bap.12 Mar.1867

GILLESPIE   Margt. : Dau.of John Gillespie, lab.and wife Margt.Reid b. at Burnside,Findon 25 Jul.bap.28 Sep.1869

GORDON   Al. : Son of Jas.Gordon and Susan Allan,Hillside b.11 Jan.1849 bap.at the Manse 23 Nov.1867

GORDON   David Graham : Burnett Gordon, Hillside and wife Mary Graham a son b.5 Sep. bap.5 Oct.1857

GORDON   John : Bap.an ill.son to Jas.Gordon, Marywell and Susan Allan,Cookston b.28 Jul. bap.15 Aug.1841

GORDON   John : Jas.Gordon and Margt.Ewen in Hill of Dronforlay an ill. son b.23 Jul.bap.9 Oct.1848

GORDON   Lewis : Burnett Gordon and wife Mary Graham, Cairngrassie a son b.13 Dec.1861 bap.28 Feb.1862

GORDON   Mary : George Gordon, overseer, Mains of Portlethen and wife Mary Lowe a dau. b.4 Jun.bap.3 Aug.1864

GORDON   Mary Ann : Philip Gordon and Margt.Henry in Cairnrobin a dau. b.31 ult.bap.22 Jul.1848

GORDON   Robert : George Gordon, Mains of Portlethen and wife Mary Low a son b.25 ult.bap.4 Mar.1866

GORDON   William : Al.Gordon, Gellybrands and Betty Anderson in Findon an ill. son b.15 ult.bap.18 Dec.1847
        (Grandfather sponsor)

GRANT   Jane : Alex.Grant,Kirkmichael and Margt.McCleanan, Hill of Portlethen an ill. dau.b.17 Feb.bap.13 May 1850

GRAY   James : Al.Gray and wife Mary Coutts a son at Evertown of Findon b.4 Oct. bap.21 Nov.1850

GREIG   George : Wm.Greig, North Mains of Findon and wife Janat Forbes a son b.22 ult.bap.13 Aug.1865

GREIG   Helen Forbes : Wm.Greig, North Mains of Findon and wife Janat Forbes a dau. b.23 ult.bap.18 Dec.1859

GREIG   James : Wm.Greig and wife Janat Forbes, North Mains of Findon a son b.24 ult. bap.19 Apr.1868

GREIG   John Nisbet Forbes : Wm.Greig, N.Mains of Findon and wife Jane Forbes a son b.6 ult.bap.25 Sep.1863

GREIG   William : Wm.Greig, farmer,North Mains of Findon and wife Janat Forbes a son b.9 ult.bap.28 Dec.1861

HALL	Barbara : Jas.Hall, Hillside and wife Barbara Milne a dau.b.25 ult.bap.15 Apr.1847
HAND	James : Mick Hand, navie, and Elspet Leiper,Portlethen an ill. son b.9 Jul.bap.10 Sep.1850
HORN	Elsy : Jas.Horn, Roadside and wife Agnes Black a dau.b.16 Apr.bap. 27 May 1843
HOWIE	Andrew : Bap.a son to Peter Howie and Jane Yule in Clashfarquhar b.4 May bap.24 May 1841
HOWIE	Betty : P.Howie, West Clashfarquhar and wife Jane Yule a dau. b.3 ult.bap.3 Nov.1845
HOWIE	George : John Howie and Helen Roger in Cairnrobin a son b.29 ult.bap.4 Apr. 1846
HOWIE	George : Peter Howie,Glashfarquhar and wife Jane Yuil a son b.21 Jun.bap.12 Aug.1853
HOWIE	Isobel : John Howie,Fiddestown and wife Helen Roger a dau.b.13 ult.bap.4 Mar.1850
HOWIE	Jane : John Howie and wife Helen Roger in Hill of Cairnrobin a dau.b.13 Jan.bap.21 Jan.1843
HOWIE	Jane : Peter Howie,Glashfarquhar and wife Jane Yule a dau.b.6 Aug.bap.25 Sep.1850
HOWIE	Jessie : Al.Howie and wife Elspet Knowles,Blackhill a dau.b.2 Feb.bap.18 Mar.1854
HOWIE	Margt.Yule : P.Howie,Glashfarquhar and wife Jane Yule a dau.b.27 Jul.bap.14 Aug.1843
HOWIE	Wm. : P.Howie and wife Jane Yule,Glashfarquhar a son b.9 Apr.bap.16 May 1848
HUNTER	Agnes : Wm.Jo.Hunter,Findon and wife Helen Smith a dau.b.4 Jul.bap.11 Aug.1852
HUNTER	Alex. : Geo.Hunter,Craigbite,Nigg and wife Ann Leith a son b.6 ult.bap.18 Jun.1857
HUNTER	Duncan : Wm.John Hunter,Synod's Lands and wife Helen Smith a son b.2 ult.bap.8 Feb.1846
HUNTER	Helen : Wm.Jo.Hunter and wife Helen Smith,Synod's Lands a dau.b.30 ult.bap.12 Oct.1848
HUNTER	Jamieson : Duncan Hunter,Synod's Lands and wife Christian Hunter a son b.21 ult.bap.29 Sep.1850
HUNTER	Jane : Robt. Hunter, f.s. and wife E.Donald a dau. b.26 Apr. bap.11 May 1869
HUNTER	John : Duncan Hunter, Findon and wife Catherine Duncan a son b.7 ult. bap.24 Mar.1847
HUNTER	Robert : Duncan Hunter, Hill of Findon and wife Catherine Duncan a son b.25 ult. bap.31 Dec.1844
	Ann : see Mary and Ann (twins)
HUTCHEON	Catherine Jane : D.Hutcheon, Bourtreybush and wife Helen Hunter a dau. b.5 May ult.bap.8 Jun.1862
HUTCHEON	David : Jas.Hutcheon, Findon and wife Jane Low a son b.30 ult.bap.6 Jun.1845
HUTCHEON	David : Thomas Hutcheon, Sketraw and wife Mary Christie a son b.6 Feb.bap.3 Mar.1856
HUTCHEON	David : David Hutcheon, Bourtreebush and wife Helen Hunter a son b.1 Mar. bap.5 Apr.1857
HUTCHEON	Elspet : Jas.Hutcheon, s.f. Findon and wife Jane Low a dau. b.23 Jun. bap.1 Jul.1843
HUTCHEON	Elspet : Thos.Hutcheon, s.f. and wife Mary Christie a dau. b.6 Apr. bap.8 May 1860
HUTCHEON	Helen : D.Hutcheon, Bourtreybush and wife Helen Hunter a dau. b.12 Jan. bap.24 Feb.1861
HUTCHEON	Jas. : Thos.Hutcheon and wife Mary Christie, residing at or near Cammochmore,s.f.and member of Congregation, a son b.24 Jan. bap.25 Feb.1854
HUTCHEON	Jas. : David Hutcheon and wife Helen Hunter a son b.1 Nov.bap.1 Dec.1858
HUTCHEON	Jane : Jas.Hutcheon, Findon and wife Margt.Keith a dau. b.3 Jun. bap.19 Jun.1860
HUTCHEON	Jane Low : Thomas Hutcheon s.f.Cammochmore and wife Mary Christie a dau.b.31 Oct.bap.13 Nov.1852

HUTCHEON	John : Thos.Hutcheon and Jane Reid an ill.son b.23 ult.bap.1 Mar.1851
HUTCHEON	Joseph : David Hutcheon,Bourtreybush and wife Helen Hunter a son b.14 Dec.1865 bap.26 Jan.1866
HUTCHEON	Maggy Ann : David Hutcheon,Old Bourtreybush and wife Helen Hunter a dau.b.18 ult.bap.23 May 1864
HUTCHEON	Margt. : Bap.a dau.to Jas.Hutcheon,s.f.and Jane Low in Findon b.25 Jun.bap.21 Jul.1841
HUTCHEON	Margt. : Thos.Hutcheon and wife Mary Christie,Cammochmore a dau.b.8 ult.bap.26 Apr.1862
HUTCHEON	Mary & Ann(twins) : Jas.Hutcheon,Findon and wife Jane Low twin dau.b.9 ult.bap.20 Jul.1847
HUTCHEON	Thomas Hunter : D.Hutcheon,Bourtreybush and wife Helen Hunter a son b.26 ult.bap.1 Jul.1867
HUTCHEON	Thorn Collins : Thos.Hutcheon and wife Mary Christie a dau.b.at Cammochmore 4 ult.bap.29 Jan.1865
HUTCHESON	John Richard : John Hutcheson;wife Mary A.Benson a son b.Portlethen 29 Dec.1865 bap.Badentoy 27 Jun.1866
INGRAM	James : John Ingram,Swellhead of Maryculter and wife Sophia Brown a son b.4 Jan.bap.7 Mar.1866
JAFFERY	Jessie Ann : Jas.Jaffery,Abdn.-Isobel Howie,Findon an ill.child b.14 Dec.1843 bap.4 Feb.1844-Mother sponsor
JAMIESON	Alexander : Wm.Jamieson and wife Jane Sutherland a son b.15 ult.bap.2 Mar.1850
JAMIESON	Ann : Wm.Jamieson and wife Jane Sutherland,Findon a dau.b.21 Mar.bap.27 Apr.1854
JAMIESON	Charles : Wm.Jamieson,Kirktown and wife Jane Sutherland a son b.6 Mar.bap.3 Apr.1852
JAMIESON	Elizabeth : Jo.Jamieson,E.Cookston and wife Elizabeth Walker a dau.b.20 ult.bap.27 May 1843
JAMIESON	Elizabeth : Wm.Jamieson,Riccarton,Fetteresso & Mary Stewart,Synod's Lands an ill.dau.b.3 Sep.bap.14 Oct.1855
JAMIESON	Jane : John Jamieson and wife Elizabeth Walker,E.Cookston a dau.b.12 ult.bap.28 Oct.1848
JAMIESON	Jane : Wm.Jamieson,Braeside of Findon and wife Mary Farquharson a dau.b.27 Dec.last bap.2 Feb.1867
JAMIESON	Jessie : Wm.Jamieson,Braeside of Findon and wife Jane Sutherland a dau.b.12 Jun.bap.20 Jul.1859
JAMIESON	John : Wm.Jamieson,Kirk Officer and wife Jane Sutherland a son b.8 ult.bap.1 Aug.1846
JAMIESON	Katherine : John Jamieson,E.Cookston and wife Elizabeth Walker a dau.b.3 Nov.bap.4 Dec.1845
JAMIESON	Margaret : Wm.Jamieson, Kirkhill and wife Jane Sutherland a dau. b.25 ult. bap.9 Mar.1844
JAMIESON	Margaret : Margaret Jamieson, Synod's Lands, an ill. dau. b.27 ult. bap.12 Aug.1866 (reputed father, Geo.Howie, sailor, Newburgh)
JAMIESON	Mary : John Jamieson, and wife Eliza Walker,E.Cookston a dau. b.20 Apr.bap.17 May 1851
JAMIESON	William : Wm.Jamieson, Kirk Officer,and Jane Sutherland a son b.30 Apr. bap.8 May 1842
JAMIESON	William : Wm.Jamieson, Braeside of Findon and wife Mary Farquharson a son b.2 ult. bap.28 Sep.1868 at Manse
JOHNSTON	Alexander Gibb : Wm.Johnston and wife Ann Gibb,Portlethen a son b.12 Feb.ult. bap.13 Mar.1852
JOHNSTON	Alexander Milne : Mary Johnston,Burnside an ill.son b.19 Dec.ult.bap.8 Mar.1863 reputed father,Al.Milne,Abdn.

JOHNSTON   Alexandrina Ewen : Wm.Johnston, Hill of Portlethen and wife Ann Gibb a dau. b.22 ult.bap.16 Nov.1845 in presence of Congregation.

JOHNSTON   Ann : Wm.Johnston, Hill of Portlethen and wife Ann Gibb a dau. b.30 Apr. bap.20 May 1854
JOHNSTON   Barbara : Wm.Johnston, Portlethen and wife Ann Gibb a dau.b.24 Apr. bap.10 May 1856
JOHNSTON   David Silver : Wm.Johnston, Damhead and wife Ann Gibb a son b. and bap. 27 Aug.1860
JOHNSTON   Elizabeth : Bap. a dau. to Wm.Johnston and Mary Thomson, Hill of Findon 27 Oct.1840
JOHNSTON   George Hardy : Wm.Johnston and wife Ann Gibb, Damhead a son b.2 Sep.ult. bap.15 Oct.1864
JOHNSTON   Hugh Robert Donald Brown : Wm.Fiddes Johnston,Damhead and wife Ann Gibb a son b.22 Jul.ult. bap.29 Sep.1866
JOHNSTON   Isabella Mathewson Law : Wm.Johnston, Portlethen and Ann Gibb his wife, a dau. b.16 Jul. bap.22 Jul.1843
JOHNSTON   James : Bap. a son to Wm.Johnston and Magdalene Officer in Backhill of Portlethen b.10 Mar. bap.20 Mar.1841
JOHNSTON   James Collie : Margaret Johnston, Portlethen an ill. son b.29 Sep. ult.bap.10 Nov.1867 at Manse, (Grandfather sponsor)

JOHNSTON   Jas.Forbes : Jas.Johnston f.h. Mains of Findon and wife Jane Omens, a son b.18 May bap.28 Jul.1849
JOHNSTON   Jane Gordon : Bap.a dau.to Wm.Johnston and Ann Gibb in Hill of Portlethen b.18 Aug.bap.29 Aug.1841
JOHNSTON   John : Wm.Johnston and wife Ann Gibb, Hill of Portlethen a son b.11 ult. bap.28 Aug.1858
JOHNSTON   Margaret : Wm.Johnston, shoemaker, Roadside, and Mary Thomson a dau. b.28 Jan. bap.10 Feb.1842
JOHNSTON   Margaret Adam : Wm.Johnston and wife Ann Gibb a dau. b.1 Feb. bap.11 Mar.1848 at his house,Hill of Portlethen
JOHNSTON   Mary Air : Wm.Fiddes Johnston, Damhead of Portlethen and wife Ann Gibb a dau. b.28 ult. bap.2 Jun.1862
JOHNSTON   William : Wm.Johnston, Portlethen and wife Ann Gibb a son b.18 ult. bap 13 Apr.1850

KANE   Alexander : Al.Kane and wife Jessie Reid, W.Cookston a son b.2 Feb. bap.18 Mar.1854
KANE   Alexander : Joseph Kane, Hillside and wife Mary Patterson a son b.16 ult.bap.24 Apr.1863
KANE   Elizabeth : Al.Kane and wife Jessie Reid, E.Cookston a dau.b.29 Jun. bap.14 Jul.1851
KANE   Elspet : Issabella Kane, Moss-side, an ill. dau.b.16 Feb.last bap.1 Sep.1862 (brother in law sponsor)
KANE   Helen : Alex.Kane, W.Cookston and wife Jessie Reid a dau. b.14 Nov. bap.21 Nov.1844
KANE/GEDDES   Henry : Henry Geddes and Elspet Kane, E.Cookston an ill. son b.17 Dec.1861 bap.2 Mar.1862
KANE   Jas. : Alex.Kane, E.Cookston and wife Janat Reid a son b.4 Jan.ult. bap.20 Feb.1859
KANE   Janat : Al.Kane, Cookston and wife Jessie Reid a dau.b.29 ult.bap.8 Dec.1846
KANE   Joseph : Joseph Kane and wife Eliza Stewart, Gallowhill a son b.30 ult. bap.20 Apr.1861
KANE   Mary Robertson : Jas.Kane and Margt.Silver, Moss-side of Findon a dau. b.20 ult. bap.19 Jan.1862
KANE   Wm. : Joseph Kane, Gallowhill and wife Mary Stewart a son b.3 May ult. bap.at the Manse 20 Jun.1863
KEAN   Jane : Jos.Kean, Gallowhill and wife Mary Ann Stewart a dau. b...ult. bap.5 May 1865
KEAN   Margt. : Dau.of Wm.Kean s.f. b.at Cammochmore Cottage 22 Sep. bap.3 Nov.1869

| KEAN | Mary : Wm.Kean and wife Helen Kean,Carmochmore Cottage a dau. b.17 ult. bap.at the Manse 11 Sep.1867 |

| KEILTY / KELPY | Isabella : Neil Kelpy alias Keilty, navie, and Margt.Wood in Downies an ill.dau. b.7 Jul. bap.18 Dec.1850 (P.sponsor) |

| KEITH | Jane : Jas.Keith, farmer's son Loggie, Parish of Fetteresso and Helen Reid, Moss-side of this Parish, an ill. dau. b.4 Jun. bap.17 Nov.1857 |

KEMP	Robt. : Jas.Kemp, Redmyre and wife Margt.Stott a son b.30 May last bap.20 Jul.1861
KENN	..... : Jas.Kenn, farmer, Redmyre and wife Margt.Dempster a dau. b.17 Jan.1869 bap.18 Feb.1869
KENN	David Silver : Jas.Kenn and wife Margt.Silver a son b.20 ult. bap.at Haremoss 14 Feb.1864
KENN	Geo. : Jas.Kenn, Redmyre and wife Margt.Dempster a son b.23 ult. bap.10 Nov.1866
KENN	Jane Patterson : Joseph Kenn, Hillside and wife Mary Patterson a dau. b.29 ult. bap.16 Jun.1867
KENN	Joseph : Joseph Kenn and wife Mary Patterson, Hillside a son b. 6 ult. bap.12 Mar.1865
KENN	Robt. : Jas.Kenn,Redmyre and wife Margt.Dempster a son b.5 Jul.bap.7 Aug.1864
KENNEDY	Geo. : Wm.Kennedy,Afforthies and wife H.Elrick a son b.6 Nov.bap.23 Dec.1844
KENNEDY	John : Wm.Kennedy,lab.Afforthies and wife Harriet Elrick a son b.16 May bap.13 Jun.1842
KINMUND	Ann : Alex.Kinmund,blacksmith,Hillside(from Ruthven) and wife Ann Lindsay,Mains of Findon a dau.b.16 Oct.bap.14 Nov.1855

KNIGHT	Mary Ann Stewart : Wm.Knight,Hillside and Ann Stewart,Badentoy an ill.dau.b.18 Nov.ult.bap.21 Dec.1857
KNOWLES	Agnes : Jo.Knowles w.f.Downies and wife Margt.Knowles a dau.b.18 ult.bap.8 Sep.1849
KNOWLES	Alex. : Geo.Knowles w.f.22 Downies and wife Jane Wood a son b.4 Dec.1850 bap.4 Jan.1851
KNOWLES	Alex. : Geo.Knowles w.f.22 Downies and wife Jane Wood a son b.4 ult.bap.27 Dec.1856
KNOWLES	Alex.Cormack : Jas.Knowles w.f.Findon and wife Agnes Leiper a son b.6 Jun.bap.10 Jul.1852
KNOWLES	Andrew : Al.Knowles,Clochandighter and wife Jane Anderson a son b.1 ult.bap.20 Jul.1847
KNOWLES	Ann : Bap.an ill.dau.to Geo.Knowles in Downies and Jane Wood in Portlethen 29 Dec.1840
KNOWLES	Ann : Geo.Knowles w.f.22 Downies and wife Jane Wood a dau.b.21 ult.bap.28 Oct.1843
KNOWLES	Ann : John Knowles w.f.3 Downies and wife Margt.Knowles a dau.b.2 ult.bap.18 Nov.1843
KNOWLES	Ann : Jas.Knowles w.f.27 Downies and wife Jane Main a dau.b.--ult.bap.4 Oct.1856
KNOWLES	David : Al.Knowles,Badentoy and wife Jane Anderson a son b.14 bap.29 Jun.1844
KNOWLES	Eliz. : Jas.Knowles w.f.Findon and wife Agnes Leiper a dau.b.21 ult.bap.14 Nov.1846
KNOWLES	Eliz. : Jas.Knowles w.f.27 Downies and wife Jane Main a dau.b.7 ult.bap.26 Feb.1866
KNOWLES	Elspet : Jas.Knowles w.f.27 Downies and wife Jane Main a dau.b.13 Aug.bap.13 Sep.1854
KNOWLES	Elspet Argo : Bap.a dau.to David Knowles and Elspet Walker in Charleston of Nigg 13 May 1842
KNOWLES	Elspet Hunter : John Knowles and Christian Hunter,Findon an ill.dau.b.7 Dec.1854 bap.16 Jan.1855
KNOWLES	Geo. : Geo.Knowles w.f.Downies and wife Jane Wood a son b.20 ult.bap.6 Aug.1847

KNOWLES   Geo. : John Knowles w.f.3 Downies and wife Margt.Knowles a son b.13 Feb.bap.29 Mar.1856
KNOWLES   Geo. : Jas.Knowles w.f.27 Downies and wife Jane Main a son b.12 ult.bap.7 Dec.1861
KNOWLES   Isobel : Geo.Knowles w.f.23 Downies and wife Jane Wood a dau.b.20 ult.bap.4 May 1861
KNOWLES   Isobel : John Knowles,Blackhill of Findon and wife Elspet Donald a dau.b.16 Nov.bap.26 Nov.1842
KNOWLES   Jas. : Geo.Knowles w.f.Findon and Agnes Leiper a son b.11 ult.bap.7 Oct.1849
KNOWLES   Jas. : Jas.Knowles 27 Downies and wife Jane Main a son b.17 Mar.bap.10 Apr.1852
KNOWLES   Jas.Alex. : Al.Knowles,Clochandighter and wife Jane Anderson a son b.30 ult.bap.15 Jun.1850
KNOWLES   Janat : Geo.Knowles and wife Jane Wood a dau.b.5 May bap.17 Jun.1854
KNOWLES   Jane : Bap.a dau.to Alex.Knowles and Jane Anderson in Badentoy 30 Aug.1840
KNOWLES   Jane : Bap.a dau.to John Knowles w.f.and Margt.Knowles in Downies 16 Oct.1840
KNOWLES   Jane : Bap.a dau.to Jas.Knowles w.f.and Agnes (Leiper) in Findon --Nov.1840
KNOWLES   Jane : Jas.Knowles jun.,w.f.Downies and Jane Main there an ill.dau.b.9 ult.bap.20 Sep.1845
KNOWLES   Jane : Geo.Knowles,seaman,Findon and Isobel Wood,Portlethen an ill.dau.b.1 ult.bap.9 Sep.1850
KNOWLES   Jane : John Knowles w.f.Findon and Margt.Wood there an ill.dau.b.26 Oct.bap.28 Dec.1867
KNOWLES   Jessie : Jas.Knowles w.f.27 Downies and wife Jane Main a dau.b.5 ult.bap.26 Dec.1863
KNOWLES   John : Jas.Knowles w.f.Findon and wife Agnes Leiper a son b.18 Jun.bap.6 Jul.1844
KNOWLES   John : John Knowles w.f.3 Findon and wife Margt.Knowles a son b.1 bap.26 Dec.1846
KNOWLES   Joseph : Al.Knowles and wife Jane Anderson,Clochandighter a son b.27 Apr.bap.31 May 1852
KNOWLES   Margt. : John Knowles w.f.3 Downies and wife Margt.Knowles a dau.b.19 Jun.bap.24 Jul.1852
KNOWLES   Margt. : Jas.Knowles and Jane Main,Downies a dau.b.9 May ult.bap.11 Jun.1859
KNOWLES   Margt. : Dau.of Wm.Knowles,merchant and Ann Leiper b.at Portlethen 10 Oct.bap.26 Oct.1869
KNOWLES   Wm. : John Knowles,Blackhill of Findon and wife Elspet Donald a son b.12 ult.bap.6 Mar.1847
KNOWLES   Wm.B. : Son of Jas.Knowles w.f. and Jane Main his wife b.at 27 Downies 21 May bap.17 Jun.1869

KNOX /
MILNE   Jas. : Jannet Knox,England of Pitcaple an ill.son b.31 Mar.1864 bap.at Glen of Redmyre 6 Mar.1865
                 Mrs.Milne,Mill of Monquick sponsor

LAING   Child : Bap.18 Feb.1843 at Cove Parish of Nigg
LAING   Mary Ann : David Laing,Nigg and Christn.Bridgeford,Portlethen an ill.dau.b.11 May ult.bap.11 Aug.1858
LAIRD   Alex. : Peter Laird and wife Mary Wilson,Heathfield a son b.16 Sep.ult.bap.1 Nov.1865
LAIRD   Peter : Peter Laird f.s.Redmyre and wife Mary Wilson a son b.13 Sep.bap.6 Oct.1867
LAMB   Eliz.Ann Rae : Dau.of Robt.Lamb,lab.and wife Isabella Milne b.at Moss-side,Findon 16 Aug.bap.26 Sep.1869
LAMB   Robt. : Jas.Lamb and Agnes Wood in Portlethen an ill.son b.31 Jan.ult.bap.10 Mar.1844

LAMMOND	Alex.	: Wm.Lammond,Backburn,Fetteresso and wife Isabella Petrie a son b.30 ult.bap.26 Feb.1866
LAMOND	John	: Wm.Lammond and wife Isobel Petrie,near Cammochmore a son b.10 ult.bap.31 May 1861
LAMONT	Geo.	: Wm.Lamont and wife Is.Petrie,Cammochmore a son b.22 ult.bap.7 Mar.1864
LAWSON	Alex.	: Bap.a son to Alex.Lawson and Ann Milne at Balquhain-parties domicile in Fetteresso-14 Mar.1841
LEIGHTON	Eliz.	: Will.Leighton,Ban.Ter.and Is.Walker,Badentoy an ill.dau.b.13 Aug.bap.31 Dec.1856
LEIPER	Agnes	: Jo.Leiper w.f.38 Findon and wife Elspet Craig a dau.b.28 Sep.bap.10 Nov.1855
LEIPER	Alex.	: Bap.a son to John Leiper and Jane Wood w.f.Downies 6 Sep.1840
LEIPER	Alex.	: Jas.Leiper w.f.Findon and wife Ann Leiper a son b.11 bap.21 Sep.1844
LEIPER	Alex.	: Geo.Leiper w.f.Findon and wife Ann Wood a son b.29 ult.bap.13 Jun.1846
LEIPER	Alex.	: Alex.Leiper w.f.Findon and Helen Leiper there an ill.son b.14 Sep.bap.27 Dec.1849
LEIPER	Alex.	: Al.Leiper w.f.7 Downies and Jane Main 16 Downies an ill.son b.6 May bap.at Auchlee, Bishopston 27 Jun.1855
LEIPER	Alex.	: R.Leiper w.f.18 Downies and wife Jane Caie a son b.18 ult.bap.27 Feb.1858
LEIPER	Alex.	: Alex.Leiper w.f.26 Downies and wife Jane Morice a son b.20 ult.bap.11 Dec.1858
LEIPER	Alex.	: Al.Leiper w.f.Findon and wife Jane Wood a son b.21 ult.bap.30 Jun.1859
LEIPER	Alex.	: Al.Leiper w.f.Downies and Margt.Wood,Findon an ill.son b.21 Jun.ult.bap.27 Jul.1862
LEIPER	Alex.	: Al.Leiper w.f.21 Portlethen and wife (----)Leiper a son b.9 ult.bap.14 Aug.1864
LEIPER	Alex.	: Geo.Leiper w.f.66 Portlethen and wife Margt.Main a son b.19 ult.bap.31 Dec.1864
LEIPER	Alex.	: Geo.Leiper w.f.8 Findon and wife Agnes Craig a son b.14 ult.bap.30 Dec.1866
LEIPER	Alex.Milne	: Moses Leiper and Margt.Wood,Findon an ill.son b.10 ult.bap.16 Mar.1848-Wm.Wood sponsor
LEIPER	Andrew	: Wm.Leiper w.f.Findon and wife Is.Main a son b.14 ult.bap.27 Dec.1845
LEIPER	Andrew	: Wm.Leiper w.f.38 Findon and wife Ann Knowles a son b.9 Dec.bap.29 Dec.1867
LEIPER	Ann	: Jas.Leiper w.f.6 Downies and wife Ann Christie a dau.b.7 bap.10 Jun.1843
LEIPER	Ann	: Robert Leiper w.f.Portlethen and wife Elspet Leiper a dau.b.17 Nov.bap.6 Dec.1845
LEIPER	Ann	: John Leiper ---- Portlethen and wife Margt.Knox a dau.b.26 ult.bap.15 Dec.1848
LEIPER	Ann	: Wm.Leiper w.f.Findon and wife Is.Main a dau.b.13 Jan.bap.23 Feb.1850
LEIPER	Ann & Helen	: Geo.Leiper w.f.38 Findon and wife Ann Wood twin daus.b.and bap.3 Jul.1851
LEIPER	Ann	: Jo.Leiper w.f.17 Downies and wife Jane Wood a dau.b.18 Sep.bap.15 Oct.1853
LEIPER	Ann	: Alex.Leiper w.f.Findon and wife Jane Wood a dau.b.6 ult.bap.28 Feb.1857
LEIPER	Ann	: Alex.Leiper w.f.33 Findon and wife Is.Leiper a dau.b.17 ult.bap.2 Jun.1857
LEIPER	Ann	: Robert Leiper w.f.Findon and Eliza Wood an ill.dau.b.14 ult.bap.26 Feb.1859
LEIPER	Ann	: Wm.Leiper w.f.Burnbanks,Nigg and Ann Wood,Findon an ill.dau.b.16 ult.bap.27 Apr.1861
LEIPER	Ann	: Al.Leiper w.f.28 Portlethen and Jane Leiper,Findon an ill.dau.b.22 ult.bap.31 May 1862
LEIPER	Ann	: Andrew Leiper w.f.Findon and wife Jessie Leiper a dau.b.24 ult.bap.30 Jul.1864

LEIPER	Ann :	John Leiper w.f.3 Downies and wife Eliz.Leonard a dau.b.19 ult.bap.29 Oct.1864
LEIPER	Ann :	Joseph Leiper w.f.24 Downies and wife Jessy Main a dau.b.26 ult.bap.27 Mar.1865
LEIPER	Ann :	Wm.Leiper w.f.28 Findon and wife Margt.Leiper a dau.b.17 ult.bap.6 Jul.1865
LEIPER	Ann :	Geo.Leiper w.f.66 Portlethen and wife Margt.Main a dau.b.7 ult.bap.8 Apr.1868 at the Manse
LEIPER	Ann :	Al.Leiper w.f.44 Findon and wife Ann Wood a dau.b.13 ult.bap.24 Sep.1868
LEIPER	Ann Christie :	John Leiper and wife Is.Craig w.f.21 Downies a dau.b.11 Mar.bap.12 Apr.1851
LEIPER	Ann Craig :	Robt.Leiper w.f.21 Portlethen and Jane Craig there (dead) an ill.dau.b.11 May bap.14 Jun.1855
LEIPER	Ann Wood :	Al.Leiper w.f. 19 Portlethen and Janat Wood, Findon (pro secund) an ill. dau. bap.22 Jul.1855 in School of Findon.
LEIPER	Arthur :	Bap. a son to Arthur Leiper w.f. Findon and Jane Main b.19 Oct.bap.21 Oct.1841
LEIPER	Arthur :	John Leiper w.f. 22 Downies and wife Elspet Craig a son b.6 ult. bap.3 Apr.1847
LEIPER	Arthur :	Arthur Leiper w.f. and Jane Main a son (18th child) b.9 Nov. bap.27 Dec.1849
LEIPER	Arthur Christie :	Wm.Christie w.f.Sketraw and Christian Leiper,Findon an ill. son b.19 Sep.ult.bap.4 Nov.1863
LEIPER	Bell :	Bap. a dau.to Al.Leiper w.f. and Ann Wood,Downies 16 Oct.1840
LEIPER	Betty :	Al.Leiper w.f. Findon and wife Jane Leiper a dau.b.8 Sep. bap.28 Oct.1854
LEIPER	Christina Middleton :	Jessy Leiper, serv. 2 Findon an ill. dau. b.at Findon bap.at Manse 5 Jul.1868
LEIPER	Eliz. :	John Leiper w.f. Findon and wife Elspet Craig a dau.b.9 ult. bap.10 Jul.1846
LEIPER	Eliz. :	Geo.Leiper w.f. Findon and wife Eliz.Craig, 5 Portlethen an ill.dau. b.11 ult.bap.15 Jul.1865
LEIPER	Eliz. :	Robt.Leiper w.f. 52 Findon and wife Eliz.Wood a dau. b.12 Sep.ult. bap.1 Oct.1865
LEIPER	Elizabeth :	John Leiper w.f. 3 Downies and wife Eliz. Leonard a dau. b.16 ult.bap.22 Apr.1868 at the Manse
LEIPER	Elspet :	see Robert and Elspet, twins
LEIPER	Elspet :	Bap.a dau. to John Leiper w.f. and Elspet Craig in Findon 16 Aug.1840
LEIPER	Elspet :	Al.Leiper, Hillside Cottage and wife Elspet Thomson a dau. b.17 ult. bap.20 Oct.1843
LEIPER	Elspet :	Arthur Leiper w.f. Findon and wife Jane Main a dau. b.25 ult. bap.20 Jan.1848
LEIPER	Elspet :	Wm.Leiper w.f. and wife Isobel Main, Findon a dau. b.16 ult. bap.29 Jan.1848
LEIPER	Elspet and Margaret twins :	Janat Leiper, had twin daus. b.and bap. 28 Oct.1849
LEIPER	George :	Bap. a son to Jas. Leiper and wife Margaret Main in Findon b.25 Aug. bap.3 Sep.1842
LEIPER	George :	Geo. Leiper w.f. Findon and wife Ann Wood a son b.19 Jun. bap.22 Jun.1843
LEIPER	George :	Arthur Leiper w.f. Findon and wife Jane Main a son b.14 ult. bap.23 Dec.1843
LEIPER	George :	Jas. Leiper w.f. 15 Findon and wife Ann Knowles a son b.26 Jun. bap.9 Jul.1853
LEIPER	George :	Geo. Leiper w.f. Portlethen and wife Margt.Main a son b.29 ult. bap.11 Oct.1856
LEIPER	George :	Geo. Leiper w.f. Findon and wife Agnes Craig a son b.27 ult. bap 8 Nov.1860
LEIPER	George :	Al. Leiper w.f. Findon and wife Jane Wood a son b.25 ult. bap.31 May 1862
LEIPER	George :	Robt.Leiper w.f 52 Findon and wife Eliza.Leiper a son b.12 ult. bap.20 Apr.1863

LEIPER	George :	Wm.Leiper w.f. Findon and Ann Knowles, Downies an ill. son b.24 ult. bap.at the Manse 14 Jun.1863
LEIPER	George :	Jas. Leiper w.f. 25 Findon and wife Jane Wood a son b.17 ult. bap.12 Mar.1864
LEIPER	Geo. :	Al.Leiper w.f. 31 Portlethen and wife Jessy Wood a son b.3 ult. bap.5 Jul.1864
LEIPER	Geo. :	Alex.Leiper w.f.12 Downies and wife Jane Main a son b.26 Feb.ult. bap.1 Mar.1866
LEIPER	Geo. :	Andrew Leiper w.f. 11 Findon and wife Jessy Leiper a son b.17 ult. bap.23 Jun.1867
LEIPER	Geo. :	Jas. Leiper w.f. 19 Portlethen and wife Eliz. Leiper a son b. 10 Sep. bap. at the Manse 20 Sep.1868
LEIPER	Helen :	Al.Leiper w.f. 7 Downies and wife Ann Wood a dau. b.21 ult. bap 30 Jan 1844
LEIPER	Helen :	Jas.Leiper w.f. Findon and wife Ann Knowles a dau. b.17 ult. bap.28 Jul.1845
LEIPER	Helen :	Al.Leiper w.f. Findon and wife Is.Leiper a dau. b.11 ult. bap 13 Aug.1848
LEIPER	Helen :	see Ann and Helen, twins.
LEIPER	Helen :	Alex.Leiper w.f. 19 Portlethen and Janat Wood, Findon an ill. dau. b.26 Dec.1851 bap.4 Mar.1852
LEIPER	Helen :	Geo.Leiper w.f. 24 Portlethen and wife Margt.Main a dau. b.20 Apr. bap.1 May 1852
LEIPER	Helen :	Robt.Leiper w.f. 22 Findon and wife Eliz.Wood a dau. b.23 Dec. bap.at the Manse 28 Dec.1867
LEIPER	Isabel :	Al.Leiper w.f. Findon and Helen Leiper, Findon an ill. dau. b.1 Sep. bap.6 Nov.1852
LEIPER	Isabel :	Al.Leiper w.f. Findon and wife Helen Leiper a dau. b.15 Jun. bap.5 Jul.1856
LEIPER	Isabella :	Al.Leiper w.f. Findon and wife Isobel Leiper a dau.b.29 ult. bap.15 Sep.1849
LEIPER	Isabella :	Wm.Leiper w.f. Findon and wife Isabel Main a dau. b.23 Jul. bap.6 Aug.1852
LEIPER	Isabella :	Jas.Leiper w.f. 19 Portlethen and wife Elspet Leiper a dau. b.25 ult. bap.3 Aug.1861
LEIPER	Isabella :	Jas.Leiper w.f. 14 Findon and wife Christian Robertson a dau. b.13 ult. bap.5 May 1866
LEIPER	Isabella :	Geo.Leiper w.f. 60 Findon and wife Jane Craig a dau. b.31 Dec. last bap.2 Jan.1867
LEIPER	Isobel :	Bap.an ill. dau.to Geo.Leiper w.f. Findon and Ann Wood b.24 Oct. bap.5 Nov.1841
LEIPER	Isobel :	Jas. Leiper w.f. Findon and wife Margt.Main a dau. b.7 bap.22 Mar 1845 (Leiper's father sponsor)
LEIPER	Isobel :	Jo.Leiper w.f. 9 Downies and wife Ann Leiper a dau.b.22 ult. bap.31 Jan.1846
LEIPER	Isobel :	Jo.Leiper w.f. 17 Downies and wife Jane Wood a dau. b.28 Jul. bap.9 Sep.1851
LEIPER	Jas. :	Jas.Leiper w.f. and Ann Knowles, Findon a son b.9 Jun. bap.17 Jun.1841
LEIPER	Jas. :	Bap. a son to Al. Leiper w.f. Portlethen and Agnes Leiper b.29 Jun. bap.3 Jul.1841
LEIPER	Jas. :	Bap. a son to Wm. Leiper w.f. Findon and Isobel Main b.12 Oct. bap.21 Oct.1841
LEIPER	Jas. :	John Leiper w.f. 9 Downies and Ann Leiper a son b.3 Jan. bap.8 Jan.1842
LEIPER	Jas. :	Jo.Leiper w.f. 9 Downies and wife Ann Leiper a son b.21 bap.28 Jan.1844
LEIPER	Jas. :	Jas.Leiper w.f. Findon and wife Ann Knowles a son b.11 ult. bap.7 Jul.1848
LEIPER	Jas. :	John Leiper w.f. 21 Downies and wife Is.Craig a son b.5 Jun. bap. 6 Jul.1849
LEIPER	Jas. :	Al.Leiper w.f. 31 Findon and wife Janat Wood a son b.27 Oct. bap. 20 Nov.1852
LEIPER	Jas. :	Jo.Leiper w.f. Findon and wife Elspet Craig a son b.20 Mar. bap.23 Apr.1853

LEIPER	Jas.	: Geo.Leiper w.f. Findon and wife Agnes Craig a son b.19 ult. bap.29 Dec.1858
LEIPER	Jas.	: Geo.Leiper w.f. Findon and wife Ann Wood a son b.21 ult. bap.5 Feb.1859
LEIPER	Jas.	: Al.Leiper w.f. Downies and wife Jane Main a son b.29 ult. bap.25 May 1860
LEIPER	Jas.	: Robt.Leiper w.f. Findon and wife Eliz.Wood a son b.8 ult. bap.22 Sep.1860
LEIPER	Jas.	: Wm.Leiper w.f Findon and Margt.Leiper,there,an ill. son b.18 ult.bap.20 Oct.1860
LEIPER	Jas.	: Robt.Leiper w.f. 18 Downies and wife Jane Caie a son b.26 ult. bap.at the Manse 11 Jun.1863
LEIPER	Jas.	: Jas.Leiper w.f. 19 Portlethen and wife Eliza Leiper a son b.19 ult. bap.13 Sep.1863
LEIPER	Jas.	: Jas.Leiper w.f. Findon and Christian Robertson, there an ill. son b.and bap. 7 Nov.1863
LEIPER	Jas.	: Al.Leiper w.f. 21 Portlethen and wife Jane Leiper a son b.27 ult. bap.11 Nov.1865
LEIPER	Jas.	: Jas.Leiper w.f. Findon and wife Jane Wood a son b.15 Jun. bap.18 Jun.1866
LEIPER	James	: Jas.Leiper w.f. 25 Findon and wife Jane Wood a son b.9 ult. bap.21 Jul.1867
LEIPER	James	: Alex.Leiper and wife .... Wood a male child b.7 Jan. bap. by me at Portlethen 11 Jan.1869
LEIPER	Jane	: Bap.a dau.to James Leiper w.f. and Ann Leiper in Findon b.and bap.20 Mar.1841
LEIPER	Jane	: John Leiper w.f. Findon and wife Elspet Craig a dau. b.10 inst. bap.13 Dec.1843
LEIPER	Jane	: Jo.Leiper w.f. 17 Downies and wife Jane Wood a dau. b.20 Mar. bap.13 Apr.1844
LEIPER	Jane	: John Leiper, Portlethen and wife Margt.Knox a dau. b.12 ult. bap.24 Nov.1845
LEIPER	Jane	: John Leiper,Elder,Portlethen and wife Margt. Knox a dau. b.7 ult. bap.23 Jan.1851
LEIPER	Jane	: Al. Leiper w.f. 26 Downies and wife Jane Caie a dau. b.7 Sep. bap.15 Oct.1853
LEIPER	Jane	: Robt.Leiper w.f. Downies and Jane Caie, there an ill.dau.b.4 Jul.bap.29 Oct.1853
LEIPER	Jane	: Geo.Leiper w.f. and wife Ann Wood 38 Findon a dau.b.3 Aug. bap.23 Sep.1854
LEIPER	Jane	: Wm.Leiper w.f. Findon and wife Isobel Main a dau. b.23 ult. bap.7 Feb.1857
LEIPER	Jane	: James Leiper w.f. Portlethen and wife Elizabeth Leiper a dau. b.1 ult. bap.26 Jun.1859
LEIPER	Jane	: Ann Leiper, Findon an ill. dau. b.14 Aug. ult. bap.6 Oct.1860 (Grandmother sponsor)
LEIPER	Jane	: Geo.Leiper w.f. O.Portlethen and wife Margt.Allan a dau. b.5 ult. bap.6 May 1862
LEIPER	Jane	: John Leiper w.f. 3 Downies and wife Eliza Leonard a dau. b.7 ult. bap.26 Sep.1862
LEIPER	Jane	: Alex.Leiper w.f. 31 Portlethen and wife Jessy Wood a dau. b.2 ult. bap.3 Jan.1867
LEIPER	Jane	: Alex.Leiper w.f. 21 Portlethen and wife Jane Leiper a dau.b.12 ult.bap.31 Oct.1868 at the Manse
LEIPER	Jane	: Alex.Leiper w.f. 12 Downies and wife Jane Main a dau. b.29 Jan. bap.14 Feb.1869
LEIPER	Jane	: Ill.dau. of Agnes Wood 16 Findon and Robert Leiper,Downies b.24 Jul. bap.21 Sep.1869
LEIPER	Jane Wood	: Geo.Leiper w.f. 8 Findon and wife Agnes Craig a dau. b.7 ult. bap.22 Dec.1864
LEIPER	Janat	: Bap.a dau.to George Leiper and Helen Craig in Portlethen 27 Sep.1840
LEIPER	Janet	: Al.Leiper w.f. Portlethen and wife Ann Leiper a dau. b.19 ult.bap.2 Dec.1843
LEIPER	Jessie	: Arthur Leiper w.f. Findon and wife Jane Main a dau. b.2 Aug. bap.6 Sep.1845
LEIPER	John	: Bap.a son to Robert Leiper and Elizabeth Leiper in Portlethen 19 Aug.1840

LEIPER	John : John Leiper w.f. Findon and wife Elspet Craig a son b.12 Aug. bap.11Aug.1842
LEIPER	John : John Leiper w.f. Findon and wife Ann Knowles a son b.13 Jun. bap.22 Jun.1843
LEIPER	John : John Leiper w.f.21 Downies and Isobel Craig ,there an ill. son b.11 ult. bap.20 Feb.1844
LEIPER	John : Geo.Leiper w.f. 37 Findon and wife Ann Wood a son b.27 ult. bap.23 Sep.1848
LEIPER	John : Jas.Leiper w.f. Findon and wife Ann Leiper a son b.23 ult. bap.23 Dec.1848
LEIPER	John : John Leiper w.f. 48 Findon and wife Margt.Leiper a son b.and bap. 3 Apr.1850
LEIPER	John : Jo.Leiper w.f. Findon and wife Elspet Craig a son bap.22 Mar.1851
LEIPER	John : Alex.Leiper w.f. 26 Downies and wife Jane Morice a son b.7 Sep. bap.12 Oct.1852
LEIPER	John : John Leiper w.f. and Eliza Leonard in Downies an ill. son b.3 Oct. last bap.1 Dec 1857
LEIPER	John : Al.Leiper w.f. 34 Findon and wife Jane Wood a son b.9 ult. bap.25 Jun.1858
LEIPER	John : Geo.Leiper w.f. O.Portlethen and wife Margt.Main a son b.14 ult. bap.3 Dec.1859
LEIPER	John : Al.Leiper w.f. 12 Downies and wife Jane Main a son b.9 ult. bap.20 Sep.1862
LEIPER	John : Geo.Leiper w.f. 8 Findon and wife Agnes Craig a son b.9 ult. bap.22 Apr.1863
LEIPER	John : Al.Leiper 31 Findon and wife Jane Wood a son b.3 ult. bap.10 Sep.1864
LEIPER	John : Joseph Leiper w.f. 24 Downies and wife Jessy Main a son b.3 ult. bap.5 Feb.1867
LEIPER	John : Moses Leiper, Burnside and wife Eliz.Leiper a son b.22 ult. bap.20 Apr.1867
LEIPER	Joseph : Bap.a son to Joseph Leiper w.f. and Ann Christie in Downies 16 Jan.1841
LEIPER	Joseph : Wm.Leiper w.f. Findon and wife Isobel Main a son b.3 ult. bap.12 Oct.1843
LEIPER	Joseph : Arthur Leiper w.f. Findon and wife Jane Main a son b.19 Dec.1953 bap.8 Feb.1854
LEIPER	Joseph : George Leiper w.f. 8 Findon and wife Agnes Craig a son b.8 Mar. bap.17 Mar.1869
LEIPER	Joseph : Joseph Leiper w.f. Downies and wife .... Main a son b.at Downies 7 Jul. bap.11 Jul.1869
LEIPER	Lilly : Jo.Leiper w.f. 21 Downies and wife Isobel Craig a dau.b.8 Mar. bap.9 Apr.1853
LEIPER	Margaret : see Elspet and Margaret, twins
LEIPER	Margaret : Bap.a dau.to John Leiper,shoemaker,and Margaret Knox in Portlethen b.30 Aug. bap.2 Sep.1841
LEIPER	Margaret : Geo.Leiper w.f. Portlethen and wife Margaret Main a dau. b.4 May bap.24 Jun.1854
LEIPER	Margaret : Al.Leiper w.f. 31 Findon and wife Jane Wood a dau. b.9 Nov. bap.3 Dec.1854
LEIPER	Margaret : Alex.Leiper w.f. Findon and wife Is.Leiper a dau. b.20 Aug. bap.1 Sep.1855
LEIPER	Margaret : Al.Leiper w.f. 26 Downies and wife Jane Morice a dau. b.26 May bap.8 Jun.1856
LEIPER	Margaret : Robt.Leiper w.f. Downies and wife Jane Caie a dau. b.20 ult. bap.13 Oct.1860
LEIPER	Margaret : Alex.Leiper w.f. 31 Portlethen and wife Jessy Wood a dau. b.27 ult. bap.30 Dec.1861
LEIPER	Margaret : Jas.Leiper w.f. 19 Portlethen and wife Eliz.Leiper a dau. b.17 ult. bap.18 Oct.1866
LEIPER	Margaret : Wm.Leiper w.f. 28 Findon and wife Margt.Leiper a dau.b.10 ult. bap.12 Aug.1868 at the Manse
LEIPER	Margaret : James Leiper 15 Findon and wife Christina Robertson a dau. b.9 Dec. bap.30 Dec.1868 at Findon
LEIPER	Margt.Allan : Geo.Leiper w.f. 60 Findon and wife Jane Craig a dau.b.17 Dec. bap.20 Dec.1868 at the Manse

LEIPER	Nancy : Wm.Leiper w.f. and Js.Main, Findon a dau. b.15 Jul. bap.19 Aug.1854
LEIPER	Rachel Nicol : W.Leiper w.f. Findon and wife Isabella Leiper a dau. b.28 ult. bap.11 Jun.1861
LEIPER	Robert : Jo.Leiper w.f. 17 Downies and (John) Wood his wife a son b.31 ult. bap.27 Feb.1847
LEIPER	Robert and Elspet : Widow Al.Leiper (see loss of boat 8 Apr.1847) a son and a dau. b.2 May bap.4 May 1847
LEIPER	Robert : Robert Leiper w.f. and Jane Caie in Downies an ill. son b.16 Sep. bap.16 Nov.1850
LEIPER	Robert : Al.Leiper and wife Isabel Leiper, Findon a son b.9 ult. bap.5 Apr.1851
LEIPER	Robert : Al.Leiper w.f. and wife Jane Leiper 21 Portlethen a son b.20 ult. bap.26 Dec.1866
LEIPER	Susan : Robt.Leiper w.f. Portlethen and wife Elspet Leiper a dau. b.29 Sep. bap.2 Oct.1842
LEIPER	William : John Leiper w.f. Findon and wife Elspet Craig a son b.22 ult. bap.26 Mar.1848
LEIPER	William : John Leiper w.f. 17 Downies and wife Jane Wood a son b.24 May bap.29 Jun.1850
LEIPER	William : Jas.Leiper w.f. and Ann Knowles in Findon a son b.24 ult. bap.1 Mar.1851
LEIPER	William : Al.Leiper w.f. Downies and wife Jane Main a son b.11 Jun. bap.31 Jul.1858
LEIPER	William : Wm.Leiper w.f. 28 Findon and wife Margt.Leiper a son b.19 ult. bap.4 Apr.1863
LEIPER	William : Robt.Leiper w.f. 24 Downies and wife Jessy Main a son b.9 ult. bap.12 Sep.1863
LEIPER	William : Wm.Leiper w.f. 28 Findon and wife Ann Knowles a son b.19 ult. bap.11 Nov.1865
LEITH	William Knox : John Leiper, shoemaker, Portlethen and wife Margt.Knox a son b.2 Nov. bap.12 Nov.1843
LEITH	John : Al.Leith Jnr. and Helen Main, Lands of Portlethen an ill. son b.13 Jul. bap.15 Aug.1854
LEONARD	William : Laurence Leith f.s. Mains of Portlethen and wife Jane Stewart a son b.28 Dec.1865 bap.4 Feb.1866
	Georgina Morison : Jas.Leonard, E.Cookston and wife Jane Simm a dau. b.1 ult. bap.8 Nov.1843 in presence of the Congregation assembled in the New Church for the first time.
LEONARD	Isabella : Jas.Leonard and wife Eliza.Petrie, Craighead a dau. b.20 Jan. bap.14 Mar.1868 at the Manse
LEONARD	James : Jas.Leonard, Cookston and wife Eliza.Petrie a son b.4 Jan. bap.19 Mar.1866
LINDSAY	Robert : P.Lindsay seaman, Aberdeen and Ann Craig in Portlethen a natural son b.18 Sep.last bap.4 Nov.1846
LINDSAY	Susan Robertson : Robert Lindsay, Railway Station,Portlethen and wife Jane Robertson a dau. b.14 ult. bap.29 Mar.1850
LIVINGSTON	George : John Livingston, Portlethen and wife Elspet Craig a son b.13 ult. bap. 30 Mar.1849
LIVINGSTON	Isobel : John Livingston, lab.,Portlethen and wife Elspet Craig a dau. b.28 Jun. bap.10 Jul.1852
LIVINGSTON	James : Jo.Livingston and wife Elspet Craig a son b.27 Jun. bap.at 21 Carmelite St.Aberdeen 23 Jul.1864
LIVINGSTON	John : John Livingston and wife Elspet Craig,residing in Aberdeen a son b.19 May bap.11 Jun.1854
LOBBAN	Jemima Malcom : Jas.Lobban,teacher,Portlethen and wife Ann Fowler a dau.b.5 May bap.14 Jul.1849
LOBAN	William Chalmers : James Loban and wife Ann Fowler in Portlethen a son b.7 May bap.17 May 1852
LONGMUIR	Son : Bap.a son to Js.Longmuir in Newhall, for Mr Thomson, Fetteresso 17 Feb.1844
LONGMUIR	Elizabeth : James Longmuir, Hillside and wife Margt.Pithie a dau. b.24 Apr. bap.28 Apr.1842

LOW — Catherine : Wm.Low and Is.Mitchell, Kincardine O'Neil an ill. dau.b.1 Mar.1851 bap.22 Sep.1853 (Wm.Low's mother,sponsor,Hill of Findon)

LOW — Elspet : John Low s.f. Peterhead and wife Jane Hutcheon,Aberdeen a dau. b.4 May bap.at Findon 19 Jun.1860

LOW — James : Eliza Low, Hill of Findon a son b.12 Jan. bap.8 Mar. 1855 (reputed father,Alex.Kane,Badentoy)

LOW — Tiresha Maitland : William Low and Barbara Maitland, Synod's Lands an ill. dau. b.15 May bap.at Moss-side of Findon 1 Aug.1849

LOW — William : Jane Reid, Cairnrobin and Wm.Low (deceased) an ill. son b.12 ult. bap.11 Aug.1858

McALPINE — Mary Jane : Daniel McAlpine and wife Mary Walker, W.Cookston a dau. b.4 Aug. bap.18 Sep.1856

McBEITH — John : Al.McBeith,navie and Jane Craig both in Portlethen Village an ill. son b.6 Oct. bap.10 Dec.1850 (Wm.Main w.f. 58 Portlethen,sponsor)

McCALLUM — Mary Ann : Christina Beattie and Jas.McCallum, Cairngrassie a dau.b.19 May bap.at the Manse 4 Aug.1867

McCLAUCIN ? — Jane Cushnie : Wm.McClaucin,Moss-side of Portlethen and wife Jane Cushnie a dau.b.4 Dec.1842 bap.1 Jan.1843

McCLEAN — James : James McClean s.f.Downies and wife Is.Ewan a son b.15 Apr.bap.20 May 1860

McCLEARAN — Henrietta Polson : Elizabeth McClearan,Hill of Portlethen an ill.dau.b.16 Aug.ult.bap.3 Jan1865 reputed father Patrick Polson,parish of New Machar

McCLOUD — Christian : Norman McCloud,Portlethen and wife Elspet Wood a dau.b.16 ult.bap.9 Sep.1848

McCLOUD — George Wood : Norman McCloud w.f. and Elspet Wood in 14 Portlethen a son b.30 ult.bap.25 May 1850

McCLOUD — John : Norman McCloud w.f.14 Portlethen and wife Elspet Wood a son b.20 Oct.bap.28 Dec.1853

McCLOUD — John : John McCloud and wife Mary Smart,Redmyre a son b.5 Mar.bap.10 May 1862

McCLOUD — Margaret : Norman McCloud w.f.14 Portlethen and wife Elspet Wood a dau.b.30 Nov.bap.29 Dec.1855

McCLOUD — Mary Ann : Allan McCloud,Redmyre and wife Mary Smart a dau.b.2 Mar.bap.30 Apr.1856

McCLOUD — Norman : Norman McCloud 14 Portlethen and wife Elspet Wood a son b.8 Aug. bap.20 Sep.1851

McCOLL — Isobel : Jas. McColl, railway lab.,Rumleygowan and wife Is.Sinclair a dau.b.20 ult. bap.30 Sep.1847 (by certificate from Greenock)

McCONNACHIE — Ann : Jas.McConnachie, Hillside and Ann Wyse, Cairngrassie,Fetteresso a dau.b.22 Mar.bap.18 May 1856 at Manse

McCROBBIE — Helen Anderson : Jas.McCrobbie and Jessie Chisholm, Cairnrobin a dau.b.17 ult. bap.6 Nov.1865

McCROBBIE — Janet : John McCrobbie, Hill of Turnemiddle and Jessie Donald,Badentoy an ill.dau. b.2 Apr. bap.at the Manse 28 May 1855

McCROBBIE — Jane Keith : James McCrobbie and Jessie Chisholm, Cassieport an ill. dau.b.1 ult.bap.26 Nov.1859

McCROBBIE — Jessie Rose : Js.McCrobbie, Greenheads and wife Jessie Chisholm a dau.b.3 ult. bap.10 Aug.1861

McCROBBIE — Mary : Jas.McCrobbie, Cairnrobin and wife Jessie Chisholm a dau. b.24 ult. bap.at Manse 3 Jul.1863

McDONALD — Ann : Ronald McDonald,railway lab.,Cairnrobin and wife Isabella Murray a dau. b.5 ult. bap.16 Jul.1850

McDONALD Donald : John McDonald and wife Caroline Smith a son b.22 ult. bap.17 Sep.1845
McDONALD Duncan : Jo.McDonald, Synod's Lands and wife Margt.Colvin a son b.20 Jan. bap.28 Jan.1843
McDONALD Jane : Robert McDonald and wife Isabel Reid a dau. b.28 ult. bap.4 Feb.1851
McDONALD John : Jo.McDonald, Dyce and Mary Taylor,Afforthies an ill.son b.5 Jul. bap.20 Aug.1859
McINTOSH James : Jas.McIntosh, Hill of Portlethen and wife Ann Masson a son b.28 ult. dau.b.2 Mar.1863
McINTOSH Margaret : Angus McIntosh, Aberdeen and Isobel Blair, Cairnrobin an ill. dau. b.20 Sep. bap.3 Nov.1860
McINTYRE John : Ill.son of Jane McDonald,Auchlee and Wm.McIntyre,f.s.,b.20 Jul.at Auchlee,Portlethen bap.26 Sep.1869
McKAY Ann : John McKay, Hill of Findon and wife Elspet Taylor a dau.b.22 ult. bap.6 Apr.1844
McKAY Catherine : John McKay and wife Elspet Taylor a dau.b.5 ult. bap.14 Feb.1848
McKAY Elspet Ann : Mary McKay, Moss-side of Findon an ill. dau.b.27 Aug. bap.9 Dec.1867 at the Manse
McKAY James : Geo.McKay.lab.,Hill of Findon and wife Margt.Mitchell a son b.5 Jun. bap.23 Jul.1853
McKAY Marjory : John McKay s.f. Findon and wife Jane Duncan a dau. b.3 ult. bap.24 Sep.1868
McKAY Mary : Bap.a dau.to John McKay and Elspet Taylor, Hill of Findon b.21 Jul. bap.25 Jul.1841
MacKAY Peter : George MacKay and wife Margt. Mitchell, Synod's Lands a son b.29 Jul. bap.3 Sep.1851
McKAY William Harris : John McKay and wife Jane Duncan, Braeside of Findon a son b.8 ult. bap 27 May 1866
McKENZIE Alexander : Bap.a son to John McKenzie and Elspet Kane in East-town of Findon b.11 Aug. bap.29 Aug.1842
McKENZIE Ann Davidson Wright : Alr.McKenzie, soldier, Aberdeen and Helen Wright, Hillside an ill.dau.b.22 Apr. bap.30 Jul.1856
McKENZIE Elizabeth : Geo.McKenzie, Barclayhill and wife Christian Reid a dau.b.13 Jun.bap.12 Aug.1858
McKENZIE Hector : Duncan McKenzie,railway lab. /plate layer and wife Eliz.Nicol a son b.16 Sep.1849 at (Auchterderan) bap.2 Mar.1850
McKENZIE James : Jo.McKenzie,Findon and Ann Milne, Fintray an ill.son b.24 Jul.1859 bap.28 Feb.1863
McKENZIE William Henderson : Bap.an ill.son of Kenneth McKenzie and Margaret Reid in Balquhain, 15 Feb.1841 b.26 Nov.1840
MacKILLIGAN Robert : Bap.a son to Robert MacKilligan and Elspet Traill in the parish of Nigg 18 Dec.1841
McLAREN Helen : Margt.McLaren, Hill of Portlethen a dau. b.16 Dec. ult. bap.7 Apr.1860
McROBBIE John : Watson McRobbie, Nigg and Catherine Stewart in Drumforlay an ill.son b.28 Apr. bap.5 Jun.1848
McROBBIE Margaret Chisholm : Jas.McRobbie and wife Jessie Chisholm a dau.b.14 ult. bap.11 Jun.1867
McWILLIAM John : Daniel McWilliam, Irishman and Margt.Leiper, Portlethen an ill.son b.28 ult. bap.13 Jul.1848

MAIN	Agnes : John Main w.f.Portlethen and wife Margt.Craig a dau.b.4 Mar.bap.15 Apr.1843
MAIN	Agnes : Geo.Main w.f.15 Portlethen and wife Jane Wood a dau.b.21 ult.bap.6 Jul.1850
MAIN	Agnes : Jo.Main w.f.and Lilly Leiper,23 Downies a dau.b.20 Jul.bap.9 Aug.1851
MAIN	Agnes : Andrew Main w.f.19 Downies and wife Agnes Leiper a dau.b.27 Sep.bap.19 Oct.1852(Jo.Main sponsor)
MAIN	Agnes & William : Robert Main w.f.34 Downies and wife Agnes Leiper twins male & female b.and bap.29 Jan.1866
MAIN	Alexander : Wm.Main w.f.16 Downies and Janat Main a son b.18 Dec.1841 bap.3 Jan.1842
MAIN	Alexander : Geo.Main w.f.Portlethen and wife Jane Wood a son b.23 ult.bap.28 Sep.1844
MAIN	Alexander : Robert Main w.f.11 Downies and wife Jane Main a son b.23 ult.bap.5 Jul.1845
MAIN	Alexander : John Main w.f.3 Downies and wife Lilly Leiper a son b. 4 ult.bap.3 Mar.1849
MAIN	Alexander : John Main w.f.Portlethen and wife Margt.Craig a son b.2 Apr.bap.19 May 1849
MAIN	Alexander : Wm.Main w.f.15 Downies and wife Margt.Leiper a son b.2 Mar.bap.10 Apr.1852
MAIN	Alexander : Geo.Main w.f.12 Downies and wife Helen Mitchell a son b.14 ult.bap.11 Oct.1856
MAIN	Alexander : Alex.Main w.f.and Is.Leiper 7 Downies an ill.son b.24 ult.bap.2 Sep.1865
MAIN	Alexander : Geo.Main w.f.30 Downies and wife Ann Main a son b.29 Apr.bap.3 May 1866
MAIN	Alexander : Wm.Main w.f.25 Downies and wife Eliz.Leiper a son b.17 bap.22 Jun.1867
MAIN	Alexander Leiper : John Main w.f.and Ann Leiper his wife 11 Portlethen a son b.4 inst.bap.5 Apr.1868 at Manse
MAIN	Andrew : Geo.Main w.f.Downies and wife Helen Mitchell a son b.20 Aug.bap.16 Sep.1843
MAIN	Andrew : Andrew Main w.f.31 Downies and wife Agnes Leiper a son b.27 ult.bap.14 Jan.1857
MAIN	Ann : Bap.a dau.to James Main and Betty Leiper w.f.in Downies 6 Sep.1840
MAIN	Ann : Robert Main w.f.Portlethen and wife Janat Main a dau.b.10 ult.bap.31 Dec.1843
MAIN	Ann : Geo.Main w.f.58 Portlethen and wife Jane Leiper 7 Downies an ill.dau.b.2 Apr.bap.17 May 1851
MAIN	Ann : Geo.Main w.f.13 Portlethen and wife Helen Main a dau.b.5 Jul.bap.7 Aug.1852
MAIN	Ann : John Main w.f.11 Portlethen and wife Ann Main a dau.b.22 Jan.bap.23 Feb.1856
MAIN	Ann : Robt.Main w.f.16 Downies and Agnes Leiper an ill.dau.b.26 Apr.bap.11 Jul.1856—Grandfather sponsor
MAIN	Ann : Geo.Main w.f.13 Portlethen and wife Jane Main a dau.b.11 ult.bap.28 Nov.1856
MAIN	Ann : Wm.Main w.f.24 Portlethen and wife Jane Allan a dau.b.25 ult.bap.6 Dec.1856
MAIN	Ann : Robt.Main w.f.Portlethen and wife Jane Craig a dau.b.19 ult.bap.20 Sep.1866
MAIN	Anna : Geo.and Ann Main w.f.28 Downies a dau.b.15 Sep.bap.23 Oct.1852
MAIN	Betty : Bap.a dau.to Alex.Main and Eliz.Anderson,Townhead of Portlethen 27 Sep.1840
MAIN	Betty : Robt.Main w.f.19 Downies and Elspet Leiper,there an ill.dau.b.14 bap.23 Oct.1843
MAIN	Cathrine : Widow John Main 15 Portlethen a dau.b.13 Jun.bap.21 Jul.1855
MAIN	Eliz. : Jas.Main w.f.Downies and wife Eliz.Leiper a dau.b.23 ult.bap.5 May 1849
MAIN	Eliz. : Robt.Main w.f.and wife Janat Main in Portlethen a dau.b.20 ult.bap.9 Jun.1849
MAIN	Eliz. : Wm.Main w.f.58 Portlethen and Margt.Craig there an ill.dau.b.30 Mar.bap.29 Apr.1854

MAIN	Eliz.& William : Jo.Main w.f.23 Downies and wife Lilly Main twins b.1 ult.bap.3 Jun.1863 in the Manse
MAIN	Eliz.. : Joseph Main w.f.18 Stranathra and wife Ann Leiper a dau.b.26 Feb.bap.17 Mar.1866
MAIN	Elspet : Bap.a dau.to Jas.Main w.f.and wife Eliz.Leiper in Downies b.27 Aug.bap.3 Sep.1842
MAIN	Elspet : Robt.Main w.f.Downies and wife Elspet Leiper a dau.b.27 ult bap.1 Dec.1849
MAIN	Elspet : Robt.Main w.f.59 Portlethen and wife Janat Main a dau.b.30 Sep.bap.11 Oct.1851
MAIN	Elspet : Andrew Main w.f.and wife Agnes Leiper 29 Downies a dau.b.1 Aug.bap.23 Sep.1854
MAIN	Geo. : Bap.a son to Geo.Main w.f.12 Downies and Helen Mitchell b.26 Jul.bap.31 Jul.1841
	Grandfather Geo.Main.sponsor-child's father at Fraserburgh at herring fishing
MAIN	Geo. : John Main w.f.23 Downies and wife Lilly Leiper a son b.4 ult.bap.17 Nov.1846
MAIN	Geo. : Jas.Main w.f.20 Downies and wife Eliz.Leiper a son b.9 ult.bap.29 May 1847
MAIN	Geo. : Jo.Main w.f.Portlethen and wife Ann Wood a son b.and bap.19 Apr.1849
MAIN	Geo. : Robt.Main and Janat Main 59 Portlethen a son b.27 ult.bap.8 Apr.1854
MAIN	Geo. : Geo.Main and Helen Main w.f.13 Portlethen a son b.27 ult.bap.8 Apr.1854
MAIN	Geo. : Andrew Main and Ann Leiper,Downies a son b.16 ult.bap.11 Jun.1859
MAIN	Geo. : Robt.Main w.f.51 Portlethen and wife Jane Craig a son b.16 bap.20 Aug.1864
MAIN	Geo. : Jas.Main w.f.Downies and wife Eliza Main a son b.26 ult.bap.27 Aug.1864
MAIN	Helen : Bap.an ill.dau.to Robt.Main w.f.Portlethen and Janat Main b.19 Dec.bap.22 Dec.1841
MAIN	Helen : Geo.Main w.f.30 Downies and wife Ann Main a dau.b.7 ult.bap.24 Nov.1860
MAIN	Helen : Andrew Main w.f.Downies and wife Agnes Leiper a dau.b.4 ult.bap.31 Aug.1862
MAIN	Isabella : Geo.Main w.f.30 Downies and wife Ann Main a dau.b.22 Feb.bap.5 Mar.1864
MAIN	Isabella : John Main w.f.25 Downies and wife Lilly Main a dau.b.14 ult.bap.6 Jul.1866
MAIN	Isobel : Robt.Main w.f.and wife Margt.Craig a dau.b.in Stonehaven bap.by Rev.Silver,Dunnottar 4 Feb.1845
MAIN	Isobel : Wm.Main 15 Downies and wife Margt.Leiper a dau.b.10 ult.bap.10 Feb.1849
MAIN	Jas. : Jas.Main w.f.14 Downies and wife Lilly Craig a son b.30 ult.bap.4 May 1844
MAIN	Jas. : Jas.Main w.f.20 Downies and wife Eliz.Leiper a son b.20 bap.28 Sep.1844
MAIN	Jas. : Geo.Main w.f.12 Downies and wife Helen Mitchell a son b.24 ult.bap.13 Nov.1847
MAIN	Jas. : Robt.Main w.f.51 Portlethen and wife Jane Craig a son b.16 Nov.bap.18 Dec.1851
MAIN	Jas. : Jo.Main w.f.11 Portlethen and wife Ann Wood a son b.11 Feb.bap.18 Mar.1854
MAIN	Jas. : Robt.Main w.f.Downies and wife Elspet Leiper a son b.2 May bap.16 Jun.1855
MAIN	Jas. : Jo.Main w.f.49 Portlethen and wife Margt.Craig a son b.4 Aug.bap.15 Sep.1855
MAIN	Jas. : Charles Main.Manse of Nigg and Eliza.Robbie,Redmyre an ill.son b.24 Aug.1857 bap.29 May 1858
MAIN	Jas. : John Main w.f.Downies and wife Lilly Main a son b.18 ult.bap.15 Sep.1860
MAIN	Janat : John Main w.f.and Margt.Craig in Portlethen a dau.b.9 bap.13 Mar.1841
MAIN	Janat : Jas.Main w.f.Downies and Lilly Craig a dau.b.10 Nov.bap.13 Nov.1841

MAIN	Janat :	Geo.Main w.f.13 Portlethen and wife Helen Main a dau.b.8 ult.bap.23 Feb.1850
MAIN	Janat :	Robt.Main w.f.59 Portlethen and wife Janat Main a dau.b.1 ult.bap.12 Jan.1861
MAIN	Janat :	Robt.Main w.f.41 Portlethen and wife Jane Craig a dau.b.29 ult.bap.31 May 1862
MAIN	Janat :	Wm.Main w.f. and Jane Wood,Downies an ill.dau.b.17 Nov.bap.at the Manse 18 Dec.1867
MAIN	Janet :	Wm.Main w.f.34 Downies and wife Isabella Wood a dau.b.12 Nov.bap.at the Manse 24 Nov.1867
MAIN	Jane :	Bap.a dau.to Geo.Main w.f.Portlethen and Jane Wood b.24 Oct.bap.30 Oct.1841
MAIN	Jane :	Wm.Main w.f.13 Downies and wife Ann Main a dau.b.31 Jan.bap.2 Feb.1843
MAIN	Jane :	Wm.Main w.f.Portlethen and wife Eliz.Masson a dau.b.12 ult.bap.15 Sep.1844
MAIN	Jane :	Wm.Main w.f.Portlethen and wife Jane Young a dau.b.9 bap.25 Dec.1844
MAIN	Jane :	Geo.Main w.f.Portlethen and wife Helen Main a dau.b.1 May bap.17 May 1845
MAIN	Jane :	Geo.Main w.f.12 Downies and wife Helen Mitchell a dau.b.26 ult.bap.26 Jan.1850
MAIN	Jane :	Geo.Main 16 Downies and Ann Main,Portlethen an ill.dau.b.24 Sep.bap.26 Oct.1850
MAIN	Jane :	Robt.Main and Jane Craig 51 Portlethen a dau.b.30 Mar.bap.4 Apr.1854
MAIN	Jane :	Jo.Main w.f.Portlethen No.11 and wife Ann Wood a dau.b.18 ult.bap.17 Apr.1861
MAIN	Jane :	Dau.of Wm.Main w.f.and Eliz.Leiper his wife b.at 25 Downies 20 Oct.bap.26 Oct.1869
MAIN	Jane :	Dau.of Andrew Main w.f. and Agnes Leiper his wife b.at 31 Downies 30 Oct. bap.11 Nov.1869
MAIN	Jane Low :	Jo.Main w.f. 23 Downies and wife Lilly Main a dau. b.18 ult. bap.at the Manse 4 Oct 1868
MAIN	Jessie :	Geo.and Ann Main w.f. Downies a dau. b.10 May bap.17 Jun.1854
MAIN	Jessie :	Jas.Main w.f. Downies and wife Eliza.Leiper a dau.b. 3 ult. bap.17 Jul.1858
MAIN	Jessy :	Bap.a dau. to Wm. Main w.f. and Ann Main in Downies 21 Feb.1841
MAIN	John :	John Main w.f. and Rachel Wood in Portlethen an ill.son b.6 bap.13 Mar.1841
MAIN	John :	Jo.Main w.f. Portlethen and wife Margt.Wood a son b.1 ult.bap.13 Apr.1844
MAIN	John :	Wm.Main w.f. Downies and wife Jane Main a son b.3 bap.9 Jul.1846
MAIN	John :	Wm.Main w.f.and wife Jane Young in Portlethen a son b.26 ult. bap.9 Jan.1847
MAIN	John :	Jas.Main w.f. and wife Lilly Craig 14 Downies a son b.19 ult. bap.18 Nov.1848
MAIN	John :	John Main w.f. Portlethen and wife Jane Main a son b.28 ult. bap.13 Apr.1850 (of 29 Portlethen)
MAIN	John :	Jas.Main w.f.20 Downies and wife Elspet Leiper a son b.20 Oct. bap.1 Nov.1851
MAIN	John :	John Main w.f. Downies and wife Lilly Main a son b.3 Dec.1858 bap.22 Jan.1859
MAIN	John :	Robt.Main w.f. 51 Portlethen and wife Jane Craig a son b.14 ult. bap.16 Mar.1860
MAIN	John :	Wm.Main w.f. Downies and Is.Wood ,there, an ill.son b.26 ult. bap.6 Oct.1860
MAIN	John :	Mary Main, Hillhead of Portlethen a son b.in Maryculter 8 Jul.last bap.15 Dec.1860
MAIN	Joseph :	Wm.Main w.f. Portlethen and wife Jane Young a son b.21 ult.bap.19 Apr.1849
MAIN	Joseph :	Jo.Main and wife Margt.Craig w.f. 49 Portlethen a son b.16 ult. bap.5 Apr.1851
MAIN	Joseph :	Joseph Main and wife Ann Leiper w.f. 18 Stranathra a son b.7 ult.bap.10 Sep.1864

MAIN	Lilly :	Js.Main w.f. 14 Downies and wife Lilly Main a dau. b.18 ult. bap.24 Oct.1846
MAIN	Lilly :	Jo.Main and wife Lilly Leiper 10 Downies a.dau. b.12 Aug, bap.23 Sep.1854
MAIN	Margt. :	Wm.Main w.f. 15 Downies and wife Margt.Leiper a dau. b.27 Dec. bap.28 Dec.1842
MAIN	Margt. :	Wm.Main w.f. Portlethen and wife Jane Young a dau. b.22 Jan. bap.11 Feb.1842
MAIN	Margt. :	Wm.Main w.f. 13 Downies and wife Ann Main a dau. b.23 bap.24 Apr.1845
MAIN	Margt. :	R.Main w.f. Portlethen and wife Janat Main a dau. b.9 ult. bap.25 Apr.1846
MAIN	Margt. :	Wm.Main w.f. 15 Downies and wife Margt.Leiper a dau.b.17 bap.19 Oct.1846
MAIN	Margt. :	John Main w.f. Portlethen and wife Margt.Wood a dau. b.9 ult. bap.13 Mar.1848
MAIN	Margt. :	Jas Main and wife Lilly Craig w.f. 14 Downies a dau. b.2 ult. bap.20 Mar.1851
MAIN	Margt. :	Jo.Main w.f. 29 Portlethen and wife Jane Main a dau. b.6 Jul. bap.7 Aug.1852
MAIN	Margt. :	Jo.Main w.f. 49 Portlethen and wife Margt.Craig a dau.b.6 Jun. bap.23 Jul.1853
MAIN	Margt. :	Geo.Main w.f. 13 Portlethen and wife Helen Main a dau. b.12 ult. bap.1 Oct.1859
MAIN	Margt. :	Geo.Main w.f. 30 Downies and wife Ann Main a dau.b.and bap.7 Mar.1863
MAIN	Margt. :	John Main w.f. 11 Portlethen and wife Ann Leiper a dau. b.and bap. 13 Oct.1866
MAIN	Margt. :	Andrew Main w.f. 31 Downies and wife Agnes Leiper a dau. b.28 ult. bap.8 Jul.1867
MAIN	Mary :	Isabella Main 15 Downies an ill.dau. b.15 Nov. bap.28 Dec.1868 at Downies
MAIN	Mary :	Bap.a dau.to John Main and Margt.Wood w.f. in Portlethen b.22 May bap.29 May 1841
MAIN	Mary :	Geo.Main w.f. 12 Downies and wife Helen Mitchell a dau. b.14 Aug. bap.13 Sep.1854
MAIN	Mary :	Helen Main, Hill of Portlethen an ill.dau. b.at Stonehaven 21 Mar.1857 bap.1 Apr.1860
MAIN	Robert :	Robert Main w.f. Downies and wife Jane Main a son b.10 Sep. bap.15 Sep.1842
MAIN	Robert :	Geo.Main w.f. Portlethen and wife Jane Wood a son b.18 ult. bap.25 Jul.1846
MAIN	Robt. :	Geo.Main w.f. and wife Helen Main, Portlethen a son b.17 ult. bap.6 Nov.1847
MAIN	Robt. :	Geo.Main w.f. 12 Downies and wife Helen Mitchell a son b.25 Mar. bap.10 Apr.1852
MAIN	Robt. :	Robt.Main w.f. 25 Downies and wife Elspet Leiper a son b.28 Sep. bap.16 Oct.1852
MAIN	Robt. :	Jas.Main w.f. and wife Eliz.Leiper, 20 Downies a son b.26 May bap.1 Jun.1855
MAIN	Robt. :	Robt.Main w.f. 45 Portlethen and wife Janat Main a son b.10 Feb. bap.23 Mar.1856
MAIN	Robt. :	Robt.Main w.f. 51 Portlethen and wife Jane Craig a son b.4 ult. bap.7 Oct.1856
MAIN	Robt. :	Robt.Main w.f. Downies and wife Agnes Leiper a son b.1.ult. bap.15 Sep.1860
MAIN	Robt. :	Wm.Main w.f. Downies and wife Eliza Main a son b.2 ult. bap.20 Sep.1862
MAIN	Robt. :	Robt.Main w.f. 30½ Portlethen and Jane Robertson, there, an ill.son b.19 May ult. bap.7 Jun.1868 at the Manse
MAIN	Robt. :	Wm.Main w.f. 28 Downies and Eliz.Main an ill.son b.29 Oct.bap.6 Dec.1868 at the Manse
MAIN	Robertson :	Robt.Main w.f. Downies and Elspet Leiper in Aberdeen a son b.11 ult. bap.4 Jun.1846
MAIN	Susan :	Wm.Main w.f. 63 Portlethen and wife Jane Young a dau. b.31 May bap.12 Jul.1851

MAIN   Susan : Wm.Main w.f. Portlethen and Eliz.Masson a dau. b.29 Dec.1841 bap.10 Jan.1842
MAIN   William : Geo.Main w.f. 15 Portlethen and wife Jane Wood a son b.25 ult. bap.8 Oct.1843
MAIN   William : Wm.Main w.f. 16 Downies and wife Jane Main a son b.3 bap.6 Jun.1844
MAIN   William : Geo.Main w.f.12 Downies and wife Helen Mitchell a son b.10 bap.12 Jul.1845
MAIN   William : John Main w.f.Portlethen and wife Margt.Wood a son b.22 Aug.bap.27 Sep.1846
MAIN   William : Jo.Main w.f.Portlethen and wife Margt.Craig a son b.24 ult.bap.31 Jul.1847
MAIN   William : Geo.Main w.f.Portlethen and wife Jane Wood a son b.17 ult.bap.26 Aug.1848
MAIN   William : Wm.Main w.f.Downies and wife Ann Main a son b.27 ult.bap.23 Dec.1848
MAIN   William : Robert Main w.f.49 Portlethen and wife Margaret Craig a son b.14 ult.bap.19 Jan.1850
MAIN   William : Geo.Main w.f.30 Downies and wife Ann Main a son b.11 ult.bap.29 Nov.1856
MAIN   William : R.Main w.f.25 Downies and wife Elspet Leiper a son b.13 ult.bap.27 Feb.1858
MAIN   William : Helen Main,Hill of Portlethen an ill.son b.8 Jan.bap.1 Apr.1860
MAIN   William : see Eliz.and William-twins
MAIN   William : Wm.Main w.f.34 Downies and wife Is.Wood a son b.27 ult.bap.at the Manse 29 Jun.1863
MAIN   William : Wm.Main w.f.25 Downies and wife Eliz.Leiper a son b.and bap.24 Jan.1865
MAIN   William : see Agnes and William-twins
MAIN   William : Jo.Main w.f.57 Downies and wife Eliza Main a son b.25 ult.bap.4 Jan.1867
MAIN   William : Alex.Main w.f.30 Downies and wife Is.Leiper a son b.23 ult.bap.28 Nov.1867
MAITLAND Adam Silver : Wm.Maitland and wife Rebecca Silver in Hill of Findon a son b.23 Jun.bap.30 Jul.1850
MAITLAND Charles Stewart : Wm.Maitland,N.Findon and wife Rebecca Silver a son b.29 Apr.bap.19 Jun.1854-mother sponsor
MAITLAND Elizabeth Henry : Wm.Maitland,Garioch's Lands and Rebecca Silver a dau.b.14 Dec.1841 bap.3 Jan.1842
MAITLAND Elspet : Wm.Maitland,N.Findon and wife Rebecca Silver a dau.b.31 ult.bap.14 Sep.1844
MAITLAND Joseph : Wm.Maitland,N.Findon and wife Rebecca Silver a son b.13 Feb.bap.12 Apr.1852-mother sponsor
MAITLAND Margaret Trail : Wm.Maitland,N.Findon and wife Rebecca Silver a dau.b.16 Jun.bap.7 Aug.1848
MAITLAND Rebecca : Wm.Maitland N.Findon and wife Rebecca Silver a dau.b.19 ult.bap.6 Jul.1846
MAITLAND Wm. : Wm.Maitland and wife Rebecca Silver,Hill of Findon a son b.23 Mar.bap.10 Apr.1843
MAITLAND Wm. : Wm.Maitland and wife Eliza.Byres,Mains of Portlethen a son b.27 ult.bap.28 Aug.1862-G/father sponsor
MANN   Wm. : Wm.Mann,station keeper,Portlethen and wife Euphm.Thom a son b.13 Oct.bap.1 Nov.1854
MARTIN   Alex. : John Martin,stonedresser,Cove,Nigg and wife Mary Baird Adams a son bap.at the Manse 26 Dec.1868
MASSON   Agnes : Jas.Masson,Hill of Portlethen and wife Helen Robb a dau.b.12 ult.bap.20 Apr.1844
MASSON   Alex.Fraser : Geo.Masson and Eliza Fraser.Hill of Portlethen an ill.son b.11 Oct.ult.bap.6 Nov.1859
MASSON   Ann : Al.Masson,Doghillock and Elspet Milne,Kirkstyle an ill.dau.b.11 Nov.ult.bap.4 Dec.1864
MASSON   Ann & Margt.(twins) : Daus.of Alex.Masson,farmer and wife Margt.Tough b.and bap.6 Oct.1869 at Backhill

MASSON Christian : John Masson,Broadgreens and Mary Masson,Hill of Portlethen an ill.dau.b.25 Jun.bap.26 Jul.1852
(Christian Mennie sponsor)

MASSON David : Jas.Masson and wife Jane Allan,Backhill of Portlethen a son b.22 ult.bap.7 Aug.1866
MASSON Eliz. : Jas.Masson,Backhill of Portlethen and wife Helen Robb a dau.b.30 ult.bap.21 Aug.1847
MASSON Eliz. : Robt.Masson and wife Eliz.Masson,Doghillock a dau.b.23 Apr.bap.10 May 1856
MASSON Eliz.& Helen : Al.Masson and wife Margt.Tough,Backhill of Portlethen twin daus.b.22 ult.bap.23 Jun.1866
MASSON Eliz.Burnett : Helen Masson,Langhillock an ill.dau.b.9 Apr.ult.bap.at the Manse 22 May 1863
MASSON Eliz.Lyell : Geo.Masson and wife Mary Aberdein,Langhillock a dau.b.16 ult.bap.3 Sep.1865
MASSON Eliz.Officer : Jas.Masson and wife Jane Allan,Backhill of Portlethen a dau.b.3 Dec.ult.bap.4 Jan.1863
MASSON Elspet : Jas.Masson,Hill of Portlethen and Jane Allan,Portlethen Village an ill.dau.b.2 Jan.bap.24 Feb.1855
MASSON Geo. : Geo.Masson,Wellheads and wife Susan Eddie a son b.26 ult.bap.22 May 1859
MASSON Geo. : Geo.Masson,crofter,Roadside near Glashfarquhar and wife Mary Aberdein a son b.8 Jan.bap.22 Mar.1869
MASSON Geo.Fowler : Mary Masson an ill.son b.at 173 W.North St.Abdn.2 May 1866 bap.at Hill of Portlethen,
13 Sep.1866 (uncle sponsor)

MASSON Helen : Elspet Masson,Langhillock a dau.b.6 Mar.bap.30 Apr.1856(woman's father sponsor)
MASSON Helen : Jas.Masson,Backhill of Portlethen and wife Jane Allan a dau.b.31 ult.bap.1 Jun.1865

MASSON Helen : see Eliz. and Helen, twins
MASSON Helen : William, born the next day
MASSON Jas. : Robt.Masson and wife Isobel Wood, Moss-side, a son b.1 ult. bap.2 Jan.1849
MASSON Jas. : Jas.Masson and wife Helen Robb, Hill of Portlethen a son b.25 Jun. bap.19 Jul.1851
MASSON Jas. : Jas.Masson presently residing at Carmelite St.Abdn.and wife Jane Allan a son b.17 ult.bap.10 Aug.1858
MASSON Jas. : Geo.Masson Hill of Portlethen and wife Susan Eddie a son b.24 Dec.ult. bap.8 Feb.1866
MASSON Jas. : Helen Masson, Langhillock an ill.son b.23 Feb.ult. bap.28 Apr.1866 Her father sponsor,reputed father
R.Dawson, Alford

MASSON Jane : Jas.Masson, Backhill of Portlethen and wife Ann Allan a dau.b.27 ult. bap. at the Manse 13 Oct.1867
MASSON Jane : Al.Masson, Backhill of Portlethen and wife Margt.Tough a dau.b.10 Nov.ult. bap.at Manse 21 Dec.1867
MASSON Jane Lawson : Geo.Masson Moss-side and wife Susan Eddie dau. b.16 Dec. bap.31 Dec.1867
MASSON John : Bap.a son to Jas.Masson and Helen Robb, Backhill of Portlethen b.1 Jun. bap.6 Jun.1841
MASSON John : Wm. Masson, Cairnwell and wife Ann Leiper a son b.5 Apr. bap.5 May 1842
MASSON Margt. : Mary Masson, Wallhead of Portlethen an ill.dau.b.13 Nov.1863 bap.21 Feb.1864
MASSON Margt. : Geo.Masson and wife Mary Aberdein, Lochside a dau. b.10 Dec. last, bap.at the Manse 20 Jan.1868
MASSON Margt. : see Ann and Margt. twins
MASSON Mary Helen Anna : Geo.Masson and wife Mary Aberdein, Longhillock a dau. b.31 Aug. bap.17 Oct.1863
MASSON Susan : Geo.Masson,Hill of Portlethen and wife Susan Eddie a dau.b.23 ult. bap.6 Apr.1861

MASSON	William : Geo.Masson, Moss-side and wife Susan Eddie a son b.4 ult. bap.at the Manse 19 Jul.1863
MASSON	William : Jas.Masson and wife Jane Allan, Backhill of Portlethen a son b.and bap.1 Jun.1865 (Eleven hours after the birth of twin, Helen, born the previous day)
MASSON	William Smith : Agnes Masson, Langhillock a son b.5 Apr. bap.at the Manse 26 Jul.1868
MATHER	Helen : Jo.Mather and wife Jane Nicol,Hillside of Findon a dau. b.26 Oct. bap.7 Nov.1842
MAVER	George : Robt.Maver, Newpark and wife Agnes Wattie a son b.21 Nov. bap.25 Dec.1852
MAVOR	Jane : Robert Mavor, Newpark and wife Agnes Wattie, Newpark a dau. b.22 ult. bap 14 Apr.1851
MAVOR	Robert : Bap.a son to Robert Mavor and Agnes Wattie in Newpark, b.3 May bap.22 May 1841
MAVOR	Robert Grubb : Robt.Mavor Jnr. and Jane Grubb, Newpark an ill.son b.13 Oct. bap.5 Nov.1860
MAVOR	William : R.Mavor Esq. Newpark and wife Agnes Wattie a son bap.3 Nov.1849
MENNIE	Christian : Wm.Mennie s.f. Downies and wife Ann Christie a dau. b.1 Jun. bap.14 Jul.1855
MENNIE	Isobel : Wm.Mennie and wife Ann Christie in Downies a dau.b.20 ult. bap.27 Dec.1847
MENNIE	James Hutcheon : James Mennie and wife Ann Christie, Downies a son b.28 Sep. bap.31 Oct.1857
MENNIE	John : Wm.Mennie and wife Ann Christie a son b.4 ult. bap.15 Feb.1851
MENNIE	John Leiper : Wm.Mennie and Ann Christie in Downies a son b.22 Dec.1852 bap.6 Feb.1853
MIDDLETON	Alexander : Robt.Middleton, Bourtreybush and wife Mary Adam a son b.5 Jul. bap.31 Oct.1864
MIDDLETON	Alexander Masson : Geo.Middleton, Lunatic Asylum, Aberdeen and wife Ann Masson a son b.at Backhill of Portlethen 9 Apr. bap.15 May 1854
MIDDLETON	George : Al.Middleton, Birse and Margt.Yule, Haremoss an ill.son b.6 ult. bap.29 Jan.1860
MIDDLETON	Isabella : Ann Midleton, Sauchenshaw an ill.dau. b.13 Aug.1862 and bap.at Haremoss 5 Mar.1864 (father – Jas.McDonald)
MIDDLETON	Jane : Wm.Middleton, railway timekeeper. Perth and wife Jane Massie a dau.b.at Perth 27 May 1866 bap.at Carr's Croft 1 Jun.1866
MILNE	Child : Bap.in Nigg 21 Mar.1843
MILNE	Agnes : John Milne and Elspet Craig, Skettraw Shore.Fetteresso a dau. b.16 Aug. bap.9 Sep.1841
MILNE	Agnes : Ill.dau.of Elsie Milne, crofter's dau.,Kirk Croft Portlethen, b.9 Jul. bap.12 Sep.1869
MILNE	Alexander : Alex.Milne,Roadside of Findon and wife Mary Garden a son b.11 bap.23 Dec.1844
MILNE	Alexander : P.Milne near Bourtreybush and wife Eliz.Davidson a son b.18 ult.bap.9 Nov.1850
MILNE	Ann : Al.Milne,parish of Fordoun and Jane Leiper in Findon an ill.dau.b.15 Nov.1842 bap.21 Jan.1843
MILNE	Ann : Wm.Milne and wife Eliz.Walker in Woodside of Bourtreybush a dau.b.24 Jul.bap.8 Aug.1842
MILNE	Ann : John Milne,Hill of Portlethen and wife Elspet Craig a dau.b.31--bap.30 Aug.1846 before Congregation
MILNE	Ann Elisa : Geo.Milne,Hillside and wife Mary Walker a dau.b.28 Sep.bap.3 Dec.1865
MILNE	David : George Milne,Barclayhill and wife Mary Glennie a son b.6 ult.bap.27 Jun.1860
MILNE	Elspet : Al.Yuil,Nigg and Isabella Milne,Moss-side,Portlethen an ill.dau.b.16 Jan.bap.5 Mar.1865

MILNE   George : see James and George - twins
MILNE   George : James Milne and Margt.Shirres,Fetteresso an ill.son b.11 Dec.1854 bap.13 Jan.1855
MILNE   Helen : Peter Milne near Berryhill and wife ---- Davidson a dau.b.5 ult.bap.3 Feb.1858
MILNE   Isobel : John Milne and Elspet Craig in Hill of Portlethen a dau.b.24 Sep.bap.8 Dec.1844
MILNE   James & George : Bap.twin sons to James Milne and Ann Howie,Cammochmore,Fetteresso b.22 Aug.bap.25 Aug.1841
MILNE   James : Jas.Milne and Helen Leiper in Findon an ill.son bap.11 Jan.1847-Grandfather sponsor
MILNE   James : Al.Milne,Hillside and wife Mary Gairn a son b.23 ult.bap.2 Jun.1847
MILNE   James : George Milne,Findon and wife Mary Glennie a son b.15 ult.bap.7 Sep.1862

MILNE or
KNOX

MILNE   James : see Knox or Milne James
MILNE   James : Thos.Milne and Elspet Wood.Findon an ill.son b.at 39 Findon.11 ult.bap.13 Feb.1866-G/father sponsor
MILNE   Jane : Alex.Milne,Hill of Banchory and Helen Kane,Badentoy an ill.dau.b.6 Dec.1841 bap.22 Jan.1842
MILNE   Jane : Al.Milne and Mary Garden his wife at Hillside a dau.b.28 Oct.bap.30 Nov.1849
MILNE   Jane : Wm.Milne and wife Margt.McPherson,Burnside had a dau.b.27 Apr.bap.17 May 1856
MILNE   Jess : Wm.Milne and wife Margt.McPherson,Burnside a dau.b.20 ult.bap.12 Apr.1848
MILNE   Jessie Ann : Alex.Milne,Hillside and wife Jane Gairn a dau.b.13 Dec.1851 bap.25 Feb.1852
MILNE   Margaret : Wm.Milne,Burnside and wife Margt.McPherson a dau.b.8 ult.bap.29 Mar.1851
MILNE   Margaret : P.Milne and Eliz.Davidson,Cairngrassie a dau.b.15 Jul.bap.4 Sep.1854
MILNE   Mary : Al.Milne,Hillside and wife Mary Garden a dau.b.1 May bap.22 May 1843
MILNE   Mary Magdylene : Alex.Milne and Elspet Wood,Hill of Portlethen an ill.dau.b.19 Jan.bap.1 Mar.1846
MILNE   Peter : Peter Milne near Bourtreybush and wife Eliz.Davidson a son b.13 Apr.bap.4 May 1852
MILNE   Robert Walker : P.Milne,Hillside and wife Ann Gillespie a son b.29 ult.bap.30 Jan.1845
MILNE   William : Wm.Milne and Margt.McPherson in Burnside of Findon a son b.13 Apr.bap.3 May 1845
MILNE   William Johnston : Mary Magdilene Milne,Moss-side of Portlethen an ill.son b.26 Jul.bap.15 Sep.1867
               (Wm.Johnston sponsor)

MILTON   Jane : John Milton,Hillside and wife Eliz.Anderson a dau.b.18 Oct.1866 bap.23 May 1867
MITCHELL   Jane : Robt.Mitchell;wife Jane Gordon Gibb,Birselawrie,a dau.b.12 Jul.bap.at Hill of Portlethen 21 Sep.1862
MITCHELL   Jane : David Mitchell,P.O.Hillside and wife Helen Melvin a dau.b.16 Apr.bap.at the Manse 28 Jun.1868
MOIR   Mary Copland : David Moir,Nigg and Margt.Copland an ill.,dau.b.28 May bap.3 Sep.1859
MOIR   Robert Ewen : Andrew Moir,Maryculter and Mary Ann Bruce Ewen,Moss-side of Portlethen an ill.son,
               b.30 Oct.1864 bap.29 Jan.1865

MORICE   James Keith : Peter Morice and wife Elspet Chisholm, Cassieport a son b.8 ult. bap.28 Aug.1858
MORICE   Peter : Peter Morice, Synod's Lands and wife Elspet Chisholm a son b.16 ult. bap.20 Sep.1848

MORRICE	Agnes : Peter Morrice and wife Elspet Chisholm,Lower Badentoy (from Greyfriars parish Aberdeen), a dau.b.10 Sep.bap.9 Nov.1855
MORRIS	George : Peter Morris and wife Elspet Chisholm a son b.19 ult. bap.14 Oct.1860
MORRIS	William : Peter Morris, Findon and wife El.Chisholm a son b.3 ult. bap.19 Oct.1850
MORRISON	Eliz.Allan Welsh : Allan Morrison, Echt, and Margt.Welsh, Fiddestown an ill.dau. b.12 Oct. bap.8 Dec.1861
MORRISON	William : John Morrison and Margt.Johnston, Brunthillock a son b.1 ult. bap.19 May 1850
MUGLEN	Margt.Wright : Michal Muglen and Jane Walker,Findon,an ill.dau.b.19 Nov.ult.bap.4 Sep.1854 (Jas.Watt sponsor)
MURRAY	George : Alex.Murray and Isabel Gibbons in Hill of Findon a son b.15 ult.bap.2 Apr.1848 (G.Duncan sponsor)
MURRAY	Jessie Donald : Wm.Murray, Durris and Betty Duncan, Fiddestown an ill.dau.b.13 May bap.25 Jun.1845
MURRAY	William : Alex.Murray and wife Isabella Gibbon a son b.1 ult. bap.29 Dec.1849
MUTCH	George : Wm.Mutch, seaman and wife Jane Masson,residing at Woodside,Printfield and presently at Portlethen a son bap.17 Nov.1846
NICOL	Caroline : John Nicol and wife Caroline Masson near Westside,a dau.b.14 ult. bap.24 Mar.1851
NICOL	David : John Nicol and wife Caroline Masson, Hillhead of Portlethen a son b.8 Feb. bap.12 Apr.1848
NICOL	Elizabeth : Wm.Nicol, Netherward and wife Eliz.Mitchell a dau. b.13 Mar. bap.28 Apr. 1849
NICOL	Elizabeth : Wm.Nicol,Jellybrands and Isobel Craig,Hillhead of Portlethen an ill.dau.b.9 ult.bap.5 Apr.1857
NICOL	Jane : Wm.Nicol jnr.,Rumleygowan and Jane Main,11 Downies an ill.dau.b.4 Jul.bap.27 Sep.1856
NICOL	Jessie : Wm.Nicol,Barclayhill and wife Jessie Joss a dau.b.11 Jul.bap.14 Aug.1850
NICOL	John Falconer : Wm.Nicol,Portlethen and wife Helen Mitchell a son b.28 ult.bap.21 Feb.1846
NICOL	Margaret : Bap.a dau.to Wm.Nicol,shoemaker and Elizabeth Mitchell in Portlethen b.10 bap.31 Jul.1841
NICOL	S.C.B.Law : Wm.Nicol,Netherwadpark and wife Eliz.Mitchell a dau.b.17 Dec.1843 bap.22 Jan.1844
NORRIE	Edward : Edward Norrie,parish of Belhelvie and Margt.Leonard in Cookston an ill.son b.2 May bap.8 Jun.1845
PAPE	James : James Pape,Newmachar parish and Jane Yuile,Findon an ill.son b.17 Aug.bap.26 Sep.1859
PARK	John : Jas.Park,miller,Findon and wife Ellen Walker a son b.at Mill of Udney 10 May bap.30 Jul.1865 here
PATTERSON	---- : Bap.a child to Wm.Patterson,Lands of Ardoe for Dr.Paul 24 Sep.1859
PATTERSON	Alexander : Wm.Patterson,Hill of Turnermiddle and wife Barbara Leith a son b.19 ult.bap.31 Aug.1844
PATTERSON	Alexander : Al.Patterson,Old Bourtreybush and wife Jane Rust a son b.8 ult.bap.2 Jul.1865
PATTERSON	Alexander : Robt.Patterson,Hill of Turnermiddle and wife Jane Petrie a son b.18 ult.bap.at Manse 10 Sep.1867
PATTERSON	Andrew : see William and Andrew-twins
PATTERSON	Andrew & Mary : Wm.Patterson and Mary Mennie in W.Cookston a son and dau.b.24 bap.25 Jun.1842

PATTERSON Cathrine : Robt.Patterson,labourer,Bankhead and wife Jane Dow a dau.b.18 Jan.bap.1 Feb.1869
PATTERSON Geo. : Geo.Patterson and Isobel Leonard in Cookston an ill.son b.16 Apr.bap.7 Jul.1851
PATTERSON Geo. : Wm.Patterson,Hill of Turnermiddle and wife Barbara Leith a son b.13 Dec.1852 bap.1 Jan.1853
PATTERSON Jas. : Jas.Patterson,surfaceman,Cove Road and wife Mary Nairn a son b.8 Jun.bap.12 Jul.1865
PATTERSON Jessie : Bap.a dau.to ---- Patterson,Moss-side of Ardo in Ban.Dev. 14 Mar.1857
PATTERSON Jessie : Jas.Patterson and wife Jessie Kane,Cammochmore a dau.b.2 Mar.bap.2 May 1867
PATTERSON John : Wm.Patterson and wife Barbara Leith in Turnermiddle a son b.2 ult.bap.23 Oct.1850
PATTERSON John : Robt.Patterson,Hillside and wife Jane Petrie a son b.26 ult.bap.28 Jun.1865
PATTERSON John Souter : Al.Patterson,railway porter and wife Jane Rust a son b.18 Aug.bap.29 Sep.1867
PATTERSON Joseph : Wm.Patterson,Hill of Turnermiddle and wife Barbara Leith a son b.11 bap.27 Sep.1846
PATTERSON Margt. : Geo.Patterson and Is.Leonard in W.Cookston an ill.dau.b.9 Jun.bap.9 Aug.1853
PATTERSON Mary : see Andrew and Mary
PATTERSON Mary : Wm.Patterson,Hill of Turnermiddle and wife Barbara Leith a dau.b.20 Jan.bap.27 Feb.1855
PATTERSON Robert(Mayor) : Wm.Patterson and Rebecca Leith,Hill of Turn-the-middle a son b.8 ult.bap.21 Oct.1848
PATTERSON William & Andrew : Bap.two sons to Wm.Patterson and Mary Mennie in W.Cookston b.22 Mar.1841 bap.same day
PATTERSON William : Wm.Patterson,Turnermiddle and wife Barbara Leith a son b.13 bap.20 Aug.1842
PATTERSON William : Jas.Patterson,Cove Road and wife Mary Nairn a son b.1 ult.bap.at Manse 22 Jul.1863
PATTERSON William : Al.Patterson,Hillside and wife Jane Rust a son b.29 ult.bap.21 Aug.1863
PETRIE Ann : David Petrie and wife ---- Anderson,Heathcot a dau.b.7 Jul.bap.29 Aug.1864
PETRIE David : John Petrie,Badentoy and wife Margt.Sinclair a son b.12 Nov.bap.11 Dec.1854
PETRIE Elizabeth & Helen : Jo.Petrie and wife Margt.Sinclair,Badentoy twin daus.b.29 Apr.bap.31 May 1852
PETRIE George : David Petrie and Ann Anderson,Badentoy an ill.son b.2 ult.bap.12 Aug.1860
PETRIE Helen : see Elizabeth and Helen - twins
PETRIE Isabella : John Petrie,Badentoy and wife Margt.Sinclair a dau.b.5 bap.7 Oct.1843
PETRIE James : David Petrie and wife Ann Anderson,Hillhead of Heathcot a son b.11 May bap.19 Jul.1862
PETRIE Jane : Jo.Petrie,Badentoy and wife Margt.Sinclair a dau.b.29 ult.bap.5 Jan.1846
PETRIE Margaret : Bap.a dau.to John Petrie and Margt.Sinclair in Badentoy b.8 bap.11 May 1841
PETRIE Mary Ann : Jo.Petrie and wife Margt.Sinclair a dau.b.13 ult.bap.24 Apr.1848
PETRIE Robert Walker : Widow Petrie,E.Cookston an ill.son b.1 Mar.bap.17 Sep.1860
PETRIE William : John Petrie,Badentoy and wife Margt.Sinclair a son b.11 ult.bap.24 May 1850
PETRIE William : Margaret Petrie,Burnside an ill.son b.17 May last, bap.31 Aug.1861-Grandmother sponsor
PIRIE Elizabeth Alexander : Geo.Pirie,miller,Mill of Findon and Margt.Alexander,there an ill.dau.
b.at Mill of Findon 15 Mar.there 8 Apr.1869

PIRIE : Helen : Wm.Pirie,North Findon and wife Mary Bisset a dau.b.18 ---- bap.17 Oct.1844
PRATT : James : Forbes Pratt,Whitestone of Maryculter and wife Jane Rae a son b.16 Apr.bap.at Whitestone 20 Jun.1867

RAE : Ann : Geo.Rae,Shoanshaw,Fetteresso and wife Is.Middleton a dau.b.-- Dec.1858 bap.24 Jan.1859 there
RAE : Eliz. : Wm.Rae and Is.Blair,Cairnrobin an ill.dau.b.3 Jan.bap.26 Mar.1864
RAE : Elspet Law : Geo.Rae and Isabella Middleton,Sauchenshaw,Cookney a dau.b.2 Oct.bap.16 Nov.1861
RANKIN : Andrew : Robt.Rankin and wife Agnes Douglas,Cookstown a son b.10 Sep.bap.11 Oct.1859
REID : Child : Bap.18 Feb.1843 at Cove,Parish of Nigg
REID : Alex. : Bap.a son to Al.Reid and Margt.Milne in Moss-side b.2 Jul.bap.3 Aug.1841
REID : Andrew : Robt.Reid and wife Is.Ross,Cairngrassie a son b.10 ult.bap.8 Mar.1862
REID : Ann : Geo.Reid.N.Mains of Findon and wife Ann Porter a dau.b.4 ult.bap.12 Oct.1861
REID : Christian Falcona : Al.Reid,Moss-side and wife Margt.Milne a dau.b.24 ult.bap.27 Jan.1844
REID : Elison Jaffrey : Robt.Reid and wife Is.Ross,Backburn,Cammochmore a dau.b.5 ult.bap.27 Jul.1864 there
REID : Eliz. : Jas.Reid, Kincardine O'Neil and Eliz.Low, Hill of Findon an ill.dau. b.20 Jun. bap.18 Aug.1849
REID : Geo. : Geo.Reid, N.Findon and wife Ann Porter a son b.18 ult. bap.8 Jul.1865
REID : Isabella : Robt.Reid and Is.Ross, nr. Bourtreybush a dau.b.3 ult. bap.26 Nov.1859
REID : Jas. : Andrew Reid, wayman, C.R.Coy. and wife Agnes Mitchell a son b.30 Jun. bap.at Newtonhill 26 Jul.1867
REID : Jane : Alex.Reid, Hillside and wife Margt.Milne a dau. b.30 ult. bap.26 Aug.1848
REID : John : Mary Reid, dom.serv. Craighead, an ill.son b.4 Oct.last, bap.at the Manse 19 Jan.1868
REID : John Shepherd Wright : son of Geo.Reid,farmer,North Mains,Findon and wife Ann Porter, b.18 Jun.bap. 24 Jul.1869

REID : Joseph : Geo.Reid, Mains of Findon and wife Jessie Porter a son b.5 ult. bap.28 Feb.1863
REID : Margt. : Al.Reid,Hillside and wife Margt.Milne a dau. b.6 ult. bap.28 Mar.1846
REID : Rachel : Geo.Reid and wife Ann Porter, North Mains of Findon a dau. b.28 Jun. bap.30 Jul.1867
REID : Robert : Robert Reid, wayman, and wife Isabella Ross, Cammochmore a dau. b.12 Apr. bap.2 May 1867
REID : Robert : Andrew Reid, wayman and wife Agnes Mitchell a son b.at Newtonhill 2 May bap.7 Jun.1869
REID : William Mitchell : Andrew Reid and wife Agnes Mitchell, Cammochmore a son b.13 ult.bap.27 May 1865
REID : William Welsh : Helen Reid, Fiddestown and Alex.Lilly, Old Machar an ill.son b.26 Jun. bap.28 Jul.1860
REITHE : Isobel : Bap.a dau.to James Reithe and Isobel Cairnie at Bridge of Dee Toll b.14 bap.22 May 1841
RHIND : Alexander : Geo.Rhind, England,and wife Eliz.Bell a son b.3 Apr. bap.21 May 1852
RHIND : Elizabeth : Geo. Rhind and wife Eliz.Bell residing at Kemhill a dau. b.2 Jun. bap.13 Jul.1854
RHIND : George : George Rhind, overseer of Aberdeen Railway and wife Margt.Bell a son b.5 ult. bap.30 Oct.1850

RIACH   Alexander : Robert Riach, Bourtreybush and Ann Traill, Hill of Banchory an ill.son b.10 Sep.1862 bap.7 Mar.1863

RIACH   Robert : Robert Riach, Bourtreybush and wife Jane G.Johnston a son b.16 ult. bap.29 Mar.1863(mother sponsor)

ROBB   Elsy Walker : John Robb, Hillside and wife Margt.Riddoch a dau. b.29 Nov.ult. bap.6 Jan.1861

ROBB   Helen : John Robb and wife Mary Riddoch a dau. b.25 ult. bap.26 Dec.1858 at Hillside

ROBB   Marjory : Al.Robb and wife Ann Gordon a dau. b.at Charleston,Cairnrobin on 5 ult. bap.29 Apr.1867

ROBB   Mary Ann : John Robb,coachman,Hillside and wife Margt.Riddoch a dau. b.17 ult. bap.10 Aug.1856

ROBERTSON   Child : bap.in Nigg 21 Mar. 1843

ROBERTSON   Andrew Main : John Robertson, ploughman and Agnes Wood 41 Portlethen an ill.son b.31 Mar. bap.17 May 1868

ROBERTSON   Ann Duncan : Al.Robertson and Mary Beverly in Brunthillock a dau. b.19 ult. bap.21 Oct.1848

ROBERTSON   Ann : Thomas Robertson, E.Cookston and wife Lilly Craig a dau. b.20 Aug. bap.18 Sep.1852

ROBERTSON   Elspet Main : John Robertson and Jane Wood, 36 Portlethen an ill.dau. b.14 ult. bap.12 Dec.1863

ROBERTSON   Ewen : Son of Geo. Robertson, crofter, Hill of Portlethen b.23 May of Ann Low his wife bap.22 Jun.1869

ROBERTSON   George : Geo.Robertson, Fiddestown and wife Janat Gordon a son b.9 ult. bap.29 May 1843

ROBERTSON   George : Thos.Robertson, E.Cookston and wife Lilly Craig a son b.2 Jul. bap.5 Aug. 1843

ROBERTSON   George : Bap.a son to Geo.Robertson s.f.presently residing at Mill of Elsick and wife Jane Johnston b.23 ult. bap.3 Aug.1844

ROBERTSON   Geo.Wood : Jo.Robertson w.f. Portlethen and wife Isobel Wood a son b.12 ult. bap.17 Apr.1849

ROBERTSON   Helen Mathewson : Al. Robertson, Falkirk and wife Helen Robertson, Langhillock of Portlethen a dau.b.3 ult. bap.11 Feb.1847

ROBERTSON   Isabella : Bap.a dau.to Thomas Robertson and Lilly Craig in Cookston 21 Nov.1840

ROBERTSON   Isabella : Geo.Robertson, Hill of Portlethen and wife Ann Low a dau.b.11 Jul.ult. bap.26 Aug.1865

ROBERTSON   Jane : Thos.Robertson, E.Cookston and wife Lilly Craig a dau.b.21 Nov. bap.30 Dec.1854

ROBERTSON   Jane Henrey : Thos.Robertson, E.Cookston and Lilly Craig a dau.b.21 Jul. bap.8 Aug.1846

ROBERTSON   Jemima : Geo.Robertson and Jane Jaffrey, Findon a dau.b.11 Dec.1852 bap.16 Jan 1853

ROBERTSON   Johanna Lowies : John Robertson and wife Is.Wood a dau. b.27 Feb. bap.15 May 1847

ROBERTSON   John : John Robertson w.f. Portlethen and wife Isobel Wood a son b.at Stonehaven 4 Dec 1844 bap. by Rev.Silver, Dunnottar

ROBERTSON   John : Geo.Robertson, Hill of Portlethen and wife Ann Low a son b.12 Mar. bap.8 May 1867

ROBERTSON   Lilly : Thos.Robertson, E.Cookston and wife Lilly Craig a dau. b.25 ult bap.6 May 1850

ROBERTSON   Margaret Keith : Walter Robertson, Drill Instructor, Cammochmore Cottage,Cookney and wife Margt.Cooper a dau. b.1 May bap.7 Jul.1867

ROBERTSON   Margt. Willin : Geo.Robertson and Jane Johnston, Findon a dau. b.25 ult. bap 10 Feb.1851

ROBERTSON   Mary : Geo.Robertson s.f. Findon and wife Anne Low a dau. b.6 Apr. bap.at Berryhill 28 May 1855

ROBERTSON	Moses : John Roberson w.f. Portlethen and wife Ann Craig a son b.25 bap.29 Jun.1842
ROBERTSON	Robert : Geo.Robertson and Jane Gordon in Fiddestown a son b.26 ult. bap.16 Dec.1844
ROBERTSON	Robert Gourley : John Robertson, Findon and wife May Low a son b.16 Dec.ult. bap.25 Jan.1845
ROBERTSON	Sarah Ann : Geo.Robertson, Berryhill and wife Ann Low a dau. b.8 ult. bap.2 Apr.1859
ROBERTSON	Wm.Paterson : Geo.Robertson, Berryhill and wife Ann Milne a son b.in Aberdeen 24 ult. bap.12 May 1857
RODNEY	Ann Cruickshank : David Al.Rodney, merchant,Downies and wife Margt.Forrest a dau. b.17 ult. bap.20 Sep.1858
ROGER	John : Bap.a child of Eliz.Roger in Roadside of Cairnrobin (John Howie their sponsor) (---- Slicer reputed father) 6 Dec.1840
ROSS	Alex. : Bap.an ill.son to Alex.Ross lab.,Moss-side and Jane Reid in Moss-side b.19 Aug. bap 7 Sep.1842
ROSS	Eliza.Robertson : John Ross s.f. Findon and wife Margt.Robertson a dau.b.21 Jun. bap.5 Aug.1853
ROSS	Wm. : Bap.a natural son of Wm.Ross and Mary Anderson at Hillside 29 Aug.1846 (deserted by parents)
RUST	David : Wm.Rust and wife M.Findlay, Bankhead a son b.11 Sep. bap.31 Oct.1859
RUST	Eliz. : Wm.Rust and wife Margt.Findlay, Bankhead a dau. b.14 Oct. bap.9 Nov.1854
RUST	Geo. : Bap.a son to Wm.Rust and Margt.Findlay in Portlethen b.27 Jul. bap.9 Aug.1841
RUST	Jas.Ferguson : Wm.Rust and Margt.Findlay, Hill of Turnemiddle a son b.15 May bap.5 Jul.1852
RUST	Jessie : Wm.Rust, Bankhead and wife Margt.Findlay a dau. b.24 ult. bap.16 Apr.1857
RUXTON	Andrew Patterson : Jas.Ruxton, Hillside and wife Eliza. Patterson a son b.7 Apr. bap.12 May 1861
RUXTON	David : Jas.Ruxton, E.Cookston and wife Eliz. Patterson a son b.19 Jul. bap.6 Aug.1853
RUXTON	Eliz.P. : Eliz.Ruxton, Hillside an ill.dau. b.-- ult. bap.8 May 1863 (P.Cameron,reputed father)
RUXTON	Geo. : Jas.Ruxton, 27 James St.Aberdeen and Eliz. Patterson a son b.9 Dec.1855 bap.21 Jan.1856
SCORGIE	Alex.Ewen : Geo.Scorgie, Hill of Portlethen and wife Helen Smith a son b.21 Dec. bap.31 Dec.1842
SCORGIE	Alex. : Wm.Scorgie and wife Mary Wood, Haremoss a son b.23 ult. bap.14 Jul.1864
SCORGIE	David : Wm.Scorgie, Haremoss and wife Mary Wood a son b.25 ult. bap.23 Jul.1859
SCORGIE	Elspet : Wm.Scorgie and wife Mary Wood a dau. b.at Haremoss 4 ult. bap.24 Jan.1862
SCORGIE	Geo. : Wm.Scorgie, Hill of Portlethen and wife Mary Wood, Findon an ill.son b.17 bap.18 Mar.1844
SCORGIE	Helen : Wm.Scorgie, Haremoss and wife Magdalene Officer a dau b.7 Mar. bap.30 Apr.1856
SCORGIE	John Leiper : Andrew Scorgie, England and wife Margt.Milne a son b.5 ult. bap.29 Sep.1861
SCORGIE	Joseph : Wm.Scorgie, Haremoss and wife Mary Wood a son b.19 May bap.9 Jun.1853
SCORGIE	Mary Elspet : Wm.Scorgie and wife Mary Wood, Haremoss a dau.b.28 May bap.16 Jun.1866
SCOTT	Mathewson Law : Geo.Scorgie, Hill of Portlethen and wife Helen Smith a son b.17 ult. bap.15 Mar.1846
SCOTT	Eliza : John Scott (from Elgin),Portlethen and wife Mary Phimister a dau. b.16 ult. bap.13 Jul.1850
SCROGGIE	Andrew McClean : Andrew Scroggie, England and wife Margt.Milne a son b.28 ult. bap.21 Aug.1858

SHEPHERD	Catherine Pyne : Jas.Shepherd, Barclayhill and wife Margt.Baird a dau. b.18 bap.29 May 1843
SHEPHERD	Eliz. : Jas.Shepherd, Barclayhill and Mary Baird a dau. b.10 Jan. bap.17 Jan.1842
SHEPHERD	Helen : Mary Shepherd, Hill of Turnermiddle an ill.dau. b.12 Jan. bap.7 Mar.1867
SHEPHERD	Helen Howie : Widow Jas.Shepherd, Barclayhill a dau. b.21 ult. bap.23 Feb.1848
SHEPHERD	Jas. : Jas.Shepherd, Barclayhill and wife Mary Baird a son b.7 bap.18 Nov.1844
SILVER	David : Mr D.Silver, schoolmaster and wife M.Allan a son b.7 ult. bap.8 May 1864
SILVER	Emy Jessie : D.Silver, schoolmaster,Portlethen and wife Margt. Allan a dau. b.13 ult. bap.31 Dec.1862
SILVER	Geo.Jas. : Mr D.Silver,schoolmaster,Portlethen and wife Margt. Allan a son b.16 Dec.last, bap.7 Jan.1866
SILVER	Margt. : Mr D.Silver, schoolmaster and wife Margt.Allan a dau. b.11 Nov. bap.15 Dec.1861
SILVER	Margt.Smith : D.Silver, schoolmaster and wife Margt.Smith a dau. b.5 Jul. bap.4 Aug.1867
SIMPSON	Geo.Knowles : Robt.Simpson, Barclayhill and wife Jane Craig a son b.3 Apr. bap.14 May 1853
SIMPSON	Jas. : Bap.a son to Jas.Simpson in Hillside and Mary Leonard in Cookston b.13 Apr. bap.11 May 1841
SIMPSON	Jane : Wm.Simpson, Belhelvie and Hanna Anderson, Badentoy an ill.dau. b.25 Oct.1849 bap.8 Jan.1850
SIMPSON	Mary Eliz.: Jas.Simpson, Hillside and wife Mary Leonard a dau. b.17 Feb. bap.26 Mar.1843
SIMPSON	Wm. : Jas.Simpson, Durris and Christian Rose, Portlethen an ill.son b.7 Jan. bap.13 Mar.1854
SINCLAIR	Alex. : Robt.Sinclair, Hillside and wife Garden Adam a son b.28 ult. bap.8 Sep.1849
SINCLAIR	Eliz. : Jas.Sinclair, Mains of Portlethen and wife Eliz.Watt a son b.31 Jul. bap.23 Aug.1851
SINCLAIR	Geo. : Jas.Sinclair, Mains of Portlethen and wife Eliz.Watt a son b.19 Jan. bap.7 Feb.1856
SINCLAIR	Jas. : R.Sinclair and Garden Adam, Hillside a son b.29 Dec.1851 bap.5 Jan.1852
SINCLAIR	Mary Gairn : R.Sinclair, Hillside and wife Gairn Adam a dau. b.22 Mar. bap.26 Apr.1854
SINCLAIR	Robt.Walker : R.Sinclair, Hillside and wife Gairn Adam a son b.8 ult. bap.4 Jan.1848
SINCLAIR	Wm. : Jas.Sinclair, Mains of Portlethen and wife Eliz.Watt a son b.7 Aug. bap.30 Sep.1853
SINCLAIR	William Thomas : Robert Sinclair, E.Cookstown and Gairn Adam a son b.24 Aug. bap.26 Sep.1858
SKELTON	George : Geo.Skelton, Badentoy and wife Mary Bain a son b.9 Apr. bap.28 May 1865
SKELTON	James Watt Wright : Robert Skelton, St.Cyrus and Margt.Wright, Banchory Devenick an ill.son b.9 Jun. bap.at Hillside 29 Aug.1855
SKENE	Margaret : James Skene, lab.,Badentoy and wife Jane Hay a dau.b.11 Jan. bap.30 Mar.1853
SKENE	Mary : Jas.Skene, parish of Bervie and Catherine Jamieson, Findon an ill.dau.b.5 ult. bap.26 Jan.1862
SKENE	William : Jas.Skene, Old School, and wife Eliza.Duncan a son b.10 ult. bap.16 Nov.1850
SLICER	Alexander : Benjamin Slicer and wife Jane Ritchie, England a son b.15 Dec. 1851 bap.21 Jan.1852
SLICER	Elizabeth : Benjamin Slicer and wife Jane Ritchie, England a dau.b.7 Jan. bap.6 Feb.1854
SMITH	Andrew : Jas.Smith, Burnside of Findon and wife Jane Tough a son b.12 ult. bap.29 May 1843
SMITH	Ann : Wm.Smith and wife Margt.Wright, Hillside of Portlethen a dau.b.3 ult. bap.20 Jun.1865
SMITH	Charles : Wm.Smith and wife Margt.Wright a son b. at Turnemiddle 30 Jul.ult. bap.8 Nov.1863

|---|---|
SMITH	Elspet Ann : Frances Smith and wife Jessie Smith Milne, Redmyre a dau.b.9 Feb. bap 6 Mar. 1865
SMITH	Grace Davidson : Jas.Smith, Findon and wife Jane Tough a dau. b.21 Jun. bap.22 Jul.1845
SMITH	Helen : Wm.Smith, parish of Glenbervie and Helen Anderson, presently in this parish an ill.dau. b.9 Apr. bap.21 May 1843
SMITH	Helen Findlay : Bap.at Mill of Monquich (Smith and Milne) 20 May 1867
SMITH	Isabella : Wm.Smith, wayman and wife Margt.Wright, Tappydam a dau.b.17 Apr.ult.bap.at the Manse 28 Jul.1867
SMITH	Jas. : Jas.Smith and Jane Tough in Findon a son b.19 ult. bap.17 Oct.1847 in presence of Congregation
SMITH	Jane : Bap.an ill.dau. to Joseph Smith in Muchals and Jane Tough in Portlethen b.31 Jul. bap.9 Aug.1841
SMITH	Jane : Wm.Smith, Aberdeen and wife Margt.Kane (deceased) a dau.b.4 ult.bap.at Cairnrobin 2 Jan.1864
SMITH	John : Bap.a son to widow Smith or Still in Bieldside b.14 May bap.31 May 1841
SMITH	Margt.: Dau.of Wm.Smith,labourer and wife Margt.Wright b.at Tappydam 24 Sep.bap.14 Nov.1869 (mother sponsor)
SMITH	Margt.Masson : Wm.Smith, Glasscairn and wife Elspet Masson a dau. b.15 Oct.ult. bap.at the Manse 20 Dec.1868
SMITH	Mary Jane : Wm.Smith and wife Elspet Masson, Hill of Portlethen a dau.b.30 Jul. bap.31 Aug.1862
SMITH	Robt.: Wm.Smith f.s. Mains of Portlethen and wife Margt. Wright a son b.29 Aug. bap.18 Oct.1860
SMITH	Robt.Mavor : Wm.Smith, Hillside and wife Margt. Wright a son b.21 Jul.last bap.29 Aug.1861
SMITH	Robina Walker : Wm.Smith and wife Elspet Masson, Glasscairn a dau. b.2 Aug. bap.4 Sep.1864
SMITH	Wm. : Wm.Smith and wife Elspet Masson, Langhillock a son b.3 ult. bap.2 Jan.1859
SOUTHER	Wm. : Margt.Wright, Hillside an ill.son b.30 Jun. bap.8 Oct. 1859– Wm.Smith.father– parties since married
SOUTHER	Jas. : John Souther,Checkbar and wife Isabel Rust a son b.28 Jun.bap.10 Jul.1852 G.Rust.grandfather sponsor
SPALDING	John : Chas.Souther or Souter,Hill of Portlethen and wife Jane Sutherland a son b.25 Aug.ult.bap.20 Oct.1860
SPALDING	Anabella : Geo.Spalding and wife Elspet Kenn a dau. b.and bap.at Hillside 24 Feb.1863
SPENCE	Geo. : Geo.Spalding, Hillside and wife Elspet Kenn a son b.19 Feb. bap.20 Mar.1864
SPENCE	Charles : Wm.Spence, R.P.O. Hill of Findon and wife Margt. Murray a son b.22 Sep. bap.30 Oct.1853
STEPHEN	Margt. : Wm.Spence, Police Officer,Hill of Findon and wife Margt.Murray a dau.b.8 ult. bap.3 Oct.1856
STEWART	Mary Ann : Wm.Stephen, Bourtreybush and wife Mary Ann Strachan a dau. b.23 Aug. bap.28 Sep.1852
STEWART	Agnes : Al.Stewart, Laikshill and wife Mary A.Gordon a dau. b.4 ult. bap.16 Oct.1847
STEWART	Alex. : Alex.Stewart, Laikshill and wife Mary Ann Gordon a son b.27 Apr. bap.7 May 1842
STEWART	Alex. : Robt.Stewart and wife Margt.Davidson in Synod's Lands a son b.30 ult. bap.26 Dec.1850
STEWART	Ann : see Eliz. and Ann, twins
STEWART	Ann : Al.Stewart, Laikshill and wife Mary Ann Gordon a dau. b.18 Jul. bap.21 Aug.1859
STEWART	Charles : Jo.Stewart,L.N.E.Railway lab. and wife Jemima Kinnerd a son b.12 Sep. bap.27 Nov.1859
STEWART	Christina : Robt.Stewart, Findon and wife Margt.Davidson a dau. b.2 ult. bap.27 Jan.1844
STEWART	David : John Stewart, Badentoy and wife Ann Wright a son b.24 Apr. bap.22 May 1856
STEWART	Eliz.and Ann : Robt.Stewart, Findon and wife Margt. Davidson, twin daus. b.11 ult. bap.24 Mar.1847

STEWART Elspet : Jo.Stewart, Badentoy and wife Ann Wright a dau. b.18 Jan. bap.25 Feb.1843

STEWART Elspet : Jas.Stewart, Evertown of Findon and wife Isobel Wilson a dau. b.7 bap.12 Mar.1844

STEWART Emma : Norman Stewart, teacher, Findon and wife Mary Ann Stewart a dau. b.15 ult. bap.3 Dec.1847

STEWART Geo. : R.Stewart and wife Is.Ogston, Glashfarquhar a son b.4 Nov. bap.31 Dec.1853

STEWART Geo. : Robt.Stewart, Findon and wife Margt.Davidson a son b.20 Apr. bap.13 Jun.1857

STEWART Geo. : Chas.Stewart, Cauldseas of Nigg and wife Teriziah Maitland a son b.9 Nov.1862 bap.22 Mar.1863

STEWART Helen : John Stewart and wife Jemima -----, Backhill of Nigg a son b.28 Feb. bap.1 May 1867

STEWART Isabella : Jo.Stewart, Badentoy and wife Isobel Wilson in Evertown of Findon a dau. b.23 Jan. bap.31 Jan.1842

STEWART Jas. : Jo.Stewart, Badentoy and wife Ann Wright a dau. b.25 ult. bap.5 Apr.1845

STEWART Jas. : Forbes Stewart,Cairnrobin and wife Is.Laing a son b.1 Jun.bap.2 Jun.1845

STEWART Jas. : Al.Stewart,Laikshill and wife Mary A.Gordon a son b.22 ult.bap.16 Feb.1850

STEWART Jas. : Robt.Stewart,Glashfarquhar and wife Isobel Ogston a son b.12 ult.bap.3 Apr.1850

STEWART Jas. : Charles Stewart and wife Triesah Maitland in Bogside a son b.18 ult.bap.5 Aug.1850

STEWART Jas. : John Stewart,Badentoy and wife Ann Wright a son b.27 May bap.14 Jun.1852

STEWART Jas.Lowden : Norman Stewart,teacher,Findon and wife Margt.Lowden a son b.28 ult.bap.19 Mar.1850

STEWART Jane Jemima : Chas.Stewart,Bogside and wife Tereziah Maitland a dau.b.6 ult.bap.12 Jul.1858

STEWART Jemimah : John Stewart and Jemimah Kinaird,Backhill of Nigg a dau.b.7 Feb.bap.23 Mar.1862

STEWART Jessie : R.Stewart and wife ---- Davidson a dau.b.12 Apr.bap.at Findon 4 Jun.1854

STEWART John : R.Stewart,Findon and wife Margt.Davidson a son b.28 Aug.bap.18 Oct.1845

STEWART John : Jo.Stewart, Badentoy and wife Ann Wright a son b.25 ult. bap.6 Aug.1849

STEWART John : Alex.Stewart, Larkshill and wife Mary Gordon a son b.7 Jan. bap.9 Feb.1857

STEWART John : John Stewart,wayman,L.N.E.R.,Backhill of Nigg and wife Jemima Kinaird a son b.10 Apr.bap.18 Jun.
          1864 at the Manse

STEWART Margaret : Bap.a dau.to Al.Stewart in Laikshill and wife M.A.Gormon 3 Aug 1844 (b.19 ult)

STEWART Margaret : Chas.Stewart in Bogside and wife Tiresah Maitland a dau. b.27 ult. bap.31 Jan.1848

STEWART Mary Hunter : Jo.Stewart and Ann Wright, Badentoy a dau. b.17 Sep. bap.6 Oct.1854

STEWART May : Alex.Stewart, Larkshill and wife Mary Ann Gordon a dau. b.13 Mar. bap.3 Apr.1852

STEWART Robert : Robert Stewart in Findon and wife Isobel Thomson a son b.8 Jul.1842

STEWART Robert : Robert Stewart and wife Isobel Ogston, Glashfarquhar a son b.18 ult. bap.29 Mar.1851

STEWART Robert : Al.Stewart, Larkshill and wife Mary A.Gordon a son b.5 May bap.24 Jun.1854

STEWART Susan Allan : Al.Stewart, Hillside and wife Mary Gordon a dau. b.6 Feb. bap.11 Apr.1863

STEWART Therseah : John Stewart, railway lab. presently resid.at Blackhill of Nigg and wife Jemima Kinaird a dau.
          b.20 ult. bap.9 Aug.1856

STEWART William : John Stewart, Badentoy and wife Ann Wright a son b.11 ult. bap.31 Jul.1847

STEWART   William : R.Stewart, Glashfarquhar and wife Isobel Ogston a son b.24 Jun. bap.17 Jul.1852
STEWART   William : Robert Stewart, Synod's Lands and wife Margt.Davidson a son b.1 Jun. bap.2 Aug.1859
STEWART   William Law : James Stewart and wife Sarah Christina Bower Law (dau.of Minister) a son b.May 1861 bap.at
           Fern Cot. B.T. 6 Jun.1861

STOTT   Edward : James Stott, Whitebruntland and wife Catherine Cruickshank a son b.10 Feb. bap.16 Apr.1867
STRACHEN   Ann : Bap.in Church at Portlethen 14 Mar.1847 by Rev.Paul
STRATHDEE Helen : James Straiton,crofter,Hill of Findon and wife Isabel Mess/Meff a dau.b.22 Sep.1868 bap.18 Jan.1869
STRATTON   John : Wm.Strathdee R.P.O. and wife Janat Grant, Synod's Lands a son b.11 Aug. bap.24 Sep.1851
STRATTON   Alexander : James Stratton, Hill of Turnemiddle and wife Jessie Trail a son b.26 Oct. bap.24 Dec.1860
STRATTON   Andrew : Jas.Stratton, Turnemiddle and wife Jane Trail a son b.8 ult. bap.1 Aug.1862
STRATTON   James : David Stratton and wife Jane Trail, Turnemiddle a son b.19 ult. bap.14 Jan.1859 (possible error
           of reversed male christian names?)

STRATTON   Jessie : James Stratton and wife Jessie Trail, Hill of Turnemiddle a dau. b.25 May bap.12 Jun.1856
STRATTON   Joseph William : Jas.Stratton and wife Jessy Trail, Hill of Turnemiddle a son b.4 ult. bap.29 May 1865
STRATTON   Margaret : James Stratton, Muir's Moss and wife Jessie Trail a dau. b.23 May bap.24 Jun.1854
STUART   Charles : Charles Stuart, Bogside and wife Tereizah Maitland a son b.5 Dec.1854 bap.24 Jan.1855
STUART   Elizabeth and Isobel : Bap.twin daus.to John Stuart and Ann Wright in Badentoy 24 Oct.1840
STUART   Isobel : see Elizabeth and Isobel, twins
STUART   James : John Stewart, Bogside and Jemima Kinneff, Aberdeen an ill.son b.4 Nov. bap.27 Dec.1852
SUTHERLAND William : Bap.a son to Forbes Stuart and Isobel Laing Nov.1840
           Thomas : Thos.Sutherland and Christian Wood in Downies an ill.son b.8 ult. bap.14 Mar.1848 (Andrew Wood w.f.
           Portlethen, uncle to the child, - sponsor)

TAYLOR   Alexander : Alex.Taylor and wife Barbara Leonard in W.Cookston a son b.20 Nov. bap.26 Dec.1842
TAYLOR   Ann : Wm.Taylor and wife Isabella Jamieson Hunter, Checkbar,Portlethen a dau. b.15 ult. bap.9 Jul.1866
TAYLOR   George : Al.Taylor in W.Cookston and wife Barbara Leonard a son b.16 bap.31 May 1845
TAYLOR   Idea : Donald Taylor, Station, Portlethen, railway keeper and wife Hanna Fergusan a dau.b.12 May
           bap.13 Sep.1851

TAYLOR   Isabella : Wm.Taylor, Aquorthies and wife Isabella Strachan a dau. b.14 Sep. bap.31 Oct.1868 at Manse
TAYLOR   Isobel : Al.Taylor and wife Barbara Leonard a dau.b.14 ult.bap.27 Jan.1851
TAYLOR   James : Alex.Taylor and wife Barbara Leonard,Badentoy a son b.26 Apr.bap.17 May 1856
TAYLOR   Jane : Charles Taylor,blacksmith,E.Cookston and wife Jane Melvin a dau.b.26 ult.bap.1 Aug.1856
TAYLOR   John : Al.Taylor W.Cookston and wife Barbara Leonard a son b.29 Jul.bap.19 Aug.1853

TAYLOR   Margaret : Al.Taylor and wife Barbara Leonard,W.Cookston a dau.b.26 ult.bap.19 Jun.1849
TAYLOR   William : Al.Taylor and wife Barbara Leonard,W.Cookston a son b.5 ult.bap.22 May 1847
TAYLOR   William : Wm.Taylor,Checkbar and wife Isabella J.Hunter a son b.2 ult.bap.25 Sep.1868
THANE   Mary : Al.Thane,farmer,W.Cookston and wife Jessie Reid a dau.b.2 ult.bap.18 Jul.1849
THOM   Margaret Trail : Geo.Thom and Elspet Wood,Hill of Portlethen a dau.b.19 Dec.1848 bap.11 May 1849
THOMSON   Alexander : Al.Thomson,Hillside and wife Eliz.Stewart a son b.24 Mar.bap.29 Apr.1860
THOMSON   Alexander : Robert Thomson and wife Eliza Morrison,Bourtreybush a son b.27 ult.bap.at the Manse 22 Feb.1868
THOMSON   Alexander : Andrew Thomson,merchant,Downies and wife Elizabeth Anderson a son b.1 May bap.9 Jun.1869
THOMSON   Ann : Andrew Thomson and wife Eliz.Anderson,Downies a son b.29 Oct.bap.8 Dec.1864
THOMSON   Barbara Craigmile : John Thomson,Breadhaven and wife Margt.Donald a dau.b.7 bap.8 May.1844
THOMSON   David : Bap.a son to Alex.Thomson at Mid Toll of Jettylea 25 Jan.1850
THOMSON   Eliza Jane : Al.Thomson,Hillside and wife Eliza Stewart a dau.b.24 ult.bap.10 Jul.1858
THOMSON   George : Andrew Thomson and wife Eliza Anderson,Bourtreybush a son b.21 ult.bap.20 Apr.1862
THOMSON   George Masson : Robert Thomson,England and wife Martha Scott a son b.9 ult.bap.21 Aug.1858
THOMSON   Isabel : Andrew Thomson and wife Eliza Anderson,Bourtreybush a dau.b.16 Dec.1859 bap.4 Mar.1860
THOMSON   Jane : Andrew Thomson,Bourtreybush and wife Eliza Anderson a dau.b.23 ult.bap.29 Nov.1857
THOMSON   John : John Thomson,Redmyre and wife Mary Mouat a son b.11 Aug.bap.3 Sep.1852
THOMSON   Martha : Robert Thomson.f.s.,England and wife Margt.Scott a dau.b.5 Apr.bap.8 May 1856
THOMSON   Mary : R.Thomson and wife Martha Scott,Fiddestown a dau.b.11 Apr.bap.19 May 1861
THOMSON   Mary Ann : Bap.a dau.to John Thomson and Barbara Donald,Blackburn,Fetteresso b.8 bap.25 Aug.1841
THOMSON   Mary Ann : Andrew Thomson and wife Elizabeth Anderson,Downies a dau.b.19 ult.bap.26 Dec.1866
THOMSON   Peter : Peter Thomson in Auchlee and Margt.Reid,Balquhain an ill.son b.18 Sep.bap.3 Dec.1842
THOMSON   Robert : Robert Thomson,Bourtreybush and Eliza Morrison an ill.son b.at Gordon's Court,Schoolhill,
          Aberdeen bap.25 Aug.1866
THOW   Ann : Bap.a dau.to John Thow and Isobel Sievewright in Moss-side of Portlethen 23 Aug.1840
THOW   Annie : Dau.of Elizabeth Thow,Moss-side of Portlethen (ill.) b.16 Jan.bap.26 Feb.1866
THOW   Betty : Jo.Thow,Hill of Portlethen and wife Isobel Sievewright a dau.b.2 Dec.ult.bap.13 Jan.1844
THOW   Jane : Jas.Thow,Newhills and Mary Welsh,Fiddestown an ill.dau.b.30 May bap.30 Jul.1859
TOUGH   Isabella : David Tough,Nigg and Christian Gibb,Clochandighter an ill.dau.b.13 Oct.bap.20 Nov.1851
TOUGH   Isobel : Wm.Tough,R.P.O. and Jane Masson a dau.b.18 Mar.bap.3 Apr.1842
TOUGH   Mary : Alex.Tough,Belhelvie and Helen Howie,Findon an ill.dau.b.5 Sep.bap.2 Dec.1861
TURNER   Eliza : Jo.Turner,Findon and Helen Kane,E.Cookston an ill.dau.b.10 Jun.bap.30 Jul.1861

VALENTINE   Female : James Valentine from Nigg and Isabella Straiton an ill.dau.b.12 Sep.1868 bap.12 Apr.1869
VALENTINE   Ann : Francis Valentine,blacksmith,Charleston and wife Jane Stewart a dau.b.3 Oct.bap.7 Nov.1857
VALENTINE   David : Wm.Valentine and wife Mary Milne a son b.15 Feb.bap.at Hillside 8 Mar.1853
VALENTINE   David : Francis Valentine,Blacksmith,Charleston and wife had a son b.4 ult.bap.19 Mar.1859
VALENTINE   Elizabeth : Francis Valentine and wife Jane Stewart a dau.b.at E.Cookston 17 ult.bap.16 Dec.1864
VALENTINE   Francis : Francis Valentine,E.Cookston and wife Jane Mowat a son b.2 Mar.bap.11 Apr.1866
VALENTINE   Helen : Wm.Valentine and wife Mary Milne, Cairnrobin a dau. b.22 ult. bap.7 Nov.1857
VALENTINE   James : Wm.Valentine, Hillside and wife Mary Milne a son b.24 Jan. bap.17 Feb.1855 by Rev.Dr.Paul
VALENTINE   James : Francis Valentine, E.Cookston and wife Jane Stewart a son b.16 Apr. bap.29 Jun.1867
VALENTINE   Jane : Wm.Valentine and wife Mary Milne in Hillside a dau. b.3 Jul. bap.2 Aug.1851
VALENTINE   John Shepherd : F.Valentine, Charleston and wife Jane Stewart a son b.8 ult. bap.6 Jul.1861
VALENTINE   Robert : Robert Valentine, Banchory and Margt.Hunter, Hill of Findon an ill.son b.29 ult. bap.23 Apr.1858
VALENTINE   Mary Jane : Francis Valentine and wife Jane Stewart, E.Cookston a dau. b.19 ult. bap.at the Manse 8 Aug.1868
VALENTINE   William : Francis Valentine, Marywell and wife Jane Stewart a son b.16 Sep. bap.11 Nov.1863

WALES,   Prince of : Public thanksgiving offered up this day for the Queen's safe delivery of a Prince on 11 Nov.1841
WALKER   Annabella : R.Walker, Mains of Portlethen and wife Elspet Walker a dau. b.24 Feb. bap.11 Mar.1843
WALKER   Andrew: Bap.a son to Andrew Walker and Margt.Moir. W.Cookston b.8 bap.15 May 1842
WALKER   Ann : Andrew Walker and Susan Gerrard, Cairnrobin a dau. b.8 ult. bap.24 May 1847
WALKER   Charlotte : Jo.Walker and wife Eliz.Wood in Hillside a dau. b.18 ult. bap.4 May 1848
WALKER   Elizabeth : Wm.Walker presently resid.at Cove Road and wife Christian Anderson a dau.b.9 ult.bap.23 May 1846
WALKER   Elizabeth Duguid : R.Walker, Hill of Findon and wife Eliz.Bartlet a dau. b.16 Jun. bap.24 Jul.1847
WALKER   Elspet : Geo.Walker, Hill of Findon and wife Margt.Kerr a dau. b.14 Apr. bap.20 May 1843
WALKER   Elspet Greig : Jas.Walker and Christian Douglass, Groundlessmyres an ill.dau. b.17 Jun. bap.23 Jul.1851
WALKER   Elsy : R.Walker, Mains of Portlethen and wife Elsy Bartlet a dau. b.7 May bap.29 May 1844
WALKER   George : Andrew Walker, Redmyre and wife Margt.Moir a son b.7 Oct. bap.17 Nov.1855
WALKER   Geo. : John Walker, Labourer, Redmyre and wife Ann Tait a son b.10 Apr. bap.30 Apr.1869
WALKER   Helen : John Walker, Cairnrobin and wife Ann Tait a dau. b.4 ult. bap.30 May 1857
WALKER   Isabella and James : John Walker, Glen of Redmyre and wife Ann Tait twins b.27 ult. bap.13 Jul.1861
WALKER   James : see Isabella and James, twins
WALKER   James : John Walker and wife Ann Tait, Redmyre a son b.10 Feb. bap.17 Mar.1864
WALKER   John : Andrew Walker and wife Margt.Moir in Badentoy a son b.12 bap.20 Jul.1844
WALKER   John : John Walker and Eliz.Duncan in Findon an ill.son b.21 ult. bap.12 Apr.1848 (Wm.Duncan sponsor)

WALKER	John Tait : John Walker, Carinrobin and wife Ann Tait a son b.18 ult. bap.19 Mar.1859
WALKER	Jonathan : Jo.Walker, Hillside and wife Eliza.Wood a son b.28 ult. bap.2 Jun.1845
WALKER	Joseph : Andrew Walker, Badentoy and wife Margt.Moir a son b.10 ult. bap.20 Mar.1847
WALKER	Joseph : Andrew Walker and wife Margt.Moir in Badentoy a son b.9 ult. bap.22 May 1848
WALKER	Margaret : R.Walker, Mains of Portlethen and wife Elsy Bartlet a dau. b.15 ult. bap.2 Oct.1845
WALKER	Mary : John Walker, Badentoy and wife Ann Tait a dau.b.8 Jun. bap.at 13 Carmelite St.Abdn. 2 Jul.1855
WALKER	Mary Ann Shepherd Davidson : Jo.Walker and Eliz.Wood, Hillside a dau. b.27 ult. bap.10 Feb.1851
WALKER	Robert : Andrew Walker and wife Margt.Moir a son b.at Redmyre 10 Oct. bap 24 Nov.1852
WALKER	Robt.Shand : John Walker and wife Eliz.Wood in Hillside a son b.14 ult.bap.21 Mar.1843
WALKER	Susan : Andrew Walker and wife Susan Gerrard a dau. b.20 ult. bap.14 Feb.1849
WALKER	Wm. : Bap.a son to Geo.Walker and Margt.Kerr in Hill of Findon 29 Nov.1840
WALKER	Wm. : Bap.a son to John Walker and Eliza.Wood in Roadside of Findon b.4 Apr. bap.6 Apr.1841
WALKER	Wm. : Andrew Walker, Cairnrobin and wife Susan Gerrard a son b.12 ult. bap. 23 Jul.1845
WALKER	Wm. : John Walker and wife Ann Tait, Glen of Redmyre a son b.7 ult. bap.25 Dec.1866
WALLACE	Eliz. : Wm.Wallace, Langhillock and wife Eliza Donald a dau. b.1 Jan. bap.26 Feb.1855
WARN	John : John Warn and Margt.Reid, 38 Park St.Aberdeen an ill.son b.7 Sep.1867 bap.at Haremoss 3 Aug.1868
WATSON	Elizabeth : Andrew Watson, Maryculter and Ann Chalmers, Brunthillock an ill. dau. b.24 Nov. bap.25 Dec.1850
	Grandfather sponsor
WATSON	John James : Margt.Sim Watson, 4 Canal Terr.Aberdeen an ill.son b.12 Jul.1863 bap.at Moss-side 15 Oct.1864
WATT	Jane : Geo.Watt, Hillside and wife Christian Lennie a dau. b.25 bap.30 Apr.1842
WATT	Margt. : Bap.a dau.to Geo.Watt and Christian Lennie in Hillside 28 Nov.1840
WELSH	Agnes Law : Al.Welsh and wife Mary Milne, Fiddestown a dau. b.15 ult. bap.26 May 1849
WELSH	Isobel : Al.Welsh, Fiddestown and wife Mary Milne a dau. b.23 ult. bap.9 Jun.1846
WELSH	James : Al.Welsh and wife Margt.Milne,Fiddestown,Findon a son b.4 Aug.bap.3 Sep.1851
WELSH	James : Mary Welsh,Fiddestown an ill.son b.2 May bap.20 Aug.1865-Jas.Cramond,father sponsor
WELSH	Jessie : Al.Welsh,Fiddestown and wife Margt.Milne a dau.b.2 ult.bap.20 Mar.1858
WELSH	Jessie Taylor : Jas.Taylor and Jane Welsh,Fiddestown an ill.dau.b.9 Jan.1862 bap.at Manse 26 Jun.1863
WELSH	John (Bower) : Al.Welsh and wife Margt.Milne,Fiddestown a son b.14 Nov.bap.30 Dec.1853
WELSH	Margaret : Al.Welsh,Fiddestown and wife Mary Milne a dau.b.25 ult.bap.4 Mar.1844
WELSH	Richard Campbell : Mary Welsh,Findon an ill.son b.4 Mar.bap.at Manse 25 Apr.1868
WILSON	William Low : Mary Welsh,Fiddestown an ill.son b.25 Jun.1861 bap.22 Jun.1862
WOOD	James : Joseph Wilson,railway lab..Barclayhill and wife Eliz.Brock a son b.2 ult.bap.20 Jul.1850
WOOD	Agnes : Jo.Wood w.f.16 Portlethen and wife Margt.Leiper a dau.b.31 Aug.bap.16 Sep.1843
	Agnes : Jas.Wood w.f.10 Findon and wife Jane Leiper a dau.b.10 ult.bap.3 Dec.1847

WOOD	Agnes :	Jas.Wood w.f.39 Findon and wife Ann Wood a dau.b.10 ult.bap.8 Feb.1849
WOOD	Agnes :	James Wood w.f.Findon and wife Margt.Kay a dau.b.12 Feb.bap.29 Mar.1856
WOOD	Agnes :	James Wood w.f.Findon and wife Agnes Caie a dau.b.14 ult.bap.17 Jul.1858
WOOD	Agnes :	Moses Wood w.f.4 Findon and wife Agnes Leiper a dau.b.29 ult.bap.18 Sep.1858
WOOD	Agnes :	Jas.Wood 44 Findon and wife Agnes Caie a dau.b.9 ult.bap.26 Mar.1863
WOOD	Agnes Law :	Al.Wood w.f. and wife Jane Wood,Findon a dau.b.11 ult.bap.1 Dec.1849
WOOD	Alexander :	Bap.a son to John Wood w.f.Downies and Janat Wood b.3 Jul.bap.11 Jul.1841
WOOD	Alexander :	Al.Wood w.f.5 Downies and wife Ann Leiper a son b.25 ult.bap.11 Sep.1843
WOOD	Alexander :	Al.Wood w.f.Findon and wife Jane Wood a son b.1 ult.bap.12 Oct.1843
WOOD	Alexander :	Al.Wood w.f.Portlethen and Mary Craig there an ill.son b.3 Apr.bap.19 Jul.1847
WOOD	Alexander :	Geo.Wood w.f.Findon and wife Helen Leiper a son b.30 ult.bap.23 Nov.1850
WOOD	Alexander :	Moses Wood w.f.4 Findon and wife Agnes Leiper a son b.27 May bap.14 Jun.1856
WOOD	Alexander :	Jas.Wood w.f.23 Findon and wife Agnes Caie a son b.11 ult.bap.17 Aug.1856
WOOD	Alexander :	Alex.Wood and Ann Leiper 32 Downies a son b.1 ult.bap.20 Jun.1859
WOOD	Alexander :	Jas.Wood w.f.Findon and wife Margt.Hay a son b.and bap.2 Dec.1859
WOOD	Alexander :	Moses Wood w.f.Downies and wife Betty Leiper a son b.26 Feb.bap.7 Apr.1860
WOOD	Alexander :	James Wood w.f. and wife Jane Wood,Findon a son b.28 ult.bap.30 Nov.1861
WOOD	Alexander :	Joseph Wood w.f.Downies and wife Ann Main a son b.18 ult.bap.26 Jul.1862
WOOD	Alexander :	Andrew Wood w.f.1 Downies and wife Jane Wood a son b.29 ult.bap.25 Jun.1864
WOOD	Alexander & William :	Jas.Wood w.f.9 Downies and wife Is.Wood twins b.10 ult.bap.12 Dec.1864
WOOD	Alexander :	John Wood w.f.40 Downies and wife Mary Christie a son b.6 ult.bap.9 Jul.1865-G/father sponsor
WOOD	Alex.Masson :	Andrew Wood w.f.36 Portlethen and Janat Masson,5 Sketraw an ill.son b.29 ult.bap.24 Sep.1864
WOOD	Andrew :	John Wood w.f.Portlethen and wife Elspet Wood a son b.19 May bap.28 May 1842
WOOD	Andrew :	Andrew Wood w.f.Portlethen and wife Elspet Main a son b.18 Dec.1842 bap.23 Jan.1843
WOOD	Andrew :	Al.Wood w.f.Portlethen and wife Margt.Wood a son b.21 Jun.bap.1 Jul.1843
WOOD	Andrew :	Geo.Wood w.f.Portlethen and wife Janat Leiper a son b.25 ult.bap.3 Oct.1846
WOOD	Andrew :	Alex.Wood w.f.23 Portlethen and wife Margt.Craig a son b.5 Jul.bap.16 Aug.1851
WOOD	Andrew :	Andrew Wood w.f.Downies and Jane Wood,Findon an ill.son b.31 ult.bap.12 Nov.1860
WOOD	Andrew :	G.Wood w.f.14 Findon and wife Is.Wood a son b.6 ult.bap.9 Aug.1863
WOOD	Andrew :	Jas.Wood w.f. and wife Isabella Wood 9 Downies a son b.18 Feb.bap.at Manse 18 Mar.1868
WOOD	Ann :	Geo.Wood w.f.40 Findon and Ann Wood a dau.b.and bap.10 Jun.1843
WOOD	Ann :	Geo.Wood w.f.Findon and Margt.Craig in Portlethen an ill.dau.b.4 bap.10 Aug.1844
WOOD	Ann :	Jas.Wood w.f.Findon and wife Jane Leiper a dau.b.24 ult.bap.13 Sep.1845
WOOD	Ann :	Wm.Wood w.f.Findon and Helen Wood there an ill.dau.b.26 ult.bap.10 Oct.1845

WOOD Ann : Alex.Wood w.f.Findon and wife Jane Main a dau.b.14 ult.bap.24 Apr.1847
WOOD Ann : John Wood w.f.Findon and wife Eliz.Craig a dau.b.20 Feb.bap.23 Mar.1850
WOOD Ann : Andrew Wood w.f.4 Downies and wife Agnes Twigg a dau.b.25 ult.bap.7 Sep.1850
WOOD Ann : Geo.Wood w.f. and wife Isobel Leiper,Findon a dau.b.13 Feb.bap.12 Mar.1853
WOOD Ann : Alex.Wood w.f. 32 Downies and wife Ann Leiper a dau. b.10 ult. bap.4 Apr.1857
WOOD Ann : Moses Wood w.f. 6 Downies and wife Eliza.Leiper a dau. b.25 ult. bap.26 Sep.1857
WOOD Ann : Al.Wood w.f.27 Portlethen and Ann Craig there an ill.dau. b.7 Jun. bap.7 Aug.1859
WOOD Ann : John Wood w.f. 17 Portlethen and wife Ann Main a dau. b.11 ult. bap.19 Aug.1860
WOOD Ann : Geo.Wood w.f. 36 Findon and wife Margt.Craighead a dau. b.25 ult. bap.1 Feb.1861
WOOD Ann : Geo.Wood w.f. 21 Downies and wife Ann Wood a dau. b.5 ult. bap.4 May 1861
WOOD Ann : James Wood w.f. and wife Helen Leiper, Findon a dau.b.22 ult. bap.30 Nov.1861
WOOD Ann : Al.Wood w.f. Downies and Isobel Craig, Portlethen an ill.dau. b.16 ult. bap.26 Dec.1863
WOOD Ann : Joseph Wood w.f. Downies and wife .... a dau. b.21 ult. bap.22 Sep.1864
WOOD Ann : Al.Wood w.f. 36 Downies and wife Margaret Wood a dau. b.23 Aug. bap.2 Sep.1866
WOOD Ann : Jas.Wood w.f. 10 Findon and wife Susan Leiper a dau. b.21 ult. bap.24 Sep.1868
WOOD Ann : Dau.of Joseph Wood w.f. and wife Ann Main b.at 35 Downies 29 Jul. bap.8 Aug.1869
WOOD Bell : Moses Wood Jnr. w.f. Downies and Elspet Knowles an ill.dau. b.30 Nov.1843 bap.9 Jan.1844
WOOD Betsy : Geo.Wood w.f. Findon and wife Margt.Craig a dau. b.17 Sep. bap.30 Oct.1855
WOOD Betty : John Wood w.f. Portlethen and wife Agnes Craig a dau. b.11 ult. bap.18 Sep.1847
WOOD Catherine Shepherd : Alex.Wood w.f. Findon and wife Jane Wood a dau. b.22 ult. bap.8 Jul.1846
WOOD Elizabeth : Jas. Wood w.f.10 Findon and wife Jane Leiper a dau. b.19 bap.28 Jan.1843
WOOD Elizabeth : Geo.Wood w.f. Portlethen and wife Janat Leiper a dau. b.19 Feb. bap.25 Mar.1843
WOOD Elizabeth : Geo.Wood w.f. Findon and wife Ann Wood a dau. b.12 bap.25 Aug.1845
WOOD Elizabeth : John Wood w.f.45 Findon and wife Eliz.Craig a dau. b.2 ult. bap.17 Apr.1847
WOOD Elizabeth : Geo.Wood and Helen Wood in Findon an ill.dau. b.5 ult. bap.19 Oct.1848
WOOD Elizabeth : Jas. and Ann Wood w.f. 39 Findon a dau. b.3 ult. bap.19 Apr.1851
WOOD Elizabeth : Wm.Wood and wife Helen Wood in Findon a dau. b.22 Jun. bap.6 Jul.1851
WOOD Elizabeth : Al.Wood w.f. Findon and wife Jane Main a dau. b.29 Jan. bap.9 Feb.1856
WOOD Elizabeth : Jas. Wood w.f. Findon and wife Agnes Caie a dau. b.17 ult. bap.6 Oct.1860
WOOD Elizabeth : Moses Wood w.f. 4 Findon and wife Agnes Leiper a dau. b.21 ult. bap.27 May 1861
WOOD Elizabeth : Jas.Wood w.f. Findon and wife Margt.Robertson a dau. b.8 ult bap.12 Jul.1862
WOOD Elizabeth : Wm.Wood w.f. 53 Findon and wife Helen Craig a dau. b.12 bap.22 Jan.1863
WOOD Elizabeth : Wm.Wood w.f. 53 Findon and wife Helen Craig a dau. b.11 ult. bap.24 Jan.1864
WOOD Elizabeth : Moses Wood w.f. 6 Downies and wife Elizabeth Leiper a dau. b.15 ult. bap.11 Mar.1867

WOOD	Elspet	: Andrew Wood w.f. Portlethen and wife Elspet Main a dau. b.4 ult. bap.12 Feb.1848
WOOD	Elspet	: Alex.Wood w.f. Findon and wife Jane Main a dau. b.29 ult. bap.16 Apr.1849
WOOD	Elspet	: Alex.Wood w.f. Portlethen and wife Margt.Craig a dau. b.8 Apr. bap.25 Jun.1849
WOOD	Elspet	: Andrew w.f. 36 Portlethen and wife Elspet Main a dau.b.22 ult. bap.30 Mar.1850
WOOD	Elspet	: Geo.Wood w.f. and Isabella Leiper in Findon an ill.dau. b.7 Sep. bap.25 Oct.1851
WOOD	Elspet	: Geo.Wood w.f. 36 Findon and wife Margt.Craig a dau. b.10 ult. bap.26 Mar.1859
WOOD	Elspet	: Al.Wood w.f. Findon and wife Helen Wood a dau. b.20 ult. bap.24 Aug.1861
WOOD	Elspet	: Andrew Wood w.f. 45 Portlethen and wife Janat Masson a dau. b.1 ult. bap.9 Oct.1867
WOOD	George	: John Wood w.f. Portlethen and wife Ann Craig a son b.23 bap.31 Jul.1842
WOOD	George	: James Wood w.f. Findon and wife Ann Wood a son b.11 Nov. bap.17 Nov.1842
WOOD	George	: Geo.Wood w.f. Portlethen and wife Jane Knowles a son b.8 ult. bap.17 Jun.1843
WOOD	George	: Alex.Wood w.f. 5 Downies and wife Ann Leiper a son b.7 ult. bap.16 Dec.1845
WOOD	George	: Geo.Wood w.f. Findon and wife Helen Leiper a son b.6 bap.20 Jun.1846
WOOD	George	: Jas.Wood w.f. 44 Findon and wife Jane Leiper a son b.24 ult. bap.5 Dec.1846
WOOD	George	: Geo.Wood w.f. and wife Margt.Craig a son b.18 ult. bap.3 Mar.1848
WOOD	George	: Andrew Wood w.f. 36 Portlethen and wife Elspet Main a son b.29 May bap.5 Jun.1852
WOOD	George	: Joseph Wood w.f.Downies and wife Jane Leiper a son b.15 May bap.3 Jun.1853 - Moses Wood, sponsor
WOOD	George	: George Wood w.f. 46 Findon and wife Elspet Leiper a son b.7 ult. bap.11 Aug.1856
WOOD	George	: Geo.Wood w.f. Findon and wife ... Leiper a son b.5 ult. bap.6 Jul.1860
WOOD	George	: Al.Wood w.f. 3 Portlethen and wife Margt.Wood a son b.10 ult. bap.29 Jun.1861
WOOD	George	: Geo.Wood w.f. 14 Findon and wife Isobel Wood a son b.21 ult. bap.27 Sep.1861
WOOD	George	: Moses Wood w.f. Downies and wife Eliza Leiper a son b.30 Sep. bap.15 Nov.1862
WOOD	George	: Jo.Wood w.f. 26 ? Downies and wife Agnes Wood a son b.17 ult. bap.2 Apr 1864
WOOD	George	: Jas.Wood w.f. 3 Findon and wife Jane Wood a son b.10 ult. bap.29 Oct.1864
WOOD	George	: Geo.Wood w.f. 21 Downies and wife Ann Wood a son b.18 ult. bap.27 Mar.1865
WOOD	George	: Jas.Wood w.f. 16 ? Findon and wife Margaret Robertson a son b.1 ult. bap.3 Apr.1866
WOOD	George	: Jas.Wood w.f. 49 Findon and wife Margt.Caie a son b.9 Jan. bap.2 Feb.1867
WOOD	George	: Joseph Wood w.f. 35 Downies and wife Ann Main a son b.13 and bap.18 May 1867
WOOD	George	: John Wood w.f. 20 Downies and wife Agnes Wood a son b.3 ult. bap.at the Manse 11 Apr.1868
WOOD	George	: Al.Wood w.f. 36 Downies and wife Margt.Wood a son b.9 ult. bap.at the Manse 23 Aug.1868
WOOD	George	: John Wood w.f. 40 Downies and wife Mary Christie a son b.9 ult. bap.at the Manse 25 Oct.1868
WOOD	Helen	: Al.Wood w.f. Portlethen and Margt.Craig there, an ill.dau. b.31 ult. bap.9 Nov.1844
WOOD	Helen	: Jas.Wood w.f. Findon and wife Ann Wood a dau. b.22 ult. bap.3 Jul.1847
WOOD	Helen	: Wm.Wood w.f. 36 Findon and wife Helen Leiper a dau. b.9 ult. bap.22 Jun.1850

WOOD Helen : Wm.Wood w.f. 47 Findon and wife Helen Wood a dau. b.20 Jun. bap.1 Jul.1853
WOOD Helen : Geo.Wood w.f. Findon and wife Helen Leiper a dau. b.2 Apr. bap.5 May 1855
WOOD Helen : Geo.Wood w.f. Findon and wife Helen Leiper a dau. b.19 Jun. bap.5 Jul.1856
WOOD Helen : Jas.Wood w.f. 4 Downies and ... Wood 8,there, an ill.dau. b.3 ult. bap.4 Feb.1858
WOOD Helen Craig : Wm.Wood w.f. Findon and Helen Craig there, an ill. dau. b.17 Dec.1852 bap.21 Jan.1853
WOOD Helen Leiper : Jas.Wood w.f. 51 Findon and wife Helen Leiper a dau. b.17 ult. bap.29 Aug.1867
WOOD Hellen : Alex.Wood w.f. 36 Downies and wife Margt.Wood a dau. b.8 ult. bap.18 Sep.1864
WOOD Isabel : Geo.Wood w.f. 36 Findon and wife Margt.Craig a dau. b.13 ult. bap.29 Apr.1865
WOOD Isabel : Geo.Wood w.f. Findon and wife Is.Leiper a dau. b.1 Feb. bap 3 Mar.1855
WOOD Isabella : Jas.Wood w.f. Downies and wife Isabella Wood a dau. b.28 Feb. at 78 Shiprow,Aberdeen bap. there
12 Apr.1862
WOOD Isabella : Al.Wood w.f. 32 Downies and wife Ann Leiper a dau. b.4 ult. bap.16 Jan.1864
WOOD Isabella : Jas.Wood w.f. 8 Downies and wife Helen Main a dau. b.31 Dec.ult. bap.at the Manse 23 Jan.1868
WOOD Isabella Law : Geo.Wood w.f. Findon and wife Helen Leiper a dau. b.20 Mar. bap 30 Apr.1859
WOOD Isabella Law : Al.Wood w.f. Findon and Elspet Cay an ill.dau. b.22 Dec.1861 bap.23 Feb.1862
WOOD Isobel : Andrew Wood w.f. 4 Downies and wife Agnes Twigg a dau. b.19 ult. bap.1 Aug.1846
WOOD Isobel : Al.Wood w.f. 23 Portlethen and wife Margt.Craig a dau. b.9 Jan. bap.25 Feb.1854
WOOD Isobel : Geo.Wood w.f. Findon and wife Elspet Leiper a dau. b.27 Nov. bap.23 Dec.1854
WOOD Isobella and Mary : Jas.Wood s.f. 1 Downies and wife Mary Findlay, twins b.18 Feb. bap.29 Mar.1856
WOOD Jas. : Bap.a son to Geo.Wood w.f. Portlethen and Janat Craig b.6 Nov. bap.11 Nov.1841
WOOD Jas. : Alex.Wood w.f. 41 Findon and wife Jane Main a son b.6 and bap.7 Jul.1842
WOOD Jas. : Geo.Wood w.f. Findon and wife Helen Leiper a son b.20 ult. bap.28 Oct.1843
WOOD Jas. : Jas.Wood w.f. Findon and wife Jane Leiper a son b.6 and bap.9 Nov.1844
WOOD Jas. : Moses Wood w.f. 6 Downies and wife Elspet Knowles a son b.29 ult. bap.11 Sep.1847
WOOD James : Geo.Wood w.f. Findon and wife Ann Wood a son b.6 ult. bap.12 Mar.1848
WOOD James : Geo.Wood w.f. Findon and wife Margt.Craig a son b.8 ult. bap.29 Sep.1849
WOOD James : Al.Wood w.f. 5 Downies and wife Ann Leiper a son b.and bap.11 Dec.1849
WOOD James : Jo.Wood w.f. 2 Downies and wife Janat Wood a son b.9 Oct. bap 27 Nov.1852
WOOD James and Margaret : James Wood w.f. Village of Findon and wife Margt.Caie, twins b.4 Nov. bap.5 Dec.1853
WOOD James : Moses Wood w.f. Findon and wife Agnes Leiper a son b.15 Sep. bap.28 Oct.1854
WOOD James : Jas.Wood w.f. 23 Findon and wife Agnes Caie a son b.17 Nov. bap.16 Dec.1854
WOOD James : James Wood w.f. Findon and wife Margt.Robertson a son b.19 Jul. bap.25 Aug.1855
WOOD James : Al.Wood w.f. 32 Findon and wife Helen Wood a son b.2 Mar. bap.19 Apr.1856
WOOD James : James Wood w.f. 49 Findon and wife Margt.Caie a son b.10 ult. bap.27 Feb.1858

WOOD James : Geo.Wood w.f. 14 Findon and wife Is.Wood a son b.22 ult. bap.26 Feb.1859
WOOD James : Jas.Wood w.f. Downies and Helen Main there, an ill.son b.29 ult. bap.1 Oct.1859
WOOD James : James Wood w.f. Downies and wife Isabel Wood a son b.31 ult. bap.19 Jan.1860
WOOD James : Al.Wood w.f. 23 Portlethen and wife Margt.Craig a son b.and bap.9 May 1864
WOOD James : Jas.Wood w.f. 8 Downies and wife Helen Main a son b.14 ult. bap 17 Apr.1865
WOOD James : Geo.Wood w.f. 2 Downies and Jane Knowles there, an ill.son b.1 Sep. bap.5 Oct.1866
WOOD James : Geo.Wood w.f. 9 Findon and wife Isabella Leiper a son b.22 ult. bap.5 Jul.1868
WOOD James : Jas.Wood w.f. 22 Portlethen and wife Isabella Craig a son b.9 Nov. bap.28 Nov.1868
WOOD James : Andrew Wood w.f. Downies and wife Jane Wood a son b.30 Dec.1868 bap.31 Jan 1869
WOOD James and Jane : Twin children of James Wood w.f. and wife Susan Leiper b.at 10 Findon 25 Nov.bap.28Nov.1869
WOOD Jas. Chisholm : Wm.Wood w.f. Findon and wife Isobel Crow a son b.20 ult. bap.31 Aug.1844
WOOD Jas. Stewart : Jas.Wood, Hill of Portlethen and wife Mary Findlay a son b.3 inst. bap.6 Mar.1844
WOOD James Coutts : Wm.Wood w.f. 47 Findon and wife Helen Wood a son b.3 ult. bap.4 Oct. 1857
WOOD James Farquharson : Son of James Wood and wife Margt.Caie b.at Findon 12 Jan. bap.29 Jan.1869
WOOD Janat : John Wood w.f. 2 Downies and wife Janat Wood a dau. b.6 and bap.9 Jan.1844
WOOD Janat : Andrew Wood w.f. 36 Portlethen and wife Elspet Main a dau. b.17 ult. bap.4 Feb.1860
WOOD Janat : Andrew Wood, 1 Downies and wife Jane Wood a dau. b.23 Sep. bap.21 Oct.1865
WOOD Jane : Bap.a dau.to Geo.Wood w.f. and Ann Wood in Findon b.14 bap.20 Mar.1841
WOOD Jane : Moses Wood w.f. 6 Downies and wife Elspet Knowles a dau. b.and bap.18 Oct.1845
WOOD Jane : Andrew Wood w.f. Portlethen and wife Elspet Main a dau. b.27 ult. bap.29 Nov.1845
WOOD Jane : Jo.Wood w.f. 2 Downies and wife Janat Wood a dau. b.3 ult. bap.13 Dec.1847
WOOD Jane : Al.Wood w.f. Portlethen and wife Margt.Wood a dau. b.22 ult. bap.1 Feb.1846
WOOD Jane : Wm.Wood w.f. 38 Findon and wife Helen Wood a dau. b.4 Aug. bap.23 Sep.1848
WOOD Jane : Geo.Wood w.f. 22 Findon and wife Helen Leiper a dau. b.27 ult. bap.23 Sep.1848
WOOD Jane : Jas.Wood w.f. and wife Jane Leiper 44 Findon a dau.b.10 ult.bap.4 Oct.1848
WOOD Jane : Alex.Wood w.f.Findon and wife Helen Wood a dau.b.14 ult.bap.15 Feb.1859
WOOD Jane : Al.Wood w.f.Portlethen and wife Margt.Craig a dau.b.11 ult.bap.1 Oct.1859
WOOD Jane : Joseph Wood w.f.Downies and wife Jane Leiper a dau.b.24 ult.bap.8 Jun.1861
WOOD Jane : Al.Wood w.f.32 Downies and wife Ann Leiper a dau.b.15 ult.bap.3 Aug.1861
WOOD Jane : Jas.Wood w.f.Downies and Helen Main there an ill.dau.b.2 ult.bap.28 Sep.1862
WOOD Jane : Andrew Wood w.f.1 Downies and wife Jane Wood a dau.b.9 ult.bap.22 Mar.1863
WOOD Jane : Geo.Wood w.f.9 Findon and wife Isabella Leiper a dau.b.4 ult.bap.26 Mar.1863
WOOD Jane : Jas.Wood w.f.51 Downies and wife Ann Leiper a dau.b.4 ult.bap.at the Manse 6 Sep.1863
WOOD Jane : Moses Wood w.f.Findon and wife Agnes Leiper a dau.b.6 ult.bap.26 Mar.1864

WOOD	Jane :	Geo.Wood w.f.21 Downies and wife Ann Wood a dau.b.10 ult.bap.at the Manse 19 Jul.1868
WOOD	Jane :	see James and Jane
WOOD	Jessie :	Geo.Wood w.f.22 Portlethen and wife Jessie Stephen there an ill.dau.b.1 ult.bap.22 Aug.1858
WOOD	Jessie :	John Wood w.f.17 Portlethen and wife Ann Main a dau.b.31 ult.bap.10 Feb.1866
WOOD	John :	John Wood w.f.Portlethen and wife Elspet Wood a son b.10 bap.16 Mar.1844
WOOD	John :	John Wood w.f.45 Findon and wife Elspet Craig a son b.9 ult.bap.20 Oct.1845
WOOD	John :	Moses Wood w.f.6 Downies and wife Elspet Knowles a son b.15 ult.bap.1 Dec.1849
WOOD	John :	Jo.Wood w.f.1 Portlethen and wife Ann Craig a son b.23 ult.bap.30 Mar.1850
WOOD	John :	Geo.Wood w.f.Findon and wife Helen Leiper a son b.29 Jan.bap.26 Feb.1853
WOOD	John :	Andrew Wood 36 Portlethen and wife Elspet Main a son b.16 ult.bap.26 May 1857
WOOD	John :	Jas.Wood w.f.Findon and wife Margt.Robertson a son b.24 ult.bap.31 Dec.1859
WOOD	John :	Wm.Wood w.f.47 Findon and wife Helen Wood a son b.25 ult.bap.13 Apr.1861
WOOD	John :	Andrew Wood w.f.1 Downies and wife Jane Wood a son b.22 ult.bap.4 Jan.1862
WOOD	John :	Al.Wood w.f. and wife Margt.Craig 23 Portlethen a son b.24 ult.bap.30 Aug.1862
WOOD	John :	John Wood w.f.17 Portlethen and wife Ann Main a son b.18 ult.bap.1 Nov.1862
WOOD	John :	Geo.Wood w.f.Findon and wife Margt.Craig a son b.15 ult.bap.20 Nov.1862
WOOD	John :	Jas.Wood w.f.Findon and wife Margt.Caie a son b.15 ult.bap.22 Nov.1862
WOOD	John :	Joseph Wood w.f.35 Downies and wife Ann Wood a son b.13 ult.bap.15 Dec.1864
WOOD	John :	Jas.Wood w.f.44 Findon and wife Agnes Caie a son b.22 ult.bap.28 Jul.1865
WOOD	John :	John Wood w.f. 20 Downies and wife Agnes Wood a son b.29 Dec.1865 bap.14 Jan.1866
WOOD	John :	John Wood w.f. 40 Downies and wife Mary Christie a son b.6 ult. bap.16 Feb.1867
WOOD	John :	Jas.Wood w.f. 3 Findon and wife Jane Wood a son b.31 ult. bap.21 Sep.1867
WOOD	John :	Geo.Wood w.f. 41 Downies and wife .... a son b.20 Jan. bap 22 Jan.1869
WOOD	John Leiper :	Bap.a dau.to Alex.Wood w.f. and Ann Leiper in Downies b.10 Jun. bap.19 Jun.1841
WOOD	Joseph :	Jas.Wood, Hill of Portlethen and wife Mary Findlay a son b.8 ult. bap.25 Jul.1846
WOOD	Joseph :	Andrew Wood w.f. 4 Downies and wife Agnes Twigg a son b.15 ult. bap.3 Sep.1848
WOOD	Joseph :	Geo.Wood w.f. 9 Findon and wife Isobel Leiper a son b.11 ult. bap.29 Jan.1858
WOOD	Joseph :	Wm.Wood w.f. Findon and wife Helen Craig a son b.20 ult. bap.3 Jul.1858
WOOD	Joseph :	Joseph Wood w.f. 29 Downies and wife Jane Leiper a son b.31 ult. bap.1 Feb.1867
WOOD	Lilly :	Geo.Wood w.f. and Jane Knowles in Portlethen a dau. b.3 bap.13 Mar.1841
WOOD	Margt. :	Bap.a dau.to Geo.Wood w.f.and Helen Leiper in Findon 12 Jan.1841
WOOD	Margt. :	Al.Wood w.f. and wife Margt.Wood in Portlethen a dau. b.and bap.12 Mar.1841
WOOD	Margt. :	Alex.Wood w.f. Findon and wife Jane Wood a dau. b.in Aberdeen 9 Dec.1840 bap.6 Dec.1842
WOOD	Margt. :	Moses Wood w.f. Portlethen and wife Margt.Craig a dau.b.5 and bap.8 Mar.1845

WOOD Margt. : Geo.Wood w.f. and wife Margt.Craig, Findon a dau. b.4 Feb. bap.5 Apr.1851
WOOD Margt. : see James and Margt.,twins
WOOD Margt.Knowles and Moses : Moses Wood w.f. 6 Downies and wife Elspet Knowles, twins b.15 Jan. bap 16 Feb.1853
WOOD Margt. : Al.Wood w.f. 23 Portlethen and wife Margt.Craig a dau. b.11 Jun. bap.12 Jul.1856
WOOD Margt. : Joseph Wood w.f. Downies and wife Jane Leiper a dau. b.24 ult. bap.8 Nov.1856
WOOD Margt. : John Wood w.f. Findon and wife Eliza.Craighead a dau. b.24 ult. bap.2 Nov.1861
WOOD Margt. : Jas. Wood w.f. 51 Findon and wife Helen Leiper a dau. b.10 Aug. bap.16 Sep.1865
WOOD Martha : Andrew Wood w.f. 4 Downies and wife Agnes Twigg a dau. b.22 bap.30 Mar.1844
WOOD Mary : see Isobella and Mary, twins
WOOD Mary Ferguson : Geo.Wood w.f. Findon and wife Elspet Leiper a dau. b.22 ult. bap.3 Jan.1859
WOOD Moses : Wm.Wood w.f. Findon and wife Isobel Crow a son b.20 May bap.28 May 1842
WOOD Moses : Jo.Wood w.f. 2 Downies and wife Janat Wood a son b.11 ult. bap.16 Aug.1845
WOOD Moses : Jo.Wood w.f. 2 Downies and wife Janat Wood a son b.13 ult. bap.26 Jan.1850
WOOD Moses : see Margt.Knowles and Moses, twins
WOOD Moses : Geo.Wood w.f. Findon and wife Margt.Craig a son b.4 Nov. bap.5 Dec.1853
WOOD Moses : Jas.Wood and wife Jane Wood, 21 Downies a son b.28 May bap.19 Jul.1856
WOOD Moses : Wm.Wood w.f. 55 Findon and wife Helen Craig a son b.16 ult. bap.5 Jul.1866
WOOD Moses : Moses Wood w.f. 4 Findon and wife Agnes Leiper a son b.5 ult. bap.at the Manse 25 Oct 1868
WOOD Rachel : Geo.Wood w.f. 36 Findon and wife Margt.Craig a dau. b.8 Dec. bap.29 Dec.1867
WOOD Robt. : Alex.Wood w.f. Findon and wife Jane Main a son b.25 ult. bap.4 nov.1844
WOOD Robt. : Andrew Wood w.f. 36 Portlethen and wife Elspet Main (since dead) a son b.29 ult. bap.at the Manse 31 May 1863
WOOD Sally : Al.Wood w.f. 32 Findon and wife Helen Wood a dau. b.24 Dec.1854 bap. 20 Jan.1855
WOOD Simpson : Al.Wood w.f. Findon and wife Jane Main a dau. b.16 Jun. bap.28 Jun.1851
WOOD Susan : Jas.Wood w.f. 39 Downies and wife Ann Wood a dau. b.26 ult.bap.14 Jun.1845
WOOD Wm. : Bap. an ill.son of Wm.Wood and Isobel Crow, 1 Feb.1841
WOOD Wm. : Andrew Wood w.f. 4 Downies and wife Helen Twigg a son b.18 Oct. bap.22 Oct.1842
WOOD Wm. : Al.Wood w.f. 5 Downies and wife Ann Leiper a son b.1 ult. bap 15 Feb.1848
WOOD Wm. : Moses Wood w.f. and Agnes Leiper, Findon an ill.son b.10 ult. bap.5 Apr.1851
WOOD Wm. : Andrew Wood w.f. 36 Portlethen and wife Elspet Main a son b.11 ult. bap.21 Oct.1854
WOOD Wm. : Wm.Wood w.f. Findon and wife Helen Craig a son b.24 Sep. bap.20 Oct.1855
WOOD Wm. : Wm.Wood w.f. 47 Findon and wife Ellen Wood a son b.24 Jun. bap.4 Jul.1855
WOOD Wm. : Wm.Wood w.f. 35 Downies and wife Ann Main a son b.14 ult. bap.23 Mar.1860
WOOD Wm. : see Alex and Wm.,twins

WOOD : Wm. : Geo.Wood w.f. 9 Findon and wife Is.Leiper a son b.11 Jan. bap.3 Feb.1866

WOOD : Wm. : John Wood w.f. 17 Portlethen and wife Ann Main a son b.23 ult. bap.at the Manse 9 Oct.1868

WOOD : Wm.Craig : Is.Wood, presently residing at Sketraw and Wm.Craig, Cammochmore, an ill.son b. at Sketraw and bap.at the Manse of Portlethen 10 Nov.1867

WOOD : Wm.Stewart : John Wood w.f. 1 Portlethen and wife Ann Craig a son b.7 Jan. bap.12 Feb.1853

WRIGHT : Ann : John Wright,railway lab.,and wife from Northumberland,residing at Rumleygowan a dau.b.there 24 ult. bap.upon regular certificates from Northumberland 23 Mar.1850

WRIGHT : Eliz.Barbar : Sinclair Wright,Findon and wife Mary Symon a dau.b.6 ult.bap.31 Mar.1860

WRIGHT : Jane : Margt.Wright,Hillside an ill.dau.b.20 Nov.ult.bap.4 Jun.1858

WYNNES : Jas.(----) : ill.son of Mary Ann Wynnes,servant b.at Hillside 6 Sep.bap.10 Oct.1869

YEATS : Geo. : Jo.Yeats and Jane Leonard,Badentoy a son b.25 Aug.bap.30 Sep.1854

YEATS : Jas.Leonard : Al.Thomson and Is.Yeats,E.Cookston an ill.son b.24 Jun.bap.1 Sep.1862

YEATS : John : Margt.Yeats,E.Cookston and John Knowles,Mains of Findon an ill.son b.28 Sep.bap.1 Nov.1861

YOUNG : Isabella : Murdoch Young and wife Rebecca McDonald,Cobbleboads a dau.b.26 May bap.at Manse 18 Aug.1863

YOUNG : Rebecca : Murdoch Young and wife Rebecca McDonald,Cammochmoir a dau.b.12 Nov.1859 bap.13 Feb.1860

YULE : Catherine : Bap.a dau.to Alex.Yule and Margt.Jamieson,Clashfarquhar 14 Sep.1840

YULE : David : Al.Yule,Glashfarquhar and wife Margt.Jamieson a son b.12 ult.bap.4 Jan.1851

YULE : Helen : Helen Yule,Hatton of Ban.-Dev.,an ill.dau.b.25 Jun.bap.13 Aug.1864

YULE : Jane : Al.Yule jun.,Haremoss and Mary Ronald,Inverury an ill.dau.b.4 Jan.bap.6 Apr.1865

YULE : John : Al.Yule and wife Margt.Jamieson in Clashfarquhar a son b.31 Oct.bap.5 Nov.1842

YULE : Robert : Al.Yule and wife Margt.Jamieson in Glashfarquhar a son b.12 ult.bap.22 Jan.1848

YULE : Wm. : Al.Yule,Glashfarquhar and wife Margt.Jamieson a son b.3 Apr.bap.11 Apr.1845

SECTION 1(b)
Index of Mothers by maiden name, with (SURNAME) of issue for reference to 1(a)

Aberdein Mary (MASSON)
Adam Ann (FRASER)
Adam Garden or Gairn (SINCLAIR)
Adam Jane (BAXTER)
Adam Mary (MIDDLETON)
Adams Mary (ADAMS)
Adams Mary Baird (MARTIN)
Alexander Margt. (PIRIE)
Allan Ann (CRAIG)
Allan Ann (MASSON)
Allan Christ. (CRAIG)
Allan Jane (MAIN)
Allan Jane (MASSON)
Allan Margt. (SILVER)
Allan Margt. (CRAIG)
Allan Margt. (LEIPER)
Allan Susan (GORDON)
Anderson Ann (PETRIE)
Anderson Ann (DANIEL)
Anderson Betty (GORDON)
Anderson Christian (WALKER)
Anderson Eliz. (THOMSON)
Anderson Eliz. (MAIN)
Anderson Eliz. (CHALMERS)
Anderson Eliz. (MILTON)
Anderson Hanna (SIMPSON)
Anderson Helen (SMITH)
Anderson Jane (ANDERSON)
Anderson Jane (KNOWLES)
Anderson Mary (ROSS)

Bain Mary (SKELTON)
Baird Christian (BRIDGEFORD)
Baird Margt. (SHEPHERD)
Baird Mary (SHEPHERD)
Barclay Ann (DONALD)
Bartlet Eliz./Elsy (WALKER)
Baxter Isobel (ABERCROMBY)
Beattie Agnes (CHRISTIE)
Beattie Christina (McCALLUM)
Bell Eliz. (RHIND)
Bell Margt. (RHIND)
Benson Mary Ann (HUTCHESON)
Beverly Mary (ROBERTSON)
Bisset Mary (PIRIE)
Black Agnes (HORN)
Blair Eliz. (BARRON)
Blair Eliz. (BLAIR)
Blair Isobel (McINTOSH)
Blair Is. (RAE)
Bridgeford Christian (LAING)
Brock Eliz. (WILSON)
Brown Eliz. (BROWN)
Brown Eliz. (COUTTS)
Brown Sophia (INGRAM)
Brownie Helen (CAMPBELL)
Bruce Eliz. (COUTTS)
Burnett Ann (CRABB)
Burnett Eliz. (CRAIG)
Byres Eliz. (MAITLAND)
Caie Agnes (WOOD)
Caie Jane (LEIPER)

Caie Margt. (WOOD)
Cairnie Isobel (REITHE)
Carneggie Margt. (DALE)
Cay Elspet (WOOD)
Chalmers Ann (WATSON)
Chalmers Eliz. (ALLAN)
Chisholm Elspet (MOR(R)ICE / MORRIS)
Chisholm Margt. (FERGUSON)
Chisholm Jessie (McCROBBIE)
Christie Ann (LEIPER)
Christie Ann (MENNIE)
Christie Isabella (COUTTS)
Christie Jane (CRAIG)
Christie Mary (WOOD)
Christie Mary (HUTCHEON)
Collard Margt. (ANDERSON)
Colvin Margt. (McDONALD)
Cooper Margt. (ROBERTSON)
Copland Margt. (MOIR)
Copland Margt. (COPLAND)
Copland Mary (COPLAND)
Copland Mary (DEMPSTER)
Coull Helen (CRAIG)
Couts Mary (COUTS)
Coutts Mary (BUCHAN)
Coutts Mary (GRAY)
Craig Agnes (WOOD)
Craig Agnes (LEIPER)
Craig Ann (LINDSAY)
Craig Ann (ROBERTSON)
Craig Ann (CRAIG)

Craig Ann (WOOD)
Craig Eliz. (LEIPER)
Craig Eliz. (FERGUSON)
Craig Eliz. (WOOD)
Craig Eliz. (CRAIG)
Craig Elspet (WOOD)
Craig Elspet (MILNE)
Craig Elspet (LIVINGSTON)
Craig Elspet (CRAIG)
Craig Elspet (LEIPER)
Craig Helen (LEAPER)
Craig Helen (CRAIG)
Craig Helen (WOOD)
Craig Is. (CRAIG)
Craig Isabel (NICOLL)
Craig Isabella (WOOD)
Craig Isabella (CRAIG)
Craig Isobel (WOOD)
Craig Isobel (LEIPER)
Craig Janat (WOOD)
Craig Janat (CRAIG)
Craig Jane (McBEITH)
Craig Jane (LEIPER)
Craig Jane (SIMPSON)
Craig Jane (CRAIG)
Craig Jane (MAIN)
Craig Jessie/Jessy (CRAIG)
Craig Lilly (MAIN)
Craig Lilly (CRAIG)
Craig Lilly (ROBERTSON)
Craig Margt. (MAIN)
Craig Margt. (WOOD)
Craig Margt. (CRAIG)
Craig Mary (WOOD)

Craighead Eliz. (WOOD)
Craighead Margt. (WOOD)
Crow Isobel (WOOD)
Cruickshank Catherine (STOTT)
Cumming Ann (DUNCAN)
Cushnie Jane (McGLAUCIN)
Davidson Eliz. (MILNE)
Davidson Helen (DUNBAR)
Davidson Isobel (CAIE)
Davidson Isobel (CARR)
Davidson Margt. (STEWART)
Davidson Mary (FRASER)
Dempster Margt. (KENN)
Donald Barbara (THOMSON)
Donald Eliz. (DONALD)
Donald Eliz. (WALLACE)
Donald E. (HUNTER)
Donald Elspet (KNOWLES)
Donald Jane or Janat (CHALMERS)
Donald Jessie (DONALD)
Donald Jessie (McCROBBIE)
Donald Margt. (THOMSON)
Douglas Agnes (RANKIN)
Douglass Christian (WALKER)
Dow Jane (PATERSON)
Duncan Betty (MURRAY)
Duncan Catherine (HUNTER)
Duncan Eliz. (SKENE)
Duncan Eliz. (WALKER)
Duncan Jane (ASHER)
Duncan Jane (McKAY)
Eddie Susan (MASSON)
Edward Mary (CHISOM)
Elrick Harriet (KENNEDY)

Ewan Is. (McCLEAN)
Ewen Margaret (GORDON)
Ewen Mary A. Bruce (MOIR)
Farquharson Mary (JAMIESON)
Fenton Christian (DONALD)
Ferguson Hanna (TAYLOR)
Findlay M. (RUST)
Findlay Margaret (RUST)
Findlay Mary (WOOD)
Flatt Margaret (CRAIG)
Forbes Jane/Janat (GREIG)
Forbes Margaret (CRAIG)
Forbes Mary (DUNCAN)
Forrest Margaret (RODNEY)
Fowler Ann (LOB(B)AN)
Fraser Eliz. (MASSON)
Fraser Jane Ann (COSSAR)
Gairn Jane (MILNE)
Gairn Mary (MILNE)
Garden Mary (MILNE)
Gerrard Susan (WALKER)
Gibb Ann (JOHNSTON)
Gibb Christian (TOUGH)
Gibb Hutcheon (BROWN)
Gibb Jane Gordon (MITCHELL)
Gibbon(s) Isabel(1a) (MURRAY)
Gillespie Ann (MILNE)
Glennie Mary (MILNE)
Gordon Ann (STEWART)
Gordon Ann (ROBB)
Gordon Ann (COUTTS)
Gordon Jane/Janat (ROBERTSON)
Gordon Jane (ALLAN)
Gordon Mary Ann (STEWART)

Graham Mary (GORDON)
Grant Janat (STRATHDEE)
Gregory Elspet (COUTTS)
Grubb Jane (MAVOR)
Harper Christina (FOWLER)
Hay Beatrice (COOK)
Hay Jane (SKENE)
Hay Margt. (ALEXANDER)
Hay Margt. (WOOD)
Henderson Eliz. (FINDLAY)
Henry Jane (ARCHIBALD)
Henry Margt. (GORDON)
Howie Ann (MILNE)
Howie Eliz. (DONALD)
Howie Eliz. (FINDLAY)
Howie Helen (TOUGH)
Howie Isabella (CHISHOLM)
Howie Isobel (JAFFREY)
Hunter Christian (HUNTER)
Hunter Christian (KNOWLES)
Hunter Eliz. (BURCHELL)
Hunter Helen (HUTCHEON)
Hunter Isabella J. (TAYLOR)
Hunter Margt. (BROCKIE)
Hunter Margt. (VALENTINE)
Hunter Mary (DONALDSON)
Hutcheon Eliz. (ANDERSON)
Hutcheon Isobel (BALNEVES)
Hutcheon Jane (ALEXANDER)
Hutcheon Jane (LOW)
Jaffrey Jane (ROBERTSON)
Jamieson Catherine (SKENE)
Jamieson Eliz. (CAMPBELL)
Jamieson Margt. (YULE/YUIL)

Johnston Jane (ROBERTSON)
Johnston Jane G. (RIACH)
Johnston Margt. (JOHNSTON)
Johnston Margt. (FRASER)
Johnston Margt. (MORRISON)
Joss Jessie (NICOL)
Kan Ann (COOPER)
Kane Elspet (McKENZIE)
Kane Elspet (GEDDES)
Kane Helen (TURNER)
Kane Helen (CROMBIE)
Kane Helen (MILNE)
Kane Issabella (KANE)
Kane Jane (BOOTH)
Kane Jessie (PATERSON)
Kane Margt. (SMITH)
Kane Margt. (WOOD)
Kean Helen (KEAN)
Keith Margt. (HUTCHEON)
Keith Mary (DUNBAR)
Kenn Elspet (SPALDING)
Kerr/Keer Margt. (WALKER)
Kin(n)aird Jemima (STEWART)
Kinneff Jemima (STUART)
Knowles Ann (LEIPER)
Knowles Elspet (WOOD)
Knowles Elspet (HOWIE)
Knowles Jane (WOOD)
Knowles Margt. (KNOWLES)
Knox Jannat (MILNE)
Knox Margt. (LEIPER)
Laing Isobel (STUART/STEWART)
Lamb Mary (FINDLAY)
Law S.C.B. (STEWART)

Lawson Mary (FARQUHAR)
Leiper Agnes (LEIPER)
Leiper Agnes (WOOD)
Leiper Agnes (MAIN)
Leiper Agnes (KNOWLES)
Leiper Ann (LEIPER)
Leiper Ann (KNOWLES)
Leiper Ann (MAIN)
Leiper Ann (WOOD)
Leiper Ann (MASSON)
Leiper Ann (DONALD)
Leiper Ann (CRAIG)
Leiper Betty (WOOD)
Leiper Betty (MAIN)
Leiper Christian (CHRISTIE)
Leiper Eliz. (ANDERSON)
Leiper Eliz. (BROWN)
Leiper Eliz. (LEIPER)
Leiper Eliz. (MAIN)
Leiper Eliz. (WOOD)
Leiper Elspet (LEIPER)
Leiper Elspet (BROWN)
Leiper Elspet (HAND)
Leiper Elspet (WOOD)
Leiper Elspet (MAIN)
Leiper Helen (LEIPER)
Leiper Helen (MILNE)
Leiper Helen (WOOD)
Leiper Isabella (LEIPER)
Leiper Isabella (MAIN)
Leiper Isabella (CRAIG)
Leiper Isabella (WOOD)
Leiper Janat (LEIPER)
Leiper Janat (WOOD)

Leiper Jane (CRAIG)
Leiper Jane (MAIN)
Leiper Jane (MILNE)
Leiper Jane (LEIPER)
Leiper Jane (WOOD)
Leiper Jessy / Jessie (LEIPER)
Leiper Lilly (MAIN)
Leiper Margaret (LEIPER)
Leiper Margaret (MAIN)
Leiper Margaret (WOOD)
Leiper Margaret (CRAIG)
Leiper Margaret (McWILLIAM)
Leiper Susan (WOOD)
Leith Ann (HUNTER)
Leith Barbara (PATTERSON)
Leith Rebecca (PATTERSON)
Lennie Christian (WATT)
Leonard Barbara (TAYLOR)
Leonard Eliz. (LEIPER)
Leonard Isobel (PATTERSON)
Leonard Jane (YEATS)
Leonard Margaret (NORRIE)
Leonard Mary (SIMPSON)
Lesslie Jane (FERRIER/FARRIER)
Lindsay Ann (KINMUND)
Littlejohn Jane (CAMERON)
Low Ann (ROBERTSON)
Low Eliz. (REID)
Low Jane (HUTCHEON)
Low Margt. (ALEXANDER)
Low Mary (GORDON)
Low Mary (CRAIG)
Low May (ROBERTSON)
Lowden Margt. (STEWART)

McCleanan Margt. (GRANT)
McCleran Eliz. (BANGE)
McCrobbie Jane (CAMPBELL)
McDonald Clementina (ESSELMONT)
McDonald Jane (MCINTYRE)
McDonald Martha (CRAIG)
McDonald Rebecca (YOUNG)
McKay Mary (McKAY)
McKenzie Is. (ADAM)
McKenzie Isabel (BLACK)
McLaren Margt. (McLAREN)
McPherson Margt. (MILNE)
Mackie Mary (FINNIE)
Main Ann (MAIN)
Main Ann (CRAIG)
Main Ann (WOOD)
Main Eliz. (MAIN)
Main Elspet (CRAIG)
Main Elspet (WOOD)
Main Helen (LEITH)
Main Helen (MAIN)
Main Helen (WOOD)
Main Isabella (MAIN)
Main Isobel (LEIPER)
Main Janat (MAIN)
Main Jane (KNOWLES)
Main Jane (LEIPER)
Main Jane (MAIN)
Main Jane (NICOL)
Main Jane (WOOD)
Main Jessy (LEIPER)
Main Lilly (MAIN)
Main Margt. (DUTHIE)
Main Margt. (LEIPER)

Main Mary (MAIN)
Maitland Barbara (LOW)
Maitland Tereizah (STEWART/STUART)
Mason Margt. (CUSHNIE)
Massie Jane (MIDDLETON)
Masson Agnes (DURNO)
Masson Agnes (MASSON)
Masson Ann (McINTOSH)
Masson Ann (MIDDLETON)
Masson Caroline (NICOL)
Masson Christina (CRAIG)
Masson Eliz. (MAIN)
Masson Eliz. (MASSON)
Masson Elspet (MASSON)
Masson Elspet (SMITH)
Masson Helen (MASSON)
Masson Janat (WOOD)
Masson Jane (ALLAN)
Masson Jane (MUTCH)
Masson Jane (TOUGH)
Masson Mary (MASSON)
Mess/Meff Isabella (STRATTON)
Melvin Helen (MITCHELL)
Melvin Jane (TAYLOR)
Mennie Mary (PATTERSON)
Middleton Isabella (RAE)
Milne Ann (ANDERSON)
Milne Ann (FINDLAY)
Milne Ann (LAWSON)
Milne Ann (McKENZIE)
Milne Ann (ROBERTSON)
Milne Barbara (HALL)
Milne Elsie (MILNE)
Milne Elspet (MASSON)

Milne Helen Reid/Rae (FINDLAY)
Milne Isabella (LAMB)
Milne Jessie Smith (SMITH)
Milne Margt. (REID)
Milne Margt. (SCROGGIE/SCORGIE)
Milne Margt. (WELSH)
Milne Mary Magdilene (MILNE)
Milne Mary (WELSH)
Milne Mary (VALENTINE)
Mitchell Agnes (REID)
Mitchell Eliz. (NICOL)
Mitchell Helen (MAIN)
Mitchell Helen (NICOL)
Mitchell Is. (LOW)
Mitchell Margt. (MacKAY)
Moir Barbara (CRAIG)
Moir Christian (BEATON)
Moir Margt. (WALKER)
Monro Mary (CAMPBELL)
Morrison Eliz. (THOMSON)
Morice Jane (LEIPER)
Mouat Mary (THOMSON)
Mowat Jane (VALENTINE)
Murray Isabella (McDONALD)
Murray Margt. (SPENCE)
Nairn Mary (PATTERSON)
Nicol Ann (AITKEN)
Nicol Eliz. (McKENZIE)
Nicol Jane (MATHER)
Officer Magdalene (JOHNSTON)
Officer Magdalene (SCORGIE)
Ogston Isobel (STEWART)
Omens Jane (JOHNSTON)
Park Eliz. (DONALDSON)

Patterson Ann (CARR)
Patterson Eliz. (RUXTON)
Patterson Mary (KANE/KENN)
Petrie Eliz. (LAMOND)
Petrie Eliz. (LEONARD)
Petrie Isabella (LAMMOND/LOMONT)
Petrie Jane (BEATTIE)
Petrie Jane (PATTERSON)
Petrie Margt. (PETRIE)
Phimister Mary (SCOTT)
Pithie Margt. (LONGMUIR)
Porter Ann (REID)
Porter Jessie (REID)
Rae Jane (PRATT)
Reid Christian (McKENZIE)
Reid Eliz. (BLAIR)
Reid Helen (KEITH)
Reid Isabel (McDONALD)
Reid Janat (KANE)
Reid Jane (ROSS)
Reid Jane (HUTCHEON)
Reid Jane (LOW)
Reid Jessie (KANE/THANE)
Reid Margt. (WARN)
Reid Margt. (THOMSON)
Reid Margt. (McKENZIE)
Reid Margt. (GILLESPIE)
Reid Mary (REID)
Riddoch Margt./Mary (ROBB)
Ritchie Jane (SLICER)
Robb Ann (ANDERSON)
Robb Eliz. (DURWARD)
Robb Helen (MASSON)
Robbie Eliz. (MAIN)

Robbie Eliz. (BIRD)
Robertson Ann (CHALMERS)
Robertson Christ. (LEIPER)
Robertson Helen (ROBERTSON)
Robertson Jane (LINDSAY)
Robertson Jane (MAIN)
Robertson Lilly (BLACKHALL)
Robertson Margt. (ROSS)
Robertson Margt. (WOOD)
Roger Helen (HOWIE)
Ronald Mary (YULE)
Rose Christian (EDWARDS)
Rose Christian (SIMPSON)
Ross Isabella (REID)
Rust Isabel (SOUTHER)
Rust Jane (PATTERSON)
Rust Mary Ann (BEGG)
Scorgie Eliz. (CRUICKSHANK)
Scott Margt./Martha (THOMSON)
Shepherd Ann (FRASER)
Shepherd Jane (BURNETT)
Shepherd Mary (SHEPHERD)
Shirres Margaret (MILNE)
Sievewright Isobel (THOW)
Sillver Margaret (KANE/KENN)
Silver Rebecca (MAITLAND)
Simm Jane (LEONARD)
Sinclair Is. (McCOLL)
Sinclair Margaret (ALLAN)
Sinclair Margaret (PETRIE)
Smart Mary (McCLOUD)
Smith C. (COPLAND)
Smith Caroline (McDONALD)
Smith Helen (HUNTER)

Smith Helen (SCORGIE)
Smith Jane (BRUCE)
Smith Margaret (ALLAN)
Stephen Jessie (WOOD)
Stewart Ann (KNIGHT)
Stewart Catherine (McROBBIE)
Stewart Eliz. (KANE)
Stewart Eliz. (THOMSON)
Stewart Jane (LEITH)
Stewart Jane (VALENTINE)
Stewart Margt./Mary (CRAGGIE)
Stewart Mary (CARNEGGIE)
Stewart Mary (JAMIESON)
Stewart Mary Ann (KANE/KEAN)
Stewart Mary Ann (STEWART)
Still .... (SMITH)
Stott Margt. (KEMP)
Strachan Ann (CHRISTIE)
Strachan Christian (EWEN)
Strachan Isabella (TAYLOR)
Strachan Mary Ann (STEPHEN)
Straiton Isabella (VALENTINE)
Sutherland Jane (JAMIESON)
Sutherland Jane (SOUTHER/SOUTER)
Swanson Ann (EWEN)
Swanson Jane (EWEN)
Symon Mary (WRIGHT)
Tait Ann (WALKER)
Tavendale Susan (DUTHIE)
Taylor Ann (DUTHIE)
Taylor Elspet (McKAY)
Taylor Is. (BAIN)
Taylor Isobel (FORBES)
Taylor Margt. (GIBB)

Taylor Mary (McDONALD)
Thom Euphm. (MANN)
Thomson Eliz. (GALL)
Thomson Elspet (LEIPER)
Thomson Isobel (STEWART)
Thomson Mary (JOHNSTON)
Thomson Sarah (ANDERSON)
Thow Eliz. (THOW)
Tosh Margt. (ANGUS)
Tough Jane (SMITH)
Tough Margt. (MASSON)
Trail Ann (RIACH)
Trail Elspet (MacKILLIGAN)
Trail Jane (STRATTON)
Trail Jessie/Jessy (STRATTON)
Troup Eliz. (CHRISTIE)
Troup Mary A. (CHRISTIE)
Twigg Agnes (WOOD)
Twigg Helen (WOOD)
Walker Ann (ANDERSON)
Walker Ann (DUNCAN)
Walker Eliz. (JAMIESON)
Walker Eliz. (MILNE)
Walker Ellen (PARK)
Walker Elspet (KNOWLES)
Walker Elspet (WALKER)
Walker Is. (LEIGHTON)
Walker Jane (MUGLEN)
Walker Mary (McALPINE)
Walker Mary (MILNE)
Watson Margt.Sim (WATSON)
Watt Eliz.(SINCLAIR)
Wattie Agnes (MAVOR)
Welsh Margt. (DOUGLASS)

Welsh Margt. (MORRISON)
Welsh Mary (THOW)
Welsh Mary (WELSH)
Wilson Isobel (STEWART)
Wilson Mary (LAIRD)
Wood ..... (WOOD)
Wood ..... (LEIPER)
Wood Agnes (CRAIG)
Wood Agnes (LAMB)
Wood Agnes (LEIPER)
Wood Agnes (ROBERTSON)
Wood Agnes (WOOD)
Wood Ann (CRAIG)
Wood Ann (LEIPER)
Wood Ann (MAIN)
Wood Ann (WOOD)
Wood Christian (SUTHERLAND)
Wood Eliz.(DOW)
Wood Eliz.(LEIPER)
Wood Eliz.(WALKER)
Wood Ellen (WOOD)
Wood Elspet (McCLOUD)
Wood Elspet (MILNE)
Wood Elspet (THOM)
Wood Elspet (WOOD)
Wood Helen (WOOD)
Wood Isabella (MAIN)
Wood Isabella (WOOD)
Wood Is.(ROBERTSON)
Wood Isobel (CRAIG)
Wood Isobel (KNOWLES)
Wood Isobel (MASSON)
Wood Isobel (WOOD)
Wood Janat (LEIPER)

Wood Janat (WOOD)
Wood Jane (ALLAN)
Wood Jane (KNOWLES)
Wood Jane (LEIPER)
Wood Jane (MAIN)
Wood Jane (ROBERTSON)
Wood Jane (WOOD)
Wood Jessie/Jessy (CRAIG)
Wood Jessie/Jessy (LEIPER)
Wood ....: (LEIPER)
Wood Lilly (CRAIG)
Wood Margt. (CRAIG)

Wood Margt. (KEILTY/KELPY)
Wood Margt. (KNOWLES)
Wood Margt. (LEIPER)
Wood Margt. (MAIN)
Wood Margt. (SCORGIE)
Wood Margt. (WOOD)
Wood Mary (SCORGIE)
Wood Rachel (MAIN)
Wright Ann (STEWART/STUART)
Wright Christian (CAMERON)
Wright Helen (FORBES)
Wright Helen (McKENZIE)

Wright Margt. (WRIGHT)
Wright Margt. (SKELTON)
Wright Margt. (SMITH)
Wynnes Mary Ann (WYNNES)
Wyse Ann (McCONNACHIE)
Yeats Is. (CRUICKSHANK)
Yeats Margt. (COUTTS)
Young Jane (MAIN)
Yule/Yuile Helen (YULE/YUILE)
Yule/Yuile Jane (HOWIE)
Yule/Yuile Jane (PAPE)
Yule/Yuile Margt. (MIDDLETON)

SECTION 1(c)

Index of Fathers of Illegitimate Issue with (SURNAME) of issue for reference to 1(a)

Balnevis George (BRIDGEFORD)
Cameron P. (RUXTON)
Craig Willian (WOOD)
Dawson R. (MASSON)
Howie George (JAMIESON)
Kane Alexander (LOW)

Knowles John (YEATS)
Lilly Alexander (REID)
McDonald James (MIDDLETON)
Milne Alexander (JOHNSTON)
Polson Patrick (McCLEARAN)
Slicer .... (ROGER)

Taylor James (WELSH)
Thomson Alexander (YEATS)
Thomson Andrew (BRIDGEFORD)
Yuil Alexander (MILNE)

....

Alphabeticsl list of Marriages by Male SURNAME with all given marriage information

ABERCROMBIE	John : and Helen Kane mar. at Badentoy 1 Jun. 1844
ABERCROMBY	Andrew : Maryculter parish and Isobel Baxter in this parish mar. at Cassyport 20 May 1843
ABERDEEN	Thomas : and Margaret Longmuir, Fetteresso mar. at Newhall 10 Dec. 1842
AIKEN	Andrew : Banchory Devenick and Ann Nicol in this parish mar. at Rumleygowan 28 Nov. 1863
AIR	James : Glasscairn and Elizabeth Masson, Old Machar mar. at the Manse 1 Dec. 1866
ALEXANDER	James : and Jane Brewster both in this parish mar. 3 Jan. 1857
ALLAN	---- : and ---- Robison mar. 18 Feb. 1843 at Cove Nigg
ALLAN	George : and Jane Yule, Stonehaven parish of Fetteresso mar. at Loirston, Nigg 9 Nov. 1843
ALLAN	John : precentor and Jane Wood, Findon mar. 5 May 1849
ANDERSON	Andrew : and Margaret Walker, Mid Ardo, Banchory Devenick mar. at Redmyre 12 Jul. 1862
ANDERSON	David : and Margaret Collard both in this parish mar. 21 Nov. 1856
ANDERSON	James : and Ann Walker mar. at Cookston 6 Jun. 1848
ANDERSON	James : parish of Fetteresso and Anne Pirie, this parish mar. at North Mains, Findon 22 Nov. 1851
ANDERSON	William : tinsmith, Aberdeen and Sarah Thomson, Aberdeen, late in Findon mar. at Aberdeen 31 Jan. 1857
ANDERSON	William : Newmills and Elspet Leonard, Badentoy mar. at Badentoy 16 Aug. 1851
BEATTIE	James : blacksmith, Portlethen and Mary Ann Rust, Bankhead mar. at Bankhead 5 Mar. 1869
BEGG	Patrick : Skene parish and Helen Keith this parish mar. at Westside of Portlethen 2 Jun. 1865
BERRY	George : and Isabella Craig, Old Aberdeen mar. at Hillhead of Portlethen 4 Dec. 1863
BLACK	William : Tarves and Isabella Robertson mar. at Cairnrobin (at her Father's) 17 Dec. 1863
BLACKHALL	James : white fisher, Skaterow and Helen Main, Portlethen mar. at the Manse 17 Nov. 1866
BRODIE	George : and Jane Longmuir mar. at Altens of Nigg for Rev. Fairweather on 15 Dec. 1849
BROWN	James : Foveran and Hutcheon Gibb in this parish mar. at Mains of Hillside 7 Jun. 1862
BROWN	Robert : shoemaker, Hillside and Elspet Leiper in Downies mar. in church 28 Feb. 1845
BUCHAN	James : Newmachar and Mary Coutts, Hill of Portlethen mar. at Hill of Portlethen 30 Jun. 1866
CAITHNESS	---- : Kennay and Helen Reid, daughter of P. Reid, Kincorth mar. at Kincorth, Nigg 6 Apr. 1855
CAMERON	Richard : and Christian Wright at Hillside of Findon, daughter of Jonathan Wright there, mar.10 Feb.1849
CAMPBELL	Alexander : and Elizabeth Jamieson both in this parish mar. 14 Nov. 1856
CARR	John : East Cookston and Ann Patterson, West Cookston mar. 28 Jun. 1850
CATTO	James Shirres : Cove and Ann Nicol, Rumleygowan mar. 18 Dec. 1857
CHALMERS	David : and Elizabeth Anderson, Hillside, mar. at Hillside 11 Apr. 1868

CHISHOLM	John : and Harriet Gavin, both in parish of Fetteresso mar. at Gellybrands Toll 28 Aug. 1841
CHISHOLN	William : and Isobel Howie, Findon, mar. at Findon 14 Aug. 1854 (parties, with Mother-in-Law, going to America, tomorrow)
CHRISTIE	James : Stranathra, and Margaret Craig, Portlethen, mar. in Church of Portlethen 17 Feb. 1844
CHRISTIE	Peter : w.f. Sketraw, and Janat Main, Portlethen, mar. at Portlethen 7 Nov. 1863
CHRISTIE	William : Sketraw or Newtonhill, and Elspet Main, Downies mar. at the Manse 4 Feb. 1860
CHRISTIE	William : w.f. Sketraw, and Jane Leiper, Portlethen, mar. at the Manse 29 Feb. 1868
CLAIK ?	James : and Elizabeth McBain, mar. at Bourtreybush Inn, 9 Aug. 1845
CLERIHEW	Rev. : and Miss McDonald, Printfield Woodside, mar. 4 Dec. 1850
COOPER	James : Fetteresso, and Ann Keann in this parish, mar. at the Manse 13 Jul. 1867
COSSAR	Francis : and Jane Fraser, mar. at Hill of Portlethen, 20 Mar. 1866
COUTTS	Thomas : Hill of Portlethen, and Isabella Christie mar. at Downies 23 Nov. 1861
CRAIG	Alexander : w.f. Portlethen, and Lilly Wood, mar. at Portlethen 28 Dec. 1844
CRAIG	Alexander : w.f. Portlethen, and Christina Masson, Skateraw, mar. at the Manse 26 Dec. 1868 by Rev. Wm.Bruce
CRAIG	Andrew : w.f. Portlethen, and Helen Craig there, mar. 14 Apr.1855
CRAIG	Andrew : w.f. and Ann Leiper, Portlethen, mar. at Manse 11 Oct. 1858
CRAIG	Andrew : w.f. Portlethen, and Elspet Craig, Portlethen, mar. at the Manse 28 Dec. 1867
CRAIG	George : w.f. Portlethen, and Margaret Leiper, Findon, mar. in Church of Portlethen 2 Mar. 1844
CRAIG	George : and Margaret Craig, w.f. in Portlethen, mar. 17 Nov. 1849
CRAIG	George : w.f. 6 Portlethen, and Margaret Main Allan, mar. at the Manse 2 Nov. 1850
CRAIG	George : w.f. and Ann Allan at Portlethen, mar. 26 Apr. 1851
CRAIG	George : parish of Nigg, and Jean Anderson in this parish, mar. at Cairnrobin 13 Dec. 1851
CRAIG	George : w.f. 39 Portlethen, and Ann Wood, Portlethen, mar. Portlethen 25 Sep. 1858
CRAIG	George : w.f. Portlethen, and Margaret Craig, Portlethen, mar. 30 Oct. 1858
CRAIG	George : w.f. Portlethen, and Jane Main, Portlethen, mar. at the Manse 17 Oct. 1868
CRAIG	James : w.f. Portlethen, and Margaret Leiper, Portlethen, mar. at the Manse 24 Oct. 1868
CRAIG	James : and Jean Leiper, Findon, mar. at the Manse 29 Dec. 1849
CRAIG	James : w.f. Portlethen, and Jessie Craig, dau. of 'unies janny' there, mar. 16 Jun. 1849
CRAIG	James : w.f. and Elizabeth Burnett at Portlethen, mar. 5 Oct. 1850
CRAIG	James : w.f. 54 Portlethen, and Jane Craig, Portlethen, mar. at Portlethen 13 Nov. 1852
CRAIG	James : w.f. 31 Portlethen, and Margaret Craig there, mar. at Portlethen 26 Feb. 1853
CRAIG	James : and Christian Allan, Portlethen, mar. at Portlethen Village 16 Dec. 1854
CRAIG	James : w.f. Portlethen, and Jane Wood, Findon, mar. Findon 30 Nov. 1861
CRAIG	James : w.f. 55 Portlethen, and Ann Wood, 48 Portlethen, mar. at Manse 21 Oct. 1865

CRAIG   John : w.f. Portlethen, and Margaret Flatt also there, mar. 19 Nov.1842

CRAIG   John : quarrier, and Ann Allan, mar. at the Cove 6 Oct. 1855

CRAIG   John : w.f. 25 Portlethen, and Margaret Craig, Portlethen mar. 21 Nov. 1857

CRAIG   John : w.f. 37 Portlethen, and Jessie Wood, mar. at Portlethen 30 Dec. 1866

CRAIG   Joseph : w.f. Portlethen, and Helen Coull, also in Village of Portlethen mar. 15 Oct. 1842

CRAIG   Joseph : w.f. 12 Portlethen, and Ann Leiper, Findon, mar. at the Manse 29 Sep. 1855

CRAIG   Joseph : w.f. 3 Portlethen and Ann Leiper, Portlethen mar. 24 Oct. 1857

CRAIG   Joseph : w.f. 47 Portlethen and Jane Christie, Portlethen mar. 31 Oct. 1857

CRAIG   Joseph : Village of Portlethen and Jane Wood, 14 Carmelite Street, Aberdeen mar. 30 Dec. 1864

CRAIG   Joseph : w.f. Portlethen and Lilly Craig, Portlethen Mar. at the Manse 28 Mar. 1868

CRAIG   William : white fisher Portlethen and Helen Craig there, mar. 25 Oct. 1845

CRAIG   William : w.f. Portlethen and Jane Allan, Cove, Nigg, mar. in Church 5 May 1855

CRAIG   William : w.f. Portlethen and Elizabeth Craig, Portlethen mar. at Portlethen 3 Dec. 1859

CRAIG   William : Portlethen and Isabella Leiper, Findon mar. at School of Portlethen 20 Nov. 1869

CRUICKSHANK   John : and Isabella Yeats both in this parish mar. at East Cookston 17 Jun. 1864

CUDDIE   Nicholas : brewer, Aberdeen and Jane Dianah Middleton, there, mar. at Stonehaven 30 Sep. 1846

DAVIDSON   George : and Ann Johnston at Burnthillock, both residing in this parish mar. 17 Jun. 1843

DAVIDSON   John : and Isobel Craig mar. at College Street, Aberdeen 6 Oct. 1855

DEMPSTER   George : and Mary Copland mar. at Hill of Portlethen 4 Aug. 1865

DONALD   James : and Ann Leiper both in this parish mar. at the Manse 27 Aug. 1865

DONALD   John : Fetteresso and Helen Ferrier in this parish mar. at Moss-side of Findon 16 Dec. 1865

DONALD   Robert : and Alexandrina Ewan Johnston both in this parish mar. at Damhead of Portlethen 22 Nov. 1865

DONALDSON   Smith : and Jean Howie, parish of Nigg, mar. at Hill of Findon 5 Dec. 1863

DUNBAR   James : and Mary Keith, (dau. of Jas. Keith, Eden, N.Banchory) Dunnottar, mar. at Westside 31 May 1856

DUNCAN   Mr. : and Miss Hunter, late teacher at Badentoy, mar. at Windsor Pl. Aberdeen 21 Aug. 1854

DUTHIE   David : and Mary Forbes, Hillside mar.9 Sep. 1854 (woman having left the Papists)

EWEN   John : and Elspet Craig, both in this district, mar. at Portlethen 5 Jun.1854

FARQUHAR   John : Cairnrobin, and Christina Strachan, Mains of Charleston, parish of Nigg, mar. at Charleston 29 Nov.1851

FERGUSON   James : and Mary Lawson, mar. at Hill of Portlethen, 1 Mar. 1845

FERRIER   John : surgeon, Cove, and Annie Lundie, late govrness at the Manse of Portlethen, mar. at Aberdeen 11 Mar. 1850

FINDLAY   George : and Eliza. Knowles, both in this parish, mar. at Blackhills 18 Feb. 1862

FINDLAY   John : Parish of Nigg, and Elizabeth Howie at Findon, mar. 24 Jul. 1857

FORBES   John : and Mary Lamont, both resid. at Hill of Turnemiddle, mar. in the Manse 25 Sep. 1859

FORBES   Andrew : Torry, and Margaret Caie, both in the parish of Nigg, mar. at the Cove 19 Apr. 1856

FORBES	Charles : and Helen Wright, both in this parish, mar. at Hillside 12 Jun. 1858
FORBES	John : and Agnes Milne, mar. at Thirkstyle,Portlethen 12 Dec. 1861
FRASER	Al. : Lumphaman, and Margaret Nicol in this parish, mar. at the Manse 30 May 1868
FRASER	Simon : and Jessie Fraser, Kintore, mar. at the Manse 12 Jun. 1863
FRASER	William : Brunthillock, and Ann Shepherd, Fetteresso, mar. at Jellybrands Toll, 11 Jun. 1842
GEORGE	Alexander : draper in Aberdeen and Mary Ann Salvin, dau. of Christopher Salvin, upholsterer at Richmond, mar. at Bourtreybush Inn 10 May 1843
GILL	John : Parish of Nigg, and Margaret Howie of this parish, mar. at Findon 13 Jun. 1857
GORDON	James : and Isobel Walker, mar. at Badentoy 25 Nov. 1848, before witnesses
GORDON	James : and Mary Gibb, parish of Durris, mar. at the Manse 5 Nov. 1868
GOWANS	Robert : Gourdon, and Jane Wood, Findon, mar. in the School of Portlethen 8 Oct. 1869
GRAY	Alex. : railway labourer, and May Coutts, mar. at Evertown of Findon 24 Nov. 1849
HAY	John : seaman, Aberdeen and Isabella Craig, dau. of Jas. Craig w.f. Portlethen, mar. 6 Jul. 1850 Portlethen
HIRD	James : and Margaret Masson, Echt parish, mar. Hill of Portlethen 'Glencairn' 15 Jun. 1866
HOWIE	Alexander : Parish of Nigg, and Elspet Knowles, mar. at Blackhills 2 Apr.1853
HUNTER	George : and Ann Leith, mar. at Hill of Portlethen (both members of Congregation) 10 Jan. 1856
HUNTER	Robert : and Ann Ewen Donald, both in this parish, mar. at Bishopston 14 Dec. 1867
HUTCHEON	James : Findon, and Margaret Keith, Cassieport, mar. at Cassieport 18 Jun.1859
INGRAM	John : Maryculter, and Sophia Brown, mar. at Stuels 24 Feb.1855
INNES	Andrew : and Isobel Patterson from the parish of Newhills, at Butterywells mar. 25 Jun. 1842
IRVINE	James : and Janat Ross, Downies, mar. at Footdee, Aberdeen 15 Dec. 1849
JAMIESON	William : Fetteresso, and Mary Stewart in this parish, mar. at the Manse 31 May 1856
JAMIESON	William : Hillside of Findon, and Mary Farquharson, mar. at the Manse 9 Dec. 1865
KANE	Joseph : Gallowhill, and Mary Ann Stewart, Laikshill, both in this parish, mar. at Laikshill 16 Jun. 1860
KANE	Joseph : and Mary Patterson, both in this parish, mar. at Hill of Turnermiddle 22 Feb.1862
KANE	William : Gallowhill, and Helen Kane, Woodside of Banchory D. mar. 10 Feb. 1865
KEITH	Alexander : Maryculter, and Ann Stewart in this parish, mar. at Glashfarquhar 17 Mar.1855
KEITH	John : and Jean Watt, Dunnottar, mar. there 15 Nov.1859
KEITH	William : and Jane Thomson, both in this parish, mar. at Gellybrands 21 May 1864
KIRTON	Al. : tailor, Gellybrands, and Helen Reid, Moss-side, mar. at Moss-side 24 Jul. 1851
KNIGHT	William : Hillside, and Ann Stewart, Badentoy, mar. 28 May 1858
KNOWLES	George : and Jane Wood in Downies, mar. 3 Dec. 1842 in the Chapel
KNOWLES	William : merchant, Portlethen, and Jane Leiper, Portlethen, mar. at Midtown of Portlethen 12 Jun. 1868
LAING	George : Parish of Nigg, and Susan Warrander of Old Machar, mar. at the Manse 10 Dec. 1853

LAING	Robert : Nigg and Eliza. Walker, Badentoy mar. at Badentoy 25 Mar. 1854
LAING	Robert : Nigg and Isabella Craig, Fetteresso mar. at Berryhill 26 Nov. 1861
LAMB	George : Aberdeen and Agnes Mathewson Law in this parish mar. at the Manse of Portlethen 17 Sep. 1857
LEDINGHAM	John : Newhills and Elizabeth Wright, Hillside mar. 5 Jun. 1858
LEES	James : w.f. Sketraw and Helen Wood, Downies mar. in Portlethen Church 6 Nov. 1862
LEIPER	Alexander : and Elspet Thomson both in Findon mar. at Butterywells 8 Dec. 1842
LEIPER	Al. : and Is. Leiper mar. at Findon 12 Feb. 1848
LEIPER	Alexander : Downies and Jane Morrice, Portlethen mar. at the Manse 22 Dec. 1849
LEIPER	Al. : w.f. Findon and Jane Wood, daughter of James Wood w.f. there, mar. 20 Dec. 1851
LEIPER	Alexander : w.f. and Helen Leiper mar. at Findon 11 Dec. 1852
LEIPER	Al. : w.f. Portlethen and Janat Wood, Findon mar. at the Manse 24 Nov. 1855
LEIPER	Alexander : w.f. and Jane Main both in Downies mar. 20 Mar. 1858
LEIPER	Al. : w.f. Portlethen and Jane Leiper, Findon mar. at the Manse 17 Oct. 1863
LEIPER	Al. : w.f. Downies and Margaret Caie, Cove, Nigg mar. at the Manse 11 Nov.1865
LEIPER	Al. : w.f. 12 Findon and Ann Wood 48 Findon mar. at Findon 9 Nov. 1867
LEIPER	Andrew : w.f. Findon and Jessie Leiper, Portlethen mar. at the Manse 21 Nov.1863
LEIPER	George : w.f. in Findon and Ann Wood mar. at Findon 18 Dec. 1841
LEIPER	George : w.f. and Margaret Main both in Portlethen mar. in the Church 14 Feb. 1852
LEIPER	George : w.f. 8 Findon and Agnes Craig 26 Portlethen mar. at the Manse 20 Feb. 1858
LEIPER	George : w.f. 41 Findon and Jane Craig 5 Portlethen mar. at the Manse 25 Nov. 1865
LEIPER	James : w.f. Downies and Margaret Wood, Findon mar. at the Manse 14 Oct. 1865
LEIPER	James : w.f. Findon and Christina Robertson mar. at Findon 9 Dec. 1865
LEIPER	James : w.f. Portlethen and Elizabeth Leiper, Findon mar. at the Manse 23 Oct. 1858
LEIPER	James : and Jane Wood mar. at Findon 4 Apr. 1863
LEIPER	John : and ---- ---- mar. 10 Oct. 1846 Downies
LEIPER	Jo. : w.f. Findon and Margaret Leiper, Portlethen mar. at the Manse 28 Nov. 1846
LEIPER	John : Findon and Ann Leiper, Shiprow, Aberdeen mar. at the School of Portlethen 13 Nov. 1869
LEIPER	John : w.f. Downies and Elizabeth Leonard mar. at Downies 21 Dec.1861
LEIPER	Joseph : w.f. Downies and Ann Main mar. at the Manse 7 Jun. 1862
LEIPER	Moses : and Elizabeth Leiper, Findon mar. at the Manse 3 Jun. 1865
LEIPER	Robert : w.f. Downies and Jane Caie, there mar. at Downies 5 Nov. 1853
LEIPER	Robert : w.f. Findon and Elizabeth Wood, Findon mar. at Findon 16 Apr. 1859
LEIPER	William : Parish of Peterculter and Janat Leiper, Findon mar. at Findon 6 May 1843
LEIPER	William : w.f. Findon and Ann Knowles, Downies mar. at the Manse 5 Nov. 1864

LEIPER	William : w.f. Findon and Margaret Leiper, Findon mar. at Findon 2 Nov. 1861
LEONARD	James : Craighead and Elizabeth Petrie, Maryculter mar. at Eiskeywell 7 Jan. 1865
LIVINGSTON	John : and Elspet Craig, dau. of Bell Wood in Portlethen mar. 22 Apr. 1848
LOW	John : Peterhead and Jane Hutcheon in this parish mar. 9 Oct. 1857
LUMSDEN	James : Aboyne and Ann Barclay, Old Machar mar. in Holburn Street 5 Dec. 1850
McALLAN	Arthur : Midmar and Helen Hunter, Hill of Findon mar. at Hill of Findon 10 Dec. 1869
McCLOUD	Norman : and Elspet Wood a widow in Village of Portlethen mar. 15 Apr. 1848
McCROBBIE	James : and Jessie Chisholm, Cassieport mar. at Cassieport 10 Dec. 1859
McDONALD	Duncan : and Jane Wilson both in this parish mar. at the Manse 19 Aug. 1868
McDONALD	John : and Caroline Smith mar. at Laikshill 1 Jun. 1844
McINTOSH	William : Foveran and Mary Leonard in this parish mar. at East Cookston 25 Aug.1849
MacKAY	James : and Ann Barclay, Hill of Portlethen mar. there 10 Dec. 1859
McKAY-	George : and Margaret Mitchell both in this parish mar. at Hill of Findon 20 Jun. 1851
McKENZIE	John : in this parish and Jane Duncan mar. at Cove Road 30 Oct. 1857
McKENZIE	David : and Margaret Farquharson Hutcheon mar. at Stonehaven 9 Jun. 1860
	George : Hill of Findon and Christian Reid, Twa Mile Crofts mar. there 8 Dec. 1855
	---- : and ---- Leiper in Downies mar. in Church 24 Feb.1849
MAIN	Alexander : w.f. Downies and Isabella Leiper, Downies mar. at the Manse 18 Nov. 1865
MAIN	Andrew : w.f. Downies and Agnes Leiper, Findon mar. at the Manse 6 Mar. 1852
MAIN	George : w.f. and Helen Main both in Portlethen mar. 4 Nov. 1843
MAIN	George : w.f. Downies and Ann Main, Portlethen mar. at the Manse 27 Dec. 1851
MAIN	George : Nigg and Jane Leiper, Downies mar. at Downies 14 Apr. 1855
MAIN	George : Burnbanks, Nigg and Jean Main, Downies mar. at the Manse 20 Nov. 1858
MAIN	James : w.f. Downies and Lilly Craig, Portlethen mar. at Clashfarquhar 15 Feb. 1841
MAIN	James : w.f. Downies and Elizabeth Main, Stranathra mar.at the Manse 24 Oct. 1863
MAIN	John : Downies, and Lilly Leiper, Findon, mar. at the Manse 6 Dec. 1845
MAIN	Johnn : w.f. Portlethen, and Jane Main there, mar. 28 Oct. 1848 at Portlethen
MAIN	John : w.f. 23 Downies, and Lilly Main, Stranathra, mar. in the Manse 20 Feb. 1858
MAIN	John : w.f. Portlethen, and Ann Leiper, Findon, mar. at the Manse 16 Dec. 1865
MAIN	Joseph : w.f. Fetteresso, and Margaret Craig in this parish, mar. in the Church 26 Dec. 1840
MAIN	Joseph : w.f. Stranathro, Fetteresso, and Ann Leiper, Downies, mar. in the Church 10 Feb. 1855
MAIN	Joseph : w.f. Stranathraw, Fetteresso, and Ann Leiper, Downies, mar. at the Manse 22 Feb. 1862
MAIN	Joseph : Bogton of Drum,and Elspet Nicol,Newtonhill,Fetteresso,(both in this parish) mar.at Manse 30 Dec.1865
MAIN	Robert : w.f. and Janat Main, both in Portlethen, mar. 24 May 1842

MAIN : Robert : w.f. and Ann Wood, both in Portlethen, mar. 6 Jun. 1846

MAIN : Robert : w.f. Portlethen, and Jane Craig there, mar. 30 Mar. 1849

MAIN : Robert : and Agnes Leiper, Downies, mar. at Downies 26 Nov.1859

MAIN : William : w.f. and Margaret Leiper, mar. in Downies 19 Jun. 1841

MAIN : William : w.f. and Margaret Craig, Portlethen, mar. at Portlethen Village 16 Dec. 1854

MAIN : William : and Isabel Wood, mar. at Downies 1 Dec. 1860

MAIN : William : w.f. Downies, and Elizabeth Leiper, Downies, mar. at Downies 23 Nov. 1861

MARTIN : Alex. : and Mary Smith, at Bishopston, mar. 23 Jun. 1849

MARTIN : John : stonedresser, Cove, Nigg, and Mary Bain Adams, in this parish, mar. at the Manse 25 Dec. 1868

MASSON : Alex. : Backhill of Portlethen,and Margaret Tough,11,Millburn St.Aberdeen,mar.at Hillhead of Portlethen 3 Jun. 1865

MASSON : James : and Jane Allan, both in this parish, mar. 29 Nov.1856

MASSON : John : w.f. Skateraw, and Ann Main, Portlethen, mar. at the Manse 24 Oct. 1863

MASSON : Robert Walker : and Eliz. Findlay, at Rumelygowan, mar. 3 Apr. 1854

MATCHES : Robert : Belhelvie, and Margaret Coutts, Portlethen, mar. Hill of Portlethen, 25 Nov. 1864

MAVOR : R. Esq.: of Newpark, and Agnes Wattie, both in this parish, mar. at Newpark 24 Apr. 1841

MELDRUM : Peter : parish of Kilrinny, and Jane Knowles, Downies, mar. at the Manse 2 Nov. 1867

MENNIE : William : and Ann Christie, both in tihs parish, mar. at Schoolhouse 25 Jul. 1846

MICHAEL : William : Gartly, and Jane Kelmo, Huntly, mar. at 73 Virginia St. Aberdeen, 12 Apr. 1855 on their way to America (pr. Jane Boyed on 14 inst.)

MIDDLETON : William Law : Arbroath Railway Station, and Jane Massie, Nether Burnhaugh, Fetteresso, mar. at Nether Burn 4 Feb. 1859

MILNE : Alex. : and Mary Garden, Hillside of Findon, mar. at Hillside 12 Nov. 1842

MILNE : Alex. : and Jane Leiper, residing in Findon, mar. at Findon 26 Apr. 1845

MILNE : Alex. : Hill of Banchory, and Jane Ewen, mar. at Roadside of Cairnrobin 17 Aug. 1850

MILNE : George : seaman, Aberdeen, and Mary Shepherd, Banchory, mar. at Ardo 7 Apr. 1865

MILNE : George Muir : Fetteresso, Mill of Monquick, and Harriet Findlay, Maryculter, mar. at Maskie, Maryculter 30 Sep. 1865

MILNE : Joseph : and Elsy Nicol, Newtonhill, mar. at Manse 30 Dec. 1865

MILNE : P. : and Elizabeth Davidson at Cairngrassie, mar. 9 Jun. 1849

MILNE : Robert : and Catherine Shepherd, mar. at Cairnrobin 7 Mar. 1865 by Rev.Dr.Paul Banchory Devenick

MILNE : Thomas : 44 St.Andrew Street, Aberdeen, and Elspet Wood, Findon, mar. at Findon Village 7 Apr. 1866

MILNE : William : and Margaret MacPherson, mar. at Burnside of Findon, 20 Jun. 1844

MITCHELL : Robert : and Jane Gordon Gibb, both in this parish, mar. Hill of Portlethen 13 Jul. 1861

MONROE	Donald : and Matilda Smith, servants, mar. at Bishopston 8 Dec. 1866
MORISON	Alex. : mason, and Elizabeth Joss, both in Old Machar, at Johnston mar. 8 Dec. 1840
MORRICE	Peter : and Elspet Chisholm, both in Synod's Lands, mar. 27 Nov. 1847
MORRISON	John : parish of Logie Pert, and Margaret Johnston, in this parish, mar. at Mill of Brunthillock 10 Oct. 1841
MORRISON	Thomas : Newhills and Ann C. McDonald mar. at Hareness 11 Nov. 1869
MURRAY	Alex. : and Isobel Gibbons, Hill of Findon - they having been previously married at Gretna Green, upwards of 8 months ago, mar. 2 Apr. 1848
NAPIER	Alex. : w.f. Fetteresso and Isobel Craig in this parish mar. in the Church 2 Nov. 1844
NOBLE	John : and Catherine Donald both in this parish mar. at Bishopston 26 May 1860
PATERSON	Alex. : Turniemiddle and Jane Beattie, Aberdeen mar. in the School of Portlethen 4 Dec. 1869
PATTERSON	Alex. : and Jane Rust mar. at Bankhead 6 May 1863 by Rev. Dr. Paul
PATTERSON	James : and Mary Nairn mar. at Turneymiddle 14 Jun. 1862
PETRIE	Robert : Hill of Turneymiddle and Jane Dow, Nigg mar. at the Manse 5 Dec. 1868
PHILP	Robert : and Jane Petrie both in this parish mar. at Hillside Village 10 Jun. 1865
PROUDFOOT	David : Maryculter and Ann Anderson, Badentoy mar. 10 May 1862
RAE	William : Torry and Ann Wood, 4 Downies mar. in School of Portlethen 11 Dec. 1869
RAE	David : Parish of Liff & Benvie, and Margt.McCrae Gibb, parish of Kittens mar. at Portlethen Hill 2 Mar. 1866
REID	George : and Isabella Middleton, niece of Minister, mar. at Shoanhaw, Fetteresso 4 Dec. 1858
REID	Walter : flesher, St. Vigeans, Arbroath and Helen Tough mar. at Hill of Portlethen 14 Dec. 1852
REID	Al. : Green Gates and Jane Walker, Cassieport mar. at Cassieport 7 Dec. 1855
REID	George : and Ann Porter mar. at North Mains of Findon 12 Nov. 1860
RENNIE	George : Durris and Jane McCrobbie in this parish mar. at Hill of Turniemiddle 31 Dec. 1861
RIACH	James : Kincardine O'Neil and Catherine Low, Hill of Findon mar. 1 Dec. 1849
ROBB	Joseph : and Jane Stewart, Cults, Banchory Devenick mar. at Laikshill 20 Jan. 1860
ROBERTSON	David : Craigwall, Fetteresso and Jessie Knowles in this parish mar. at Blackhill, Findon 27 May 1863
ROBERTSON	Robert : and Jane Gordon Johnston mar. at Damhead of Portlethen 28 Jun. 1862
ROBERTSON	Alexander : Parish of Nigg and Ann Gordon in this parish mar. at Charleston 9 Jun. 1865
ROBERTSON	Alexander : Falkirk and Helen Robertson in this parish mar. at Hill of Portlethen 28 Dec. 1846
ROBERTSON	George : and Jane Johnston both in this parish mar. at the Manse 24 Jun. 1843
RUXTON	George : s.f. and Annie Low, Berryhill, members of Portlethen Congregation, mar. at the Manse 10 Oct. 1853
SCORGIE	John Sinclair : and Jane Wood, Portlethen Village mar. 26 Dec. 1863
	John : w.f. Portlethen and Isobel Wood, parish of Fetteresso mar. in Church of Portlethen 10 Feb. 1844
	James : and Elizabeth Patterson both in this parish mar. at Heathrups 4 Jun. 1853
	Al. : Frederick Street, Aberdeen and Elizabeth Kane, there, mar. 16 Dec. 1865

SCORGIE William : and Mary Wood mar. at the Manse 7 Sep. 1844

SHEPHERD Alexander : Turniemiddle and Mary Shepherd, Turniemiddle mar. there 22 May 1869

SHERRET --- : Fetteresso and ---- Milne mar. at Balquhain 23 Jun. 1848 by Rev. Clerihew

SHEWAN Al. : Parish of Logie Buchan and Jane Welsh, Old Machar mar. at Fiddestown 17 Dec. 1864

SILVER David : Schoolmaster, Portlethen and Margaret Davidson Allan mar. at East Cookston 9 Feb. 1861

SIMPSON James : in Hillside and Mary Leonard in Cookston mar. and afterwards bap. a son to them 11 May 1841

SIMPSON Robert : platelayer, Railway and Jane Craig 4 Portlethen mar. at Portlethen 5 Feb. 1853

SINCLAIR William : Parish of Nigg and Sarah Ewan in this parish mar. at Roadside of Cairnrobin 17 Dec. 1842

SMITH John : Fetteresso and Margaret Leonard in this parish mar. at Badentoy 6 Jul. 1849

SMITH Joseph : s.f. and Jane Tough, Hill of Portlethen mar. 18 Jun.1842

SMITH William : and Elspet Masson mar. at Langhillock 23 Nov. 1858

SMITH William : and Margaret Wright, Hillside mar. at Hillside 12 Nov. 1859

SPALDING George : and Elspet Kane, Dunnottar mar. at Moss-side 1 Dec. 1860

STEWART Charles : and Tieresha Maitland mar. at North Findon 24 Jan. 1846

STEWART James A.M. : Banchory Ternan and Sarah Christina Bower Law mar. at Portlethen Manse 5 Nov. 1858

STEWART Jo. : Railway labourer and Jane Robertson, residing at Rumleygowan mar. 3 Nov. 1849

STEWART John : Hill of Findon and Jemima Kinnaird, 45 Virginia Street mar. 23 Mar. 1856

STEWART Robert : and Margaret Davidson both in this parish at Hill of Findon, Synod's Lands, mar. 6 Aug. 1843

STEWART Robert : and Isabella Ogston mar. at Glashfarquhar 19 Nov. 1849

STEWART William : Newpark and Lilles Reid, Bridge of Don mar. at Newpark 17 Dec. 1869

STRACHAN William : Kittybrewster, Old Machar and Mary Gordon, Fetteresso mar. at Jellybrands Toll 16 Dec.1854

TAYLOR Alexander : Maryculter and Barbara Leonard, Cookston mar. at West Cookston in this parish 5 Nov. 1842

TAYLOR William : and Isabella Jamieson Hunter mar. at Charleston 9 Jun. 1866

THOMSON Andrew : Fetteresso and Elizabeth Anderson in this parish mar. at Bourtreybush 5 Sep. 1857

THOMSON Alexander : and Elizabeth Stewart both in this parish mar. at Badentoy 6 Aug. 1857

THOMSON Robert : Bourtreybush and Elsy Morrison, 4 Schoolhill, Aberdeen mar. 6 Oct. 1866

TOD Henry jun. : 39 York Place, Edinburgh and Margaret Walker, Hillside mar. at Hillside 2 Jun. 1869

TOUGH David : Parish of Nigg, s.f. at Holy Island and Christina Gibb mar. at Clochandighter 4 Dec. 1851

VALENTINE Francis : and Jane Stewart both in this parish mar. at Cairnrobin 15 Aug. 1857

WALKER Andrew : and ---- (Gerrard) both in this parish mar. at Cairnrobin 7 Jun. 1845

WALKER Js. : and Ann Tait,Badentoy mar. at 13 Carmelite Street,Abdn.,16 Jun.1855-proclaimed in parish of Ban.-Dev.

WALKER William : and Elizabeth Jamieson mar. at Badentoy 15 Jun. 1844

WALLACE William : Fetteresso and Eliza Donald, Badentoy mar. at the Manse 1 Jul. 1854

WATT James : and Ann Wright, Skene mar. at Findon and in Hillside Lands 12 Jun. 1852

Section 2 (a)

WEBSTER James : Parish of Midmar and Isobel Craig in this parish mar. at Cruickshank's Inn, Aberdeen 22 Apr. 1841
WEBSTER James : and Elizabeth Morris mar. at Cove, Nigg 14 Apr. 1855
WOOD   Alexander : w.f. Portlethen and Margaret Craig there, mar. in the Church 25 Nov. 1848
WOOD   Al. : w.f. Findon and Helen Wood there, mar. at Findon 15 Sep. 1853
WOOD   Alexander : w.f. Downies and Ann Leiper there, mar. 3 Dec. 1853
WOOD   Al. : w.f. Downies and Margaret Wood, Findon mar. at the Manse 21 Nov. 1863
WOOD   Alexander : and Jane Knowles both in Findon mar. in the School of Portlethen 27 Nov. 1869
WOOD   Andrew : w.f. Portlethen and Elspet Main both in Portlethen mar. 22 Oct. 1842
WOOD   Andrew : w.f. Findon and Margaret Caie both in this parish mar. at Roadside of Findon 18 Dec. 1852
WOOD   Andrew : w.f. 5 Downies and Susan Wood, Downies mar. at the Manse 27 Oct. 1867
WOOD   Andrew : Gourdon and Isabella Leiper, Findon mar. in the School of Portlethen 8 Oct. 1869
WOOD   Andrew : w.f. Portlethen and Jane Masson, Fetteresso mar. at the Manse 1 Dec. 1866
WOOD   Andrew : w.f. Downies, and Mary Brodie, Skateraw, mar. at the Manse 10 Nov. 1866
WOOD   Andrew : w.f. Portlethen, and Margaret Leiper, Findon, mar at the Manse 16 Jan. 1864
WOOD   Andrew : w.f. Downies, and Jane Wood, Findon, mar. at the School 22 Dec. 1860
WOOD   George : w.f. Findon, and Margaret Craig, Portlethen, mar. in the Manse 5 Feb. 1848
WOOD   George : w.f. Findon, and Elspet Leiper there, mar. 1 Dec. 1849
WOOD   George : w.f. Findon, and Isabel Leiper, Findon, mar. at Findon 26 Jun. 1852
WOOD   George : w.f. Downies, and Elspet Main, mar. in the Manse 29 Mar. 1856
WOOD   George : w.f. Downies, and Ann Wood, Downies, mar. at Downies 10 Nov. 1860
WOOD   George : w.f. Findon, and Ann Wood, both in this parish, mar. at the Manse 30 Aug. 1865
WOOD   George : w.f. 2 Downies, and Jane Knowles, Downies, mar. at School of Downies 15 Dec. 1866
WOOD   George : w.f. Portlethen, and Elizabeth Craig, mar. at 5 Portlethen, 5 May 1867
WOOD   George : w.f. and Jessie Stephen, Portlethen, mar. at Manse 23 Oct. 1858
WOOD   George : w.f. and Isobel Wood, Findon mar. 11 Oct. 1858
WOOD   James : w.f. and Jane Leiper, both in Findon, mar. in Findon 2 Dec. 1843
WOOD   James : w.f. Findon, and Margaret Robertson, Cove, mar. at Roadside of Findon 18 Dec. 1852
WOOD   James : w.f. Findon, and Agnes Caie, Cove, mar. at Cairnrobin 29 Oct. 1853
WOOD   James : w.f. Downies, and Jane Wood, Portlethen, mar. in the Church 8 Dec. 1855
WOOD   James : w.f. 8 Downies, and Isabella Wood, 9 Downies, mar. at the Manse 30 Apr. 1859
WOOD   James : w.f. Findon, and Susan Leiper, Portlethen, mar. at the Manse 8 Feb. 1868
WOOD   James : w.f. Portlethen, and Isabella Craig, Portlethen, mar. at the Manse 16 Nov. 1867
WOOD   James : w.f. Findon, and Margaret Craig, Portlethen, mar. at the Manse 15 Feb. 1868
WOOD   James : w.f. Downies, and Helen Main, Downies, mar. at the Manse 12 Dec. 1863

WOOD   James : w.f. and Helen Leiper, mar. at Findon 2 Feb. 1861
WOOD   James : w.f. Findon, and Jane Wood, Findon, mar. at Findon 9 Feb. 1861
WOOD   John : w.f. Portlethen, and Elspet Wood, mar.16 Apr. 1842
WOOD   John : w.f. Portlethen, and Margaret Leiper, Findon, mar. 13 Nov. 1842 at the Manse, being the first
        marriage there.

WOOD   John : w.f. Findon, and Elizabeth Craig, Portlethen, mar. in the Manse 31 Dec. 1843
WOOD   John : w.f. Findon, and Elizabeth Carneggie there, mar. 20 Jun. 1846
WOOD   John : w.f. Downies, and Mary Christie, Skatraw, mar. at the Manse 11 Feb. 1865
WOOD   John : w.f. 16 Portlethen, and Ann Main, Village of Downies, mar. in the Manse 29 Oct. 1859
WOOD   John : w.f. Downies, and Agnes Wood, Findon, mar. at the Manse 21 Feb. 1863
WOOD   Joseph : w.f. Downies, and Jane Leiper there, mar. at the Manse 25 Dec. 1852
WOOD   Joseph : w.f. Downies, and Ann Main, Downies, mar. at Downies 24 Dec. 1859
WOOD   Moses : w.f. Findon, and Margaret Craig, Portlethen, mar. in the Church 26 Dec. 1840
WOOD   Moses : w.f. and Elspet Knowles, mar. 18 Oct. 1845 at Findon
WOOD   Moses : w.f. Findon, and Agnes Leiper there, mar. at the Manse 1 Jul.1854
WOOD   Moses : and Eliza Leiper, Downies, mar. at Downies 4 Nov. 1854
WOOD   Moses : w.f. Findon, and Elspet Craig, Portlethen, mar. at the Manse 1 Dec. 1855
WILLIAM : w.f. and Isobel Crow, both Findon, mar. 19 Feb. 1842
WILLIAM : w.f. Findon, and Helen Wood, mar. 13 Nov. 1847
WILLIAM : w.f. Findon, and Helen Craig there, mar. at Findon 8 Jul. 1854
WRIGHT Sinclair : and Mary Symon, both in this parish, mar. at Findon 10 Jan. 1860
YULE   ...... : .... Keith, mar. at Broadgreens, Lands of Banchory, 22 Aug. 1840

SECTION 2(b)

Index of Brides, by SURNAME with Husband's name for reference to 2(a)

ADAMS Mary Bain : John Martin
ALLAN Ann : Geo. Craig
ALLAN Ann : John Craig
ALLAN Christian : Jas. Craig
ALLAN Jane : James Masson
ALLAN Jane : Wm. Craig
ALLAN Margt.Davidson : David Silver
ALLAN Margt.Main : Geo. Craig
ANDERSON Ann : David Petrie
ANDERSON Eliz. : David Chalmers
ANDERSON Eliz. : Andrew Thomson
ANDERSON Jean : Geo. Craig
BARCLAY Ann : Jas. Lumsden
BARCLAY Ann : Jas. McIntosh
BAXTER Isobel : Andrew Abercromby
BEATTIE Jane : Alex. Paterson
BREWSTER Jane : Jas. Alexander
BRODIE Mary : Andrew Wood
BROWN Sophia : John Ingram
BURNETT Eliz. : Jas. Craig
CAIE Agnes : Jas. Craig
CAIE Jane : Robert Leiper
CAIE Margt. : Andrew Wood
CAIE Margt. : Andrew Forbes
CAIE Margt. : Al. Leiper
CARNEGGIE Eliz. : John Wood
CHISHOLM Elspet : Peter Morrice
CHISHOLM Jessie : Jas. McCrobbie
CHRISTIE Ann : Wm. Mennie
CHRISTIE Isabella : Thomas Coutts

CHRISTIE Jane : Joseph Craig
CHRISTIE Mary : John Wood
COLLARD Margt. : David Anderson
COPLAND Mary : Geo. Dempster
COULL Helen : Joseph Craig
COUTTS Margt. : Robert Matches
COUTTS Mary : Jas. Buchan
COUTTS May : Alex. Gray
CRAIG Agnes : Geo. Leiper
CRAIG Eliz. : Geo. Wood
CRAIG Eliz. : John Wood
CRAIG Eliz. : Wm. Craig
CRAIG Elspet : John Livingston
CRAIG Elspet : John Duthie
CRAIG Elspet : Moses Wood
CRAIG Elspet : Andrew Craig
CRAIG Helen : Wm. Craig
CRAIG Helen : Wm. Wood
CRAIG Helen : Andrew Craig
CRAIG Isabella : John Hay
CRAIG Isabella : Robt. Laing
CRAIG Isabella : Jas. Wood
CRAIG Isobel : Geo. Black
CRAIG Isobel : Alex. Napier
CRAIG Isobel : Jas. Webster
CRAIG Isobel : John Davidson
CRAIG Jane : Jas. Craig
CRAIG Jane : Robt. Simpson
CRAIG Jane : Robert Main
CRAIG Jane : Geo. Leiper

CRAIG Jessie : Jas. Craig
CRAIG Lilly : Jas. Main
CRAIG Lilly : Joseph Craig
CRAIG Margt. : Geo. Craig
CRAIG Margt. : Alex. Wood
CRAIG Margt. : Geo. Wood
CRAIG Margt. : Joseph Main
CRAIG Margt. : Moses Wood
CRAIG Margt. : Jas. Craig
CRAIG Margt. : Wm. Main
CRAIG Margt. : Jas. Wood
CRAIG Margt. : Geo. Craig
CRAIG Margt. : John Christie
CRAIG Mary : Jas. Christie
CROW Isobel : Wm. Wood
DAVIDSON Eliz. : P.Milne
DAVIDSON Margt. : Robt. Stewart
DONALD Ann Ewen : Robt. Hunter
DONALD Catherine : John Noble
DONALD Eliza : Wm. Wallace
DOW Jane : Robt. Patterson
DUNCAN Jane : John McKay
EWEN Jane : Alex. Milne
EWEN Sarah : Wm. Sinclair
FARQUHARSON Mary : Wm. Jamieson
FERRIER Helen : John Donald
FINDLAY Eliz. : Robt. Walker Masson
FINDLAY Harriet : Geo. Muir Milne
FLATT Margt. : John Craig
FORBES Mary : David Duncan

FRASER Jane : Francis Cossar
FRASER Jessie : Simon Fraser
GARDEN Mary : Alex. Milne
GAVIN Harriet : John Chisholm
GERRARD .... : Andrew Walker
GIBB Christina : David Tough
GIBB Hutcheon : Jas. Brown
GIBB Jane Gordon : Robt. Mitchell
GIBB Margt.McCrae : David Proudfoot
GIBB Mary : Jas. Gordon
GIBBONS Isobel : Alex. Murray
GORDON Ann : Alex. Robb
GORDON Mary : Wm. Strachan
HOWIE Eliz. : John Findlay
HOWIE Isobel : Wm. Chisholm
HOWIE Jean : Smith Donaldson
HOWIE Margt. : John Gill
HUNTER Miss : Mr Duncan
HUNTER Helen : Arthur McAllan
HUNTER Isabella Jamieson:Wm.Taylor
HUTCHEON Jane : John Low
HUTCHEON Margt.Farquharson :
                    David McKenzie

JAMIESON Eliz. : Wm. Walker
JAMIESON Eliz. : Alex.Campbell
JOHNSTON Alexandrina Ewen :
                    Robert Donald

JOHNSTON Ann : Geo. Davidson
JOHNSTON Jane : Geo. Robertson
JOHNSTON Jane Gordon : Robt. Riach
JOHNSTON Margaret : John Morrison
JOSS Eliz. : Al. Scorgie
KANE Eliz. : Alex. Morison
KANE Elspet : George Spalding

KANE Helen : John Abercrombie
KANE Helen : Wm. Kane
KEANN Ann : Jas. Cooper
KEITH .... : .... Yule
KEITH Helen : Patrick Berry
KEITH Margt. : James Hutcheon
KEITH Mary : Jas. Dunbar
KEMLO Jane : Wm. Mitchell
KINNAIRD Jemima : John Stewart
KNOWLES Ann : Wm. Leiper
KNOWLES Eliza. : Geo. Ferrier
KNOWLES Elspet : Moses Wood
KNOWLES Elspet : Alex. Howie
KNOWLES Jane : Peter Meldrum
KNOWLES Jane : Alex. Wood
KNOWLES Jane : Geo. Wood
KNOWLES Jessie : David Rennie
LAMONT Mary : John Findlay
LAW Agnes Mathewson : Geo. Lamb
LAW Sarah Christian Bower :
                    James Stewart

LAWSON Mary : Jas. Farquhar
LEIPER .... : .... Main
LEIPER Agnes : Andrew Main
LEIPER Agnes : Moses Wood
LEIPER Agnes : Robert Main
LEIPER Ann : Alex. Wood
LEIPER Ann : Joseph Craig
LEIPER Ann : Joseph Main
LEIPER Ann : Joseph Main
LEIPER Ann : Jas. Donald
LEIPER Ann : John Main
LEIPER Ann : Joseph Craig
LEIPER Ann : Wm.Knowles

LEIPER Ann : John Leiper
LEIPER Ann : Andrew Craig
LEIPER Eliz. : Moses Wood
LEIPER Eliz. : Wm. Main
LEIPER Eliz. : Moses Leiper
LEIPER Eliz. : James Leiper
LEIPER Elspet : Geo. Wood
LEIPER Elspet : Robert Brown
LEIPER Helen : Alex. Leiper
LEIPER Helen : James Wood
LEIPER Is. : Al. Leiper
LEIPER Isabel : George Wood
LEIPER Isabella : Andrew Wood
LEIPER Isabella : William Craig
LEIPER Isabella : Alex. Main
LEIPER Janat : William Leiper
LEIPER Jane : Joseph Wood
LEIPER Jane : George Main
LEIPER Jane : William Christie
LEIPER Jane : James Wood
LEIPER Jane : Alex. Milne
LEIPER Jane : Al. Leiper
LEIPER Jean : James Craig
LEIPER Jessie : Andrew Leiper
LEIPER Lilly : John Main
LEIPER Margt. : Jo. Leiper
LEIPER Margt. : George Craig
LEIPER Margt. : George Craig
LEIPER Margt. : John Wood
LEIPER Margt. : William Main
LEIPER Margt. : Andrew Wood
LEIPER Margt. : William Leiper
LEIPER Susan : James Wood
LEITH Ann : George Hunter

LEONARD Barbara : Alex. Taylor
LEONARD Eliz. : John Leiper
LEONARD Elspet : Wm. Beattie
LEONARD Margt. : John Smith
LEONARD Mary : James Simpson
LEONARD Mary : Wm. McDonald
LONGMUIR Jane : Geo. Brown
LONGMUIR Margt. : Thomas Aberdeen
LOW Annie : Geo. Robertson
LOW Catherine : James Reid
LUNDIE Annie : John Ferguson
McBAIN Eliz. : James Clark
McCROBBIE Jane : Geo. Reid
McDONALD Miss : Rev. Clerihew
McDONALD Ann C. : Thos. Morrison
MacPHERSON Margt. : Wm. Milne
MAIN Ann : Geo. Main
MAIN Ann : John Masson
MAIN Ann : Joseph Leiper
MAIN Ann : Joseph Wood
MAIN Ann : John Wood
MAIN Eliz. : James Main
MAIN Elspet : Andrew Wood
MAIN Elspet : George Wood
MAIN Elspet : William Christie
MAIN Helen : George Main
MAIN Helen : James Brodie
MAIN Helen : James Wood
MAIN Janat : Robert Main
MAIN Janat : Peter Christie
MAIN Jane : John Main
MAIN Jane : Geo. Craig
MAIN Jane : Alex. Leiper
MAIN Jean : George Main

MAIN Lilly : John Main
MAIN Margt. : Geo. Leiper
MAITLAND Tieresha : Chas.Stewart
MASSIE Jane : Wm.Low Middleton
MASSON Christina : Alex. Craig
MASSON Eliz. : James Air
MASSON Elspet : Wm. Smith
MASSON Jane : Andrew Wood
MASSON Margt. : James Hird
MIDDLETON Isabella : Geo. Rae
MIDDLETON Jane Dianah :
            Nicholas Cuddie
MILNE .... : .... Sherret
MILNE Agnes : John Forbes
MITCHELL Margt. : Geo. MacKay
MORRICE Jane : Alex. Leiper
MORRIS Eliz. : James Webster
MORRISON Elsy : Robert Thomson
NAIRN Mary : Jas. Patterson
NICOL Ann : Andrew Aiken
NICOL Ann : Jas. S. Catto
NICOL Elspet : Joseph Main
NICOL Elsy : Joseph Main
NICOL Margt. : Al. Fraser
OGSTON Isabella : Robt. Stewart
PATTERSON Ann : John Carr
PATTERSON Eliz. : Jas. Ruxton
PATTERSON Isobel : Andrew Innes
PATTERSON Mary : Joseph Kane
PETRIE Eliz. : Jas. Leonard
PETRIE Jane : Robt. Patterson
PIRIE Ann : Jas. Anderson
PORTER Ann : Geo. Reid
REID Christian : Geo. McKenzie

REID Helen : Al. Kirton
REID Helen : .... Caithness
REID Lilles : Wm. Stewart
ROBERTSON Christina : Jas. Leiper
ROBERTSON Helen : Alex. Robertson
ROBERTSON Isabella : William Blackhall
ROBERTSON Jane : Jo. Stewart
ROBERTSON Margaret : James Wood
ROBISON .... : .... Allan
ROSS Janat : James Irvine
RUST Jane : Alex. Patterson
RUST Mary Ann : James Begg
SALVIN Mary Ann : Alex. George
SHEPHERD Ann : Wm. Fraser
SHEPHERD Catherine : Robert Milne
SHEPHERD Mary : Geo. Milne
SHEPHERD Mary : Alex. Shepherd
SMITH Caroline : John McDonald
SMITH Matilda : Donald Monroe
SMITH Mary : Alex. Martin
STEPHEN Jessie : Geo. Wood
STEWART Ann : Alex. Keith
STEWART Ann : Wm. Knight
STEWART Eliz. : Alex. Thomson
STEWART Jane : Joseph Reid
STEWART Jane : Francis Valentine
STEWART Mary : Wm. Jamieson
STEWART Mary Ann : Joseph Kane
STRACHAN Christina : John Ewan
SYMON Mary : Sinclair Wright
TAIT Ann : Js. Walker
THOMSON Elspet : Alex. Leiper
THOMSON Sarah : Wm. Anderson
THOMSON Jane : Wm. Keith

TOUGH Helen : Walter Rae
TOUGH Jane : Joseph Smith
TOUGH Margt. : Alex. Masson
WALKER Ann : James Anderson
WALKER Eliz. : Robert Laing
WALKER Isobel : Jas. Gordon
WALKER Jane : Al. Reid
WALKER Margt. : Andrew Anderson
WALKER Margt. : Henry Tod jun.
WARRANDER Susan : Geo.Laing
WATT Jean : John Keith
WATTIE Agnes : R. Mavor Esq.
WELSH Jane : Al. Shewan
WILSON Jane : Duncan McDonald
WOOD Agnes : John Wood
WOOD Ann : George Leiper
WOOD Ann : Robert Main
WOOD Ann : Geo. Craig
WOOD Ann : Al. Leiper
WOOD Ann : Wm. Philip
WOOD Ann : Jas. Craig
WOOD Ann : Geo. Wood
WOOD Ann : Geo. Wood
WOOD Eliz. : Robert Leiper
WOOD Elspet : Norman McCloud
WOOD Elspet : John Wood
WOOD Elspet : Thomas Milne
WOOD Helen : Wm. Wood
WOOD Helen : Al. Wood
WOOD Helen : Jas. Lees
WOOD Isabel : Wm. Main
WOOD Isabel : Geo. Wood
WOOD Isabella : James Wood
WOOD Isobel : John Robertson

WOOD Janat : Al. Leiper
WOOD Jane : George Knowles
WOOD Jane : John Allan
WOOD Jane : Jas. Wood
WOOD Jane : Al. Leiper
WOOD Jane : Robert Gowans
WOOD Jane : Jos. Craig
WOOD Jane : John Sinclair Robertson
WOOD Jane : James Wood
WOOD Jane : James Craig
WOOD Jane : Jas. Leiper
WOOD Jane : Andrew Wood
WOOD Jessie : John Craig
WOOD Lily : Alex. Craig
WOOD Margt. : Jas. Leiper
WOOD Margt. : Al. Wood
WOOD Mary : Wm. Scorgie
WOOD Susan : Andrew Wood
WRIGHT Ann : Jas. Watt
WRIGHT Christian : Richard Cameron
WRIGHT Eliz. : John Ledingham
WRIGHT Helen : Charles Forbes
WRIGHT Margaret : Wm.Smith
YEATS Isabella : John Cruickshank
YULE Jane : George Allan

SECTION 3

Alphabetical list of Deaths / Burials by deceased's SURNAME
Married Females entered by, both SURNAME and (OTHER NAME)

ABERNETHY   Isobel : at funeral, Bourtrybush, aged 84y, 16 Jan. 1845
AIKEN   Euphemia : Redmyre, 63y, heart disease, Portlethen 26 Nov. 1869
AIR   Mary : Whitefoundland, 64y, cancer of lips, Portlethen 28 Aug. 1866
ALBERT   Prince Consort : died at Windsor 14 Dec. 1861 aged 42y.
ALEXANDER   Mrs. : at funeral Hillside 4 May 1843
ALEXANDER   James jun.: Hillside, 23y, Banchory Devenick 14 Dec. 1861
ALEXANDER   Mary (DUNCAN) : Widow Alexander, late Mill of Findon, 89y, Banchory 26 Mar. 1860
ALEXANDER   Robert : Mill of Findon, 5 months, 18 Jul. 1857
ALLAN   Ann : Portlethen, 83y, old age, Portlethen 15 Jun. 1862
ANDERSON   Widow : Old Bourtreybush, buried 7 May 1853
ANDERSON   Andrew : Cairnrobin, 43y, (F.C.), N. Banchory 10 Aug. 1861
ANDERSON   D. : Fiddestown, 72y, old age, Portlethen 28 May 1861
ANDERSON   George : buried Cove Road, Nigg 14 Nov. 1859
ANDERSON   Helen : attending funeral in Findon 13 Dec. 1843
ANDERSON   Jane (Brewster) : Widow Brewster, Fiddestown, 71y, old age, Portlethen 16 Jul. 1865
ANDERSON   Jessie : dau. of George Anderson, Elder, Bourtreybush, 15y ,19 Mar. 1859
ANNAND   Ann : Barclayhill, 70y, old age, Old Aberdeen 28 Feb. 1864
ARCHIBALD   Jane Mary : Hillside, 1 month, Banchory Devenick 23 Nov. 1862
BAIRD   Mrs. : 88y, wife of John Baird, buried at Maryculter New Church-Yard 20 May 1856
BARCLAY   ---- (MASSON) : Widow Masson, Findon, 60y, Old Machar 8 Jun. 1861
BARCLAY   Helen (BURNETT) : Widow Burnett, Clashfarquhar, 83y, 2 Jul. 1859
BARCLAY   Jo. : Hill of Portlethen, 29y, disease of brain, Old Machar 22 Aug. 1864
BATE   Eliza (BAXTER) : wife of Jo. Baxter, Hill of Findon, 76y, 28 Jul. 1857
BAXTER   Child : attended funeral of A. Baxter's child at Badentoy 15 Jun. 1841
BAXTER   Eliza (BATE)
BEATTIE   Widow : Check Bar, 79y, Durris 20 Nov. 1868
BEATTIE   George : Moss-side, 8y, typhus, Portlethen 24 Oct. 1862
BLAIR   Elspet : Dau. of Eliza Blair, Cairnrobin, 8 months, Banchory 31 Mar. 1860
BLAIR   Mary ('Blebber') : Cairnrobin, 13y 3mon., Banchory 19 May 1860

BREWSTER   Jane (ANDERSON)

BRIDGEFORD   Robert : Hill of Portlethen, 71½y, stone, Maryculter 22 Jan. 1866

BROWN   ---- (WALKER) : Widow Walker, Bourtreybush, 82y, old age, Cowie 30 Jan. 1862

BROWN   Mrs. : at William Brown's wife's funeral at Shiels 6 Jan. 1847

BROWN   Katherine Widow : Hillside, 78y, old age, Cowie 7 Mar. 1862

BROWN   William : Hillside, Cowie, 85y, (married 51y), 21 May 1860

BRUCE   William : Shiels, 75y, disease of heart, Fetteresso 3 Oct. 1865

BURNETT   Isobel (WALKER) : at William Walker's wife's funeral 29 Nov. 1842

   Helen (BARCLAY)

CAIE   Agnes (WOOD) : Widow Wood, Findon, 54y, consumption, see husband James Wood, Portlethen 3 Feb.1866

CALDER   ---- (HUTCHEON) : Mrs. Calder, Bourtreybush, 90y, Banchory Devenick 14 Jan. 1862

CAMERON   Lewis : Old School, 13½y, fever, Migvie 15 Oct. 1861

CARNIE   Ann (COLLIER) : Widow Carnie, East Cookston, died 99y, 29 Dec. 1854

CHALMERS   Al. : blacksmith, Bourtreybush, 68y, 8 Apr. 1858

CHALMERS   Jane : Hillside, 5 months, consumption, Portlethen 19 Aug. 1867

CHALMERS   Jane (DONALD) : Hillside, 37y, sore throat, Portlethen 29 Jun. 1867

CHAPMAN   Margaret : Bruntulloch, 83y, old age, Fetteresso 13 Feb. 1868

CHRISTIE   Andrew : son of Andrew Christie, Portlethen, 6½ months, small pox, Portlethen 8 May 1861

CHRISTIE   Elspet : Portlethen, upwards of 93 years died 1842

CHRISTIE   Js. : Hillside, 15y, mortification, Portlethen 7 Jan. 1863

CHRISTIE   Margaret : 63 Portlethen, 30y, 6 Sep. 1856

COLLIE   ---- (PETRIE) : Widow Petrie, Redmyre, 75y, cancer, Maryculter 11 Nov. 1867

COLLIE   Jane : Glen of Redmyre, 86y, 4 Jul. 1857

COLLIER   Ann (CARNIE)

CORMACK   ---- (FREEMAN) : Widow Freeman, died Westside of Portlethen 21 Oct. 1841

COUTTS   James : f.s. Mains of Portlethen, 24y, drowned bathing, 7 Aug. 1859

CRAGGIE   William : Mains of Portlethen, 35½y, typhus, Portlethen 30 Jan. 1862

CRAIG   .... : 54 Portlethen, 1year, 17 Aug. 1856

CRAIG   Infant : Portlethen, 2years, 19 May 1857

CRAIG   Infant daughter : of Jo. Craig, Elder, Portlethen, 1 month, 18 Jul. 1857

CRAIG   ---- (WOOD) : Widow Wood, died Portlethen, 23 Sep. 1841

CRAIG   Alexander : drowned off Cove, 18 Aug. 1848, brother of James, body found at Cove, 9 Sep. 1848

CRAIG   Andrew : 46 Portlethen, 3 years, disease of brain, Portlethen 14 Jul. 1860

CRAIG   Andrew : 10 Portlethen, 9 years 4 months, sore leg, Portlethen 10 Nov. 1865

CRAIG   Ann : 14 Portlethen, 1 year 6 months, measles, Portlethen 20 Feb. 1863
CRAIG   Ann : daughter of J.Craig, Elder, Portlethen, 1 year, teething, Portlethen 8 Sep. 1860
CRAIG   Ann : Portlethen, 9 years, enteritis, Portlethen 1 Sep. 1869
CRAIG   Ann : widow, Portlethen, 82½ years, old age, Portlethen 10 May 1865
CRAIG   Ann (WOOD) : widow of Jo. Wood, 1 Portlethen, 52 years, Portlethen 24 Dec. 1862
CRAIG   Betsy : 45 Portlethen, 1 year 2 months, Portlethen 27 Feb. 1860
CRAIG   Elizabeth (LEIPER) : Wife of J.Leiper, Findon, 41 years, 11 Oct. 1859
CRAIG   Elspet : At funeral in Portlethen 17 Sep. 1841
CRAIG   G. : Attended G.Craig's funeral, w.f. Portlethen, died at sea yesterday morning on his way home from
        Fraserburgh,from the herring fishing there,after a few days illness,left 4 children,20 Aug.1842

CRAIG   George : Funeral, 30 Sep. 1843
CRAIG   George : Infant son of William Craig, 4 Portlethen, 14 days, Portlethen 1 Apr. 1862
CRAIG   George : Portlethen, 50 years, fever, Portlethen 24 May 1869
CRAIG   Helen : Daughter of J.Craig, Portlethen, 1 year 5 months, Portlethen 1 Dec. 1862
CRAIG   Helen : 10 Portlethen, 39 years, Portlethen 17 Nov. 1865
CRAIG   Helen : 10 Portlethen, 3½ years, disease of the heart, 1 Dec. 1865
CRAIG   James : drowned off Cove, 18 Aug. 1848, brother of Alexexander, body found at Cove, 23 Aug. 1848
CRAIG   James : w.f. "Unce's Jamie ", died 22 Sep. 1852, bur. 27 Sep. 1852 in Portlethen
CRAIG   James : 36 Portlethen, 1½ years, Portlethen 12 May 1860
CRAIG   James : Infant son of John Craig, Portlethen, 1½ months, 4 Apr. 1861
CRAIG   James : 45 Portlethen, 4 years, croup, Portlethen 23 Jan. 1865
CRAIG   Jane : Portlethen, 17 years, fever, Portlethen 20 Nov. 1862
CRAIG   Jane : Infant daughter of G.Craig, 9 Portlethen, Portlethen 5 Jul. 1860
CRAIG   Jane : Daughter of "Little Johnny ", Portlethen, 38½ years, 2 Oct. 1859
CRAIG   John : (very deaf), died at Hillhead of Portlethen, 13 Oct. 1841, attending funeral 15 Oct. 1841
CRAIG   John : 16 Aug. 1841 at Portlethen seeing John Craig, attending John Craig's funeral 20 Aug. 1841
CRAIG   John : Lost at sea, 8 Apr. 1847
CRAIG   John : 8 Portlethen, 2½ years, small pox, Portlethen 20 Mar. 1860
CRAIG   John : w.f. Portlethen, 87 years, Portlethen 3 Apr. 1860
CRAIG   John : " Littlejonny ", Portlethen Village, 84 years, 18 may 1859
CRAIG   John : 5 Portlethen, 6 years 9 months, consumption, Portlethen 15 Dec. 1866
CRAIG   John : Portlethen, 11 years, hydrocephalus, Portlethen 11 Nov. 1869
CRAIG   Joseph : Lost at sea, 8 Apr. 1847
CRAIG   Joseph : Son of Jo. Craig w.f. 43 Portlethen, bur. at Portlethen 7 Nov. 1854

CRAIG   Jos. : Portlethen, 3 years 3 months, apoplexy, Portlethen 14 Jan. 1865

CRAIG   M. (FLATT) : Wife of John Craig, 45 Portlethen, 50 years. Portlethen 24 Oct. 1868

CRAIG   Margt.(MAIN) : Widow,Portlethen,died 15 Jan.1842,75 years,attended funeral at Portlethen 17 Jan.1842

CRAIG   Margaret : Portlethen, infant, Portlethen 28 Aug. 1864

CRAIG   Mary (LEES) : 56 Portlethen, 75 years, parallysis, Portlethen 16 Apr. 1865

CRAIG   Susan (LEIPER) : Widow George Leiper, late of Portlethen, died age 83 years 16 Mar. 1852

CRUICKSHANK   Jane : East Cookston, 1¾ years, scarlet fever, Banchory Devenick 12 Dec. 1866

CUSHNIE   Jane : Hill of Portlethen, 63 years, Portlethen 30 Jul. 1864

DAVIDSON   .... (ROSS) : Widow, Nr.Bourtreybush, 76 years 9 months, 20 Jul. 1859

DAVIDSON   Andrew : Cairngrassie, 78 years, 9 Aug. 1857

DAVIDSON   Catherine (SHEPHERD) : Widow Shepherd, Cairnrobin, 67 years, 12 Jan. 1859

DEMPSTER   Mrs. : Badentoy, 67 years 7 months, dropsey, B.N. (....)? 24 Aug. 1866

DEMPSTER   Widow : Redmyre, bur. 25 Aug. 1866

DEMPSTER   John : Badentoy 68 years, inflamation, Banchory (D.)? 12 Feb. 1863

DEWAR   Mrs. : Mother of Rev. Dewar, Aberdeen, died suddenly, May 1853

DONALD   Widow : Glashfarquhar, 74 years, 29 Dec. 1858

DONALD   Janat (STEWART) : Late Glashfarquhar, widow Stewart, 75 years, Portlethen, 31 May 1865 bur.3 Jun.1865

DONALD   Jane (CHALMERS)

DOUGLAS   James : Mill of Brunthillock, 22 years, consumption, Fetteresso 24 Jul. 1866

DUNCAN   George : Son of D.Duncan, Hillside, 3 years 9 months, 26 Feb. 1859

DUNCAN   George : Hill of Findon, 84 years 10 months, Banchory 4 May 1860

DUNCAN   Isabel Collie : Hillside, 4½ months, croup, Portlethen 18 Jun. 1865

DUNCAN   James : Hillside, 90 years, old age, Portlethen 13 Jan. 1869

DUNCAN   Mary : Hill of Findon, 62 years, Banchory Devenick, 18 Aug. 1866

DUTHIE   Mary (ALEXANDER)

EWEN   Ann (FINDLAY) : Widow, Bishopston, 78 years, old age, Fetteresso 20 Oct. 1866

EWEN   C.A. : schoolmaster, Portlethen, died 30 Nov. 1855 age 63 years, (43 years teacher of the district) buried in Portlethen Churchyard 4 Dec. 1855

EWEN   P. : at funeral, 22 Feb. 1845

FERGUSON   William : 56 Portlethen, 11 years, 5 Sep. 1859

FIDDES   Katherine (HOWIE) : Andrew Fiddes's wife, Old School, attended funeral 9 Dec. 1842

FINDLAY   Ann : (DUTHIE)

FINDLAY   Christian : East Cookston, died 13 Oct. 1844, funeral 15 Oct. 1844 East Cookston

FINDLAY   D. : Son of D. Findlay, Hillside, died 6 Dec. 1842, funeral 8 Dec. 1842

FINDLAY	D. : Attended funeral at D. Findlay's 4 Mar. 1843
Flatt	M. (CRAIG)
FRASER	Al. : Hill of Portlethen, 58½ years, dropsy, Portlethen 20 Oct. 1863
FRASER	George : Hill of Portlethen, 20 years, accident, Portlethen 20 Feb. 1861
FREEMAN	Widow (CORMACK)
FREEMAN	George : at funeral, Westside 24 Jun. 1843
GORDON	Barbara (MORRISON) : wife of William Morrison, Downies, 36 years, Maryculter 22 May 1861
GORDON	James : Auchlee, 82 years, old age, Fetteresso 24 Oct. 1868
GORDON	Philip : found dead near his own house on morning of Sunday last, Roadside of Cairnrobin funeral 6 Dec. 1848
GORDON	Susan : Jellybrands, 17 years, fever, Portlethen 12 Feb. 1862
GREIG	Eliza : Cairnrobin, 77 years 4 months, old age, North Banchory 24 Jul. 1861
HORN	——(STUART) : Widow Stuart, Bankhead, 67 years, 18 Dec. 1857
HOWIE	Helen : Findon, bodily infirmities, 25 years, Banchory Devenick 13 Dec. 1862
HOWIE	Jo. : Mains of Findon, 62 years, lungs, Banchory 20 Oct. 1868
HOWIE	Katherine (FIDDES)
HUNTER	Catherine : Findon, 60 years, paralysis, Portlethen 14 May 1869
HUNTER	George : Elder, Hill of Findon, 57 years, angina pectorus, Banchory Devenick 21 Aug. 1865
HUNTER	John : Hill of Findon, 79 years, old age, North Banchory 14 Sep. 1861
HUNTER	Thomas : Cairnwell, 27 years, consumption, Peterculter 6 May 1866
HUTCHEON	——(CALDER)
HUTCHEON	D. : at funeral, Bourtriebush 28 Aug. 1843
HUTCHEON	D. : Bourtreybush, 58 years, Banchory Devenick 25 Oct. 1868
HUTCHEON	G. : Bourtreybush, 57 years, appoplexy, Nigg 24 Sep. 1860
HUTCHEON	George : Findon, 24½ years, 28 Apr. 1858
HUTCHEON	James : Mains of Findon, buried 23 Apr. 1856
HUTCHEON	James : farmer, Findon, 34 years, appoplexy, Old Machar 5 Feb. 1861
HUTCHEON	Margaret : died at Bourtreybush 14 Mar. 1844, funeral 19 Mar. 1844
JAMIES	John : funeral East Cookston 3 Dec. 1842
JAMIESON	Ely : Barclayhill, 30 years, dropsy, Portlethen 26 May 1868
JOHNSTON	Ann : Damhead, 12½ years, fever, Portlethen 18 Mar. 1867
JOHNSTON	James : Hillside, 67 years, found dead, Portlethen 28 Jan. 1864
JOHNSTON	William F. : Damhead, 56 years, angina pectores, Portlethen 14 Oct. 1866
KANE	Bannerman : Gallowhill, 72 years, John Knox 26 Nov. 1860

KANE   George : 'auld waidie', Moss-side, 88 years, Portlethen 8 Mar. 1869
KANE   Helen (KEITH) : wife of John Keith, Westside of Portlethen, 58 years, 14 Feb. 1859
KANE   Joseph : at funeral, Banchory, 53 years, 27 Apr. 1846
KANE   Mary : daughter of Al. Kane, East Cookston, 9 years 2 months, 14 Feb. 1859
KANE   Peter : East Cookston, 79 years 4 months, old age, Banchory Devenick 25 Oct. 1862
KANE   William : Boghillock - at G. Masson from Aberdeen - 15 years, Portlethen 28 Jan. 1860
KEITH   ..... : Daughter of John Keith, Westside of Portlethen, 18 years, 8 Mar. 1859
KEITH   Helen : (KANE)
KEITH   James : Cassieport, Moss-side, 65 years, appoplexy, Banchory Devenick 5 Jul. 1862
KEITH   James : late of Cassieport, appoplexy (on Aug. 4th last), Banchory Devenick 1 Dec. 1862
KEITH   Mary (SMITH) : Cassieport, 59 years, 1 Oct. 1856
KEMP   George : Redmyre, 2½ years, scarlet fever, Portlethen 14 Dec. 1865
KEMP   Robert : Redmyre, 5½ years, measles, Portlethen 28 Mar. 1866
KNOWLES Mrs. : Attending burial at Findon, 26 Aug. 1841
KNOWLES Andrew : w.f. Findon, 44 years, 24 Jan. 1859
KNOWLES George : w.f. Findon, at funeral, "taken to houf" at Cowie, 8 Sep. 1855
LAMB   George Francis William Law : Minister's grandson, died at 171 Skene St. Aberdeen, disease of the lung, at 7.15 a.m. (a good boy) age 6½ years, 28 Jan. 1865

LAW   Widow : At Stonehaven, at widow Law's funeral, age 92 years, 7 Apr. 1843
LAW   Is. (WOOD) : wife of A.Wood, Findon, 63 years, old age, Portlethen 11 Sep. 1862
LAW   Isabella (MATHEWSON) : Died 17 Feb. 1855, age 57 years, bur.in New Churchyard, Maryculter 21 Feb.1855
LAW   John : My brother John, died age 44 years, at Hill of Lairney 26 Nov. 1849
LAW   Mary : daughter of D.Law, Stonehaven, bur. at Portlethen 15 Mar. 1850
LAW   William : Minister's son died of appoplexy, at Nazarah, Upper Assam, Calcutta, India 19 Jul.1864
LEES   Mary (CRAIG)
LEIGHTON Eliza : Badentoy, 2 years, 24 Aug. 1858
LEIGHTON Mary : at funeral, Downies, 9 Oct. 1844
LEIPER Alex. : Lost at sea, 8 Apr. 1847
LEIPER Al. : 14 Findon, 74 years, angina pectoris, Banchory Devenick 3 Aug. 1863
LEIPER Alex. : son of R.Leiper, Downies, 1 year 10 months, 8 Nov. 1859
LEIPER Alex. : w.f. Findon, 31 years, consumption, 18 Dec. 1858
LEIPER Alex. : Findon, son of Jo.Leiper, Elder's brother, 12 years, 2 Dec. 1858
LEIPER Alex. : see death of John Leiper 26 Apr. 1862
LEIPER Andrew : son of George Leiper, Findon, 6 years, 26 Nov. 1858

LEIPER   Andrew : Downies, 23 years, 3 Nov. 1858
LEIPER   Ann : Portlethen Village, 2 years 7 months, fever, Portlethen 26 Dec. 1864
LEIPER   Arthur : Infant son of Arthur Leiper, w.f. Findon, bur. 26 Feb. 1842
LEIPER   Betty : Findon, 72 years, old age, Portlethen 8 Oct. 1864
LEIPER   Eliz. (CRAIG)
LEIPER   Elspet : Downies, 86 years, 23 Oct. 1858
LEIPER   Elspet : Village of Portlethen, 81 years, old age, Portlethen 3 Apr. 1866
LEIPER   George : Lost at sea, 8 Apr. 1847
LEIPER   George : w.f. Portlethen, bur. 28 Dec. 1848, Father of three brothers lost 8 Apr. 1847
LEIPER   George : Findon, 83 years, old age, Banchory Devenick 26 Mar. 1863
LEIPER   George : w.f. Downies, 24½ years, consumption, Portlethen 30 Jul. 1862
LEIPER   George : Downies, 3 years 9 months, Portlethen 13 Dec. 1869
LEIPER   Isobel (WOOD) : widow Leiper, Portlethen, 58 years, Portlethen 15 Oct. 1860
LEIPER   J. : w.f. Downies, 56 years, Portlethen 30 May 1865
LEIPER   James : see death of John Leiper 26 Apr. 1862
LEIPER   James : 21 Portlethen, 6 months, Portlethen 28 Apr. 1866
LEIPER   James : son of James Leiper, Findon, 6 days, Portlethen 20 May 1866
LEIPER   James : Village of Portlethen, 4 yers, diptheria, Portlethen 17 Aug. 1867
LEIPER   James : Portlethen, 6 months, hydrocephalus, Portlethen 12 Jul. 1869
LEIPER   Jane : Portlethen, 11 months, ulceration of bowels, Portlethen 2 Sep. 1869
LEIPER   Jane (WOOD) : Portlethen, 86½ years, old age, Banchory Devenick 20 May 1867
LEIPER   Jessie : Downies, 28 years, brain disease, Portlethen 25 Sep. 1869
LEIPER   Jo. : Auchlee, funeral Downies 9 Sep. 1843
LEIPER   John : w.f. Findon, age 48 years,whose boat was wrecked on Saturday last, about 5 miles off Portlethen
         at sea, and his brother James, drowned. (crew consisting of six) was buried, 26 Apr.1862, it
         being 48 years since a similar accident from storm happened there. Note! similar entry in Death
         Register, shows brother's name as Alexander.
LEIPER   John : Downies, 83½ years, old age, Portlethen 13 Dec. 1864
LEIPER   Joseph : Findon, 82 years 4 months, influenza, Banchory Devenick 20 Dec. 1865
LEIPER   Lilly (MAIN) : 23 Downies, wife of John Main w.f.; 31 years, 13 Jan. 1857
LEIPER   Margaret : Mains of Findon, 76 years, 14 Apr. 1858
LEIPER   Margaret : Elder daughter, Portlethen, 24½ years, consumption, Portlethen 17 Apr. 1866
LEIPER   Margaret : 19 Portlethen, 1 year, Portlethen 27 Nov. 1867
LEIPER   Robert : lost at sea 8 Apr. 1847

LEIPER   Susan (CRAIG)

LEIPER   Susan : Daughter of J. Leiper, Elder, Portlethen, 19 years, 5 Jun. 1857

-LEIPER   William : w.f. Downies, 21 years, 4 Jun. 1859

LEIPER   William Knox : Elder (daughter?), Portlethen, 23 years, consumption, Portlethen 27 Oct. 1866

LEONARD   John : West Cookston, 86 years, 1 Aug. 1857

LEYS   R. : Aberdeen, buried at Portlethen 1 Apr. 1854

LONGMUIR   Ann : Shields, 86 years, old age, Banchory Devenick 6 Jun. 1867

LONGMUIR   Mary : attended funeral from Hillside 28 Apr. 1842

LOW   Alexander : Hill of Findon, 63 years, 27 Oct. 1856

LOW   William : Hill of Findon, 35 years, 13 Mar. 1858

McCLENAN   William : Hill of Portlethen, 58 years, cancer, Portlethen 31 Jul. 1867

McCROBBIE   Mary : Cairnrobin, 4 years, scarlet fever, Banchory Devenick 29 Apr. 1867

McDONALD   Isabella : Auchlee, 64 years, Portlethen 26 Nov. 1869

McDONALD   Robert : Auchlee, 56 years, bowels disease, Banchory Devenick 28 Oct. 1869

McKIDDIE   Donald : Mains of Findon, 74 years, Free Churchyard, Banchory 2 Jul. 1860

McROBBIE   ---- : Cairnrobin, 1 hour, blue gum, Banchory Devenick 21 Sep. 1869

MAIN   ---- : child, Portlethen, 2½ years, 12 May 1857

MAIN   ---- : old woman, Findon, buried 7 Jul. 1848

MAIN   Al. jun. : Hill of Portlethen, 42 years, killed on L.N.E.R. line by 5 p.m. train Wednesday last, Portlethen 7 Jan. 1865

MAIN   Al. : 7 Downies, 1 month, Portlethen 18 Sep. 1865

MAIN   Alexander : 25 Downies, 22 months, gastric irritation, 23 Apr. 1869

MAIN   Alexander : Hillhead of Portlethen, 74 years, old age, Portlethen 16 Nov. 1865

MAIN   Andrew : Hillhead of Portlethen, 80 years, old age, Portlethen 16 Mar. 1863

MAIN   Ann (WOOD) : 11 Portlethen, 43½ years, inflamation, Portlethen 26 Dec. 1864

MAIN   Eliza : daughter of P. Main, Downies, 15 years, 25 Jan. 1859

MAIN   Eliza : Downies, 1 year 1 month, teething, Portlethen 30 May 1864

MAIN   Elspet : Downies, 82 years, appoplexy, Portlethen 28 Sep. 1865

MAIN   Elspet (WOOD) : Widow of Andrew Wood, 36 Portlethen, 42 years, inflamation, Portlethen 31 May 1863

MAIN   George : 51 Portlethen, infant, Portlethen 26 Aug. 1864

MAIN   George : "Pucy", Downies, 94 years, old age, Portlethen 12 Dec. 1868

MAIN   George : Son of Andrew Main, Downies, 1 month, croup, Portlethen 1 Jul. 1860

MAIN   Jane : 13 Portlethen, 16½ years, consumption, Portlethen 7 Dec. 1861

MAIN   John : w.f. bur. at Portlethen 24 Feb. 1855 age 37 years

MAIN	John : Ill. son, Findon, 1 year 3 months, Portlethen 11 Nov. 1861
MAIN	John : Son of Mary Main, Hillhead, 8 months, small pox, Portlethen 28 Feb. 1861
MAIN	John : Haremoss, 11 months, dropsy, Portlethen 12 Aug. 1868
MAIN	Lilly (LEIPER)
MAIN	Margaret (CRAIG)
MAIN	Margaret : 19 Downies, at funeral, 19 Oct. 1844
MAIN	Margaret : Downies, 88 years, 20 Jan. 1858
MAIN	Margaret : Infant, 30 Downies, Portlethen 16 Mar. 1863
MAIN	Margaret : Hillhead of Portlethen, 40 years, inflamation, Portlethen 25 Oct. 1866
MANN	William : Blacksmith, E.Cookston, killed by lightning between 8 and 9 a.m. near Checkbar on his way to the Doctor at the Cove 26 Jun 1859
MARNIE	John : E.Cookston, 91 years, old age, Portlethen 25 Jun. 1869
MASSON	---- (BARCLAY)
MASSON	Andrew : Hillhead, brewer, Aberdeen, 60 years, appoplexy, Portlethen 19 Sep. 1861
MASSON	Ann : Hick Style, 2 months, Portlethen 9 Jan. 1865
MASSON	D. : Hillhead of Portlethen, 2½ months, consumption, Portlethen 28 Sep. 1866
MASSON	George : Doghillock, Portlethen, 67 years, appoplexy, 9 Jun. 1860
MASSON	Helen : Backhill of Portlethen, 3 months, Portlethen 5 Sep. 1865
MASSON	Isobel : Hillhead of Portlethen, 89 years, old age, Portlethen 29 Mar. 1866
MASSON	John : Langhillock, 38½ years, railway, Portlethen 16 Jan. 1865
MASSON	Margaret : Wellhead of Portlethen, 5 months, fever, Portlethen 30 Mar. 1864
MASSON	Margaret (ROSE) : Rumleygowan, 75 years, 17 Sep. 1857
MASSON	Mary : Lochside, 76 years, old age, Portlethen 31 Jul. 1869
MASSON	William : Backhill of Portlethen, 2 months, Portlethen 12 Aug. 1865
MATHEWSON	Mrs. : Died this morning at 5 o'clock, 79 years, 8 Mar. 1845 - at Mrs. Mathewson's funeral, Maryculter 13 Mar. 1845
	Isabella (LAW)
MENNIE	Christian : daughter of William Mennie, Findon, 4 years, 12 Feb. 1859
MENNIE	James : Hill of Portlethen, 47 years, appoplexy, Banchory Devenick 14 Jan. 1864
MILNE	James : Findon, Banchory Devenick, 14 years, cholera, 14 Jun. 1860
MILNE	Margaret : daughter of the late William Milne, Elder in Balquhain, died in the Parish of Dunnotter, buried in Banchory Devenick Churchyard 29 Dec. 1849
MILNE	Margaret : Moss-side, 17 years, phthisis, Portlethen 31 Oct. 1869
MILNE	Mary (SYMON) : Widow Symon, Portlethen (Midwife, Findon), 71 years, inflamation of lungs, 12 Jun.1860

MILNE   Rebecca : sister to A. Milne, Portlethen, 72 years, died 11 Jan. 1842

MORRISON   Barbara (GORDON)

MORRISON   George Rev. Dr. : Minister of the Parish died this afternoon at 3 o'clock in the 88th year of his age
           and the 62nd year of his Ministry, 56 of which in Banchory Devenick, 13 Jul.1845
           Funeral 18 Jul. 1845

NICOL   Widow : Fiddestown, 89 years 8½ months, 1843

NICOL   Eliz. : Ill., Hillhead of Portlethen, "Old P...? " , 2 years 7 months, 2 Oct. 1859

NICOLL   William : Wairds, 67 years, heart disease, Portlethen 2 Jul. 1869

PARK   James : Hillside, 2 years 8 months, water in the head, Portlethen 9 Jan, 1866

PARK   Jane (STEWART) : E.Cookston, 86 years, old age, Banchory Devenick 22 Aug. 1864

PATTERSON Agnes Dundas Blair : 89 years, old age, Portlethen, 22 Mar. 1869

PATTERSON John : Portlethen, 18 years, accidental, Portlethen 27 Nov. 1869

PATTERSON ----- : Checkbar, Charleston, 7 years, 2 Jul. 1859

PATTERSON Eliz. (RUXTON) : Hillside, 37 years, Portlethen 31 Dec. 1861

PAUL   Is. (ROBBIE) : Widow Robbie, Redmyre, 69 years, appoplexy, Banchory 10 Feb. 1861

PETRIE   Al. : At funeral, Banchory 28 Nov. 1846

PETRIE   Widow (COLLIE)

PETRIE   William : Badentoy, bur. at Maryculter Old Churchyard 17 May 1856

PIRRIE   William : Mains of Findon, 7 months, Portlethen 6 Jan. 1862

RAFFAN   William : At funeral, Loirston, on my way home from Aberdeen 17 Jun. 1843

RAFFAN   James : Died 30 Nov. 1841, attending funeral in Banchory 4 Dec. 1841

REID   Peter : Hillhead of Portlethen, 10 years, Portlethen 14 Mar. 1860

REID   ----- : Daughter of widow Reid, bur. 6 Jun. 1851

REID   Widow : Widow Joseph Reid, N.Mains, late Moss-side, Banchory 4 Apr. 1860

REID   Alex. : Fever still in the house of the late Alex. Reid, Hillside 29 Dec. 1849

REID   Christian : Hill of Findon, 81 years, old age, Banchory Devenick 18 Apr. 1864

REID   Jessie : Dau. of Widow Reid,residing in Findon,died of typhus fever,5 Jul.1845 bur.Findon 8 Jul.1845

REITH   Joseph : farmer, Findon, 80 years, bur. Banchory Devenick 8 Nov. 1854

RIDDEL   Margaret : Doghillock, 81 years, old age, Portlethen 23 Nov. 1861

RITCHIE   Helen : Hill of Portlethen, 2½ years, tubercular disease, Portlethen 28 Oct. 1869

ROBBIE   Jane Low : Servant, Manse, 66 years, 21 Apr. 1859

ROBERTSON May (TAYLOR) : wife of William Taylor, Auqhoties, 37½ years, small pox, Cowie 12 Jan. 1864

           Is. (PATTERSON)

           Ann : Findon, bur. 17 Oct. 1853, age 88 years

ROBERTSON	Jane : E.Cookston, 6 years 2 months, croup, Portlethen 26 Jan. 1861
ROBERTSON	John : alias GILLIE, w.f. Portlethen, bur. 18 Apr. 1856
ROBERTSON	Lilly : Checkbar, 13 years 8 months, fever, Portlethen 6 Nov. 1864
RODNEY	Ann Cruickshank : Downies, 3 months, 4 Nov. 1858
ROSE	Margaret (MASSON)
ROSS	Widow (DAVIDSON)
ROSS	David : son of William Ross, Hillside, 2 years 4 months, Banchory Devenick 8 Oct. 1861
RUST	George : Charleston, 87 years, old age, Durris 25 Jan. 1864
RUXTON	Elizabeth (PATTERSON)
SCORGIE	Agnes : Redmyre, 70 years, old age, Maryculter 1 Aug. 1860
SCORGIE	Caroline (WATT) : wife of George Scorgie, Redmyre, 26 years, 5 Jun. 1859
SCORGIE	Elspet : Haremoss, 2 years 9 months, disease of brain, Portlethen 3 Oct. 1864
SCOTT	William : a man from Kinneff died at Balquhain 19 Apr. 1845, buried at Portlethen 21 Apr. 1845
SHEPHERD	Ann : Cairnrobin, 45 years, cancer, Banchory Devenick 3 Nov. 1863
SHEPHERD	Cathrine (DAVIDSON) : Widow
SHEPHERD	George : Elder, Cairnrobin, 76 years, 15 Mar. 1857
SHEPHERD	Helen : Turniemiddle, 71 years, brain disease, Banchory Devenick 26 Sep. 1869
SHEPHERD	Robert : Backburn, 19 years, killed on railway, 29 Jul. 1857
SHEPHERD	William : Cairnrobin, 69½ years, old age, Maryculter 30 Dec. 1863
SILVER	---- : Schoolhouse, 1½ hours, congenital imperfection, 15 Apr. 1869
SINCLAIR	David : Findlay,Bishopston, 8 months, 12 May 1859
SINCLAIR	John : Portlethen, 67 years, paralysis, Banchory Devenick 29 Feb. 1868
SINCLAIR	William : Mains of Portlethen, 3 years, 26 Aug. 1856
SKINNER	Margaret Ann : At Findon, old woman dead, 31 Jul. 1841, attending funeral 2 Aug. 1841
SMITH	Mrs. : Minister's aunt, Wellington Place,Aberdeen, funeral 30 Sep. 1851
SMITH	Elspet Ann : Redmyre, 1½ months, Banchory 18 Mar. 1865
SMITH	Jane : Cairnrobin, 3 years, fever, Banchory Devenick 30 Dec. 1866
SMITH	John : At funeral, 24 May 1843
SMITH	Mary (KEITH)
SOUT(H)ER	Jane : Hill of Portlethen, 1 year 10 months, Portlethen 16 Feb. 1860
STEWART	---- : Synod's Lands, (infirmary) 25 years, 10 Oct. 1858
STEWART	Widow of Donald Stewart, Bogside, 84 years, 14 Mar. 1858
STEWART	Child : Daughter of John Stewart, and Jemima ...., Backhill of Nigg, bur. 1 May 1867
STEWART	Al. : Hillside, 49½ years, small pox, Portlethen 20 Jan. 1864

STEWART	Ann : at William Middleton's, Findon Mains, 7½ years, 20 Oct. 1859
STEWART	Eliza : Hillside, 21 years, after childbirth, Portlethen 18 Sep. 1861
STEWART	Isabella : Badentoy, 16 years 7 months, typhus fever, Portlethen 21 Oct. 1861
STEWART	Isobel (THOMSON) : wife of R.Stewart, Findon, funeral 21 Jul. 1842
STEWART	Janat (DONALD)
STEWART	Jane (PARK)
STEWART	William : Mains of Findon, 2½ years, consumption, Portlethen 26 Mar. 1862
STRATTON	William : Turnermiddle, 12 years, Banchory Devenick 9 Jan. 1865
STUART	Widow (HORN)
SUTHERLAND	Barbara : Redmyre, died 85 years, 1843
SYMON	Mary (MILNE)
TAYLOR	A. : Aquithery, 84 years, old age, Cowie 26 Aug. 1865
TAYLOR	James : Cairnwell, 5 years, scarlet fever, Portlethen 11 Nov. 1865
TAYLOR	John : Auquorthies, 35 years, mortification, Cowie 10 Nov. 1862
TAYLOR	May (RITCHIE)
TAYLOR	Rachel : Died, 90 years, nota – end of 1848
TAYLOR	Rebecca : Afforthies, 82 years, 16 Sep. 1858
THOMSON	---- : Cassieport, 10 years, N.Banchory 31 Dec. 1867
THOMSOM	Alex. : Bourtrybush, 31 years, consumption, Portlethen 13 Nov. 1865
THOMSON	Isobel (STEWART)
THOW	Isabella : Daughter of John Thow, Hill of Portlethen, 21 years, 3 Jan. 1857
TURNER	Alex. : Fiddestown, 11½ years, typhus, Portlethen 17 Oct.1862
TURNER	George : Langhillock, 1½ years, Portlethen 24 Jan. 1859
TURNER	Mary : Langhillock, 5 years, Portlethen 8 Jan. 1859
TURNER	William Jnr. : Langhillock, 20 years, consumption, Portlethen 21 Jul. 1860
VALENTINE	Elizabeth : East Cookston, infant, Portlethen 16 Dec. 1864
WALKER	---- (BROWN)
WALKER	Andrew : Glen of Redmyre, 77 years, cancer on face, Banchory 24 Apr. 1860
WALKER	Annabella : Daughter of R. Walker, farmer, Mains of Portlethen, died 10.10 p.m., 8 years, 21 Sep. 1851, buried 25 Sep. 1851 in Banchory Churchyard
WALKER	Isobel (BRUCE)
WALKER	James Rev. : Assisant in the Parish of Arbuthnott died this morning, son of James Walker, East Cookston, 16 Dec. 1848
WALKER	James : Son of J. Walker, Redmyre, 3½ months, croup, Banchory Devenick 20 Oct. 1861

WALKER	James : Newport, 78 years, 25 Dec. 1858
WALKER	John : East Cookston, from Fetteresso, 56½ years, 2 Jun. 1859
WATSON	Widow : Hillhead of Portlethen, died , 85 years, 10 Apr. 1848
WATT	Caroline (SCORGIE)
WEBSTER	James : at funeral, Brae of Pitfoddels, 3 Aug. 1843
WELSH	Al. : Fiddestown, 57 years, 4 Jul. 1858
WELSH	James : Fiddestown, 5 months, inflamation, Portlethen 28 Oct. 1865
WILLIAMSON	Catherine : age 35 years, attending funeral in Aberdeen 20 Jan. 1844
WOOD	Child : Findon, 2 years, 15 May 1857
WOOD	Infant : Portlethen Village, 1 year 3 months, Portlethen 8 Jan. 1863
WOOD	Widow (CRAIG)
WOOD	A. : Portlethen - attended A. Wood's funeral at East Cookston 25 Nov. 1841
WOOD	Agnes : Findon, 4 years, 28 Nov. 1859
WOOD	Agnes : Downies, 5 years, consumption, Portlethen 17 Mar. 1868
WOOD	Agnes (CAIE)
WOOD	Al. : 7 Downies, 63½ years, bodily disease, Portlethen 31 Jul. 1866
WOOD	Al. : Downies, 38 years, fever, Portlethen 20 Mar. 1864
WOOD	Andrew : (Knotty Brow), Findon, 87 years, 17 Aug. 1856
WOOD	Andrew : Son of G. Wood, Findon, 8½ Months, teething, Portlethen 14 Apr. 1864
WOOD	Andrew : Portlethen Village, 87 years 8 months, old age, Portlethen 28 Apr. 1864
WOOD	Andrew : Findon, 10 months, dropsy, Portlethen 8 Dec. 1869
WOOD	Ann : 27 Portlethen, 1 year 4 months, croup, Portlethen 16 Feb. 1861
WOOD	Ann : Infant daughter of G. Wood, Findon, 20 days, Portlethen 6 Feb. 1861
WOOD	Ann : Downies, 2 months, head disease, 29 Apr. 1868
WOOD	Ann (CRAIG)
WOOD	Ann (MAIN)
WOOD	Elizabeth : Findon, 3 months, Portlethen 20 Jan. 1863
WOOD	Elspet (MAIN)
WOOD	Elsy : Findon, 5 years 4 months, bronchitis, Portlethen 2 Feb. 1861
WOOD	George : Findon, 18 months, interred at Portlethen 11 Feb. 1842
WOOD	George : North Findon, 82 years, old age, Portlethen 25 Mar. 1865
WOOD	George : 20 Downies, 2½ years, inflamation, Portlethen 14 Jan. 1866
WOOD	George : Findon, 48½ years, consumption, Portlethen 26 Aug. 1868
WOOD	George : Portlethen, weak minded, Portlethen 12 Feb. 1869

WOOD   Is. (LAW)
WOOD   Isabel : Kirkstyle, 92 years, Portlethen 12 May 1860
WOOD   Isobel (LEIPER)
WOOD   James : alias 'King', w.f. Findon, 70 years, died 9 May, buried 12 May 1857
WOOD   James : Downies, Portlethen, teething, 23 Jun. 1860
WOOD   James : Son of James Wood, Findon, 2½ years, 22 May 1857
WOOD   James : Findon, 47 years, consumption, Portlethen 7 Jan. 1866 - see also wife Agnes Caie
WOOD   James : 29 Downies, 4 days, Portlethen 4 Feb. 1867
WOOD   James : 'Thrumsay', w.f. 10 Findon, 53 years, Portlethen 20 May 1860
WOOD   Jane : 'Charlie's Jenny', Findon, 8½ years, 13 Sep. 1859
WOOD   Jane (LEIPER)
WOOD   Jessie : Daughter of Al. Wood, Fittie, w.f. Findon, 13 years, 1 Apr. 1859
WOOD   Jo. : w.f. Portlethen - at funeral 10 May 1844
WOOD   Jo. : w.f. Findon, 27 years, suddenly at Peterhead, 17 Jul. 1857
WOOD   John : w.f. Portlethen, died age 27 years, 20 Jul. 1844
WOOD   John : Son of Moses Wood, w.f. 9 Downies, buried at Portlethen 10 Nov. 1854
WOOD   Joseph : Infant son of James Wood, w.f. Findon, 1 year 4 months, 19 May 1859
WOOD   Margaret : at Portlethen for funeral 17 Oct. 1845
WOOD   Margaret : Findon, 9 years, 10 Jun. 1858
WOOD   Margaret : Findon, 45 years, consumption, Portlethen 30 Oct. 1869
WOOD   Moses : w.f. Downies, 64 years, 20 Dec. 1857
WOOD   Rachel : Daughter of Widow Wood - attending funeral in Portlethen 29 Sep. 1841
WOOD   William : Findon, 11 months, Portlethen 7 Dec. 1866
WRIGHT ---- : Hillside, 23 years, Infirmary 17 Oct. 1858
WYNESS Sarah Ann : Hillside, 66 years, gastritis, Portlethen 25 Jul.1869
YEATS   Margaret : East Cookston, 27 years, inflamation, Banchory Devenick 25 Nov. 1865
YULE   Al. : Funeral at Glashfarquhar 9 Nov. 1851
YUIL   Jane : Haremoss, 5 months, croup, Portlethen 30 May 1865
YUIL   Robert : Haremoss, 52 years, decline, Portlethen 30 May 1865

IT WOULD APPEAR THAT MOST ENTRIES FOLLOW A SET ORDER OF - NAME, ADDRESS, AGE, CAUSE OF DEATH, THEN PLACE AND DATE OF BURIAL

MISCELLANY - HISTORICAL EVENTS

30th July 1840 - This day The Rev. The Presbytery of Aberdeen, being met after Divine Service in the Church of Portlethen by the Rev.John Bower, Minister of Maryculter, proceeded to the Ordination of Mr.William Law, parochial Schoolmaster of Maryculter,who had for upwards of 13 years officiated at Portlethen and who was cordially welcomed by the people as their Pastor

29th November 1840 - Public Thanksgiving offered up, for the Queen's safe delivery of a Princess.

5th May 1841 - Joseph Walker Esq.of Cookston, presented 540 Tokens for the Church, marked Portlethen on one side

10th May 1841 - Presented to Portlethen Chapel - 2 Communion Cups (marked 1 and 2) from George Morrison D.D. also 16 cloths, long, and 1 large cloth for table and 2 napkins.
Also, by Cathrine Smith,Cookston - Two Pewter Plates for Communion bread in Memory of her Parents

14th November 1841 - Public Thanksgiving for the Queen's safe delivery of a Prince (of Wales) b 11 Nov.

8th January 1842 - Fever still in Portlethen, 2 years past since it entered village

4th October 1842 - Present at opening of Bridge of Dee, having been made broader by 11 feet, and having been shut up for nearly 2 years from carts, carriages etc.

18 May 1843 - This day the Non-Intrusion Party in the General Assembly convened at Edinburgh after lodging Protest and Dissent in the hands of the Clerk of Assembly. Left the Assembly of the Church of Scotland, then and there assembled and renounced all further connexion with her, as by law Established, forming themselves into an assembly under the name of the "Free Church of Scotland" Number of Parochial Clergymen who left 92, Quoad Sacra's, Parliamentary and others about 200 on 28th ult. they vacated their Churches

2nd July 1843 - Intimation given,that during the time the New Church was erecting the Congregation would meet in the Church Yard, and that the Foundation Stone would be laid on Tuesday first at 2 o'clock

3rd July 1843 - Contractors commenced this day to take down the Old Chapel

4th July 1843 - Foundation Stone laid by Rev.Dr.Morison (age 85) after prayers by the Minister, and address by Rev.Mr.Paul. In a cavity in the Foundation Stone was deposited a glass bottle (hermetically sealed) containing a newspaper, list of subscribers and members of the Church Session, a good many people present. It has been ascertained that the Old Chapel had been a place of worship for upwards of 170 years, that during the last 40 years it had been regularly supplied with public worship by Licentiates of the Church of Scotland and since July 1840 by an ordained Clergyman. "God's Name be Glorified and all Her Saints Edified" was on Old Church

5th July 1843 - Tremendous storm of thunder and lightning

95

8th November 1843 – Assembled in New Church for first time, a stormy day, a good many present

27th September 1845 – I am appointed Inspector of the Poor of the parish of N.Banchory under the New Poor Law Act

30th November 1846 – (Aberdeen) Railway, operations began beside the Church

17th March 1848 – Four woman buried in the Fish Towns, died this week, after childbirth

8th September 1848 – Queen Victoria and her husband Prince Albert, with three of the Royal Family, passed through Aberdeen, for Balmoral, Deeside. It was computed that 90,000 were present

Nota end of 1848 – Pope fled from Rome and came to Gaeta in France.

4th November 1849 – Thanksgiving for abatement of Cholera in the Kingdom.

Nota end of 1850 – Cardinal Wiseman 'setup' in London this year, much to the displeasure and sorrow of many.

Preface Vol.11 – Charges for Proclamation – 3 Sundays 4/–, 2 Sundays 5/–, 1 Sunday 11/–, at Banchory.

19th October 1851 – Congregation called upon to sign a Memorial to the General Assembly for their countenance, and Support in making the District of Portlethen into a distinct Parish – The Memorial to be signed during the earlier part of the week – signed in a few hours by nearly 500.

Nota end of 1851 – 'Temple' of 'Peace' or Crystal Palace built in London in May and open for 6 months, to which millions came from all parts of the world to see.

19th March 1854 – Prayers offered up this day in reference to War with Russia.

23rd April 1854 – Proclamation by order of Queen Victoria, intimated for a day of General Humiliation and Prayer in Scotland on account of the necessary War with Russia.

26th November 1854 – A collection will be made on behalf of the wives and families of the Soldiers and Sailors, engaged in the present Russian War.

31st December 1854 – Intimated that after tomorrow, the 1st January 1855 an alteration would take place (be in force) relative to the Registration of Births, Marriages and Deaths, throughout Scotland, and that the public were warned accordingly. This alteration is by Act passed in the last session of Parliament, introduced by Lord Elcho

4th May 1856 – National Thanksgiving offered up, for Peace with Russia

13th July 1856 – Intimation – This Church with the District attached has been Erected by the Court of Teinds into a Church and Parish 'quoad sacra', called the Parish of Portlethen, comprehending the whole of the Parish of Banchory on the South side of the River Dee, with the exception of the Lands of Banchory and Ardo – that the present Minister has been admitted a Member of the Presbytery of Aberdeen and that the Presbytery have directed the Minister and the Elders, to form themselves into a Kirk Session and to hold their first meeting on Thursday 17th current for preliminary business. The Presbytery further appointed the Ministers of Banchory and Nigg to sit with the Session at their first and at any subsequent Meeting that may be necessary until an addition is made to present numbers of Elders

17th July 1856 – Session met in terms of Presbytery's appointment – Present, The Rev.Wm.Paul D.D. Banchory, The Rev.Mr.Fairweather, Nigg. – Assessors, The Rev. Wm.Law, Minister of Portlethen, John Leiper and James Keith, Elders residing in the Parish. – Mr.A.Silver, Schoolmaster was appointed Clerk pro.temp. The Session, having been constituted by The Rev. Law, Moderator, a list of certain persons was laid on the table to be proposed as Elders as soon as convenient. An excerpt from the will of the late Robert Shand Esq. of Hillside, bequeathing the current interest of £200, to those in the lands of Hillside and villages of Findon and Portlethen not on the Poors' Roll

James Wood w.f. 21 Downies, and his wife Jane Wood were admitted to Church Disipline for antenuptial fornication, were admonished and absolved. Session closed with Prayers.

31st August 1856 – The Managers of the Nether Banchory Parish Savings Bank having resolved to call in all checks issued by them and exchange them for Pass Books.

18th January 1857 – Intimation – The Precentor, Wm.Menzies would practice singing one hour before Divine Service gratis, every Lord's Day, during his engagement.

16th August 1857 – Act as to Proclamation for Marriage in Quoad Sacra as well as Civilia, read.

4th July 1858 – Petition to the House of Lords in reference to the Colledge Bill now in the House of Commons would be handed round the Parish for signature, in disapproval of said Bill, at the request of the Synod and Town Council of Aberdeen

7th July 1858 – Petition (ut supra) signed by upwards of 200 and sent to Lord Aberdeen

1st December 1858 – The R.N.Volunteers left for 28 days training/exercises for the Navy,for Leith, 44 from 3 villages

24th April 1859 – That by Royal Recommendation, Public Prayers would be offered up next Sunday for the constant and signal successes obtained by the Troops of Her Majesty in India during the late Sanguinary Mutiny and Rebellion in that Country.

25th December 1859 – Intimated – From and after 1st Jan. 1860 the Registration of Marriages, Births and Deaths would now be in the parish of Portlethen and that Mr.D.Silver, presently schoolmaster has been appointed Registrar for Portlethen. Decree of Sherriff of Kincrdineshire

27th May 1860 – Resignation of Precentor, Wm.Menzies

10th August 1860 – Al.Thomson, carpenter, Hillside, out of 12 candidates, unanimously elected Precentor

20th December 1860 – Tricentenary of the Reformation from Popery in Scotland commemorated by all Protestants in Scotland, England and Ireland (1560) "Gloria Dei"– John Knox, Scotch Reformer – 'A man who never feared the face of man'

1st April 1861 – Census of Parish of Portlethen – Males 821– Females 857– Total 1688. Deceased since last census 112. No.of houses 342 – Inhabited houses 333 – Uninhabited 12, buildings 2. Windowed rooms 765 Children between 5–15 at school 280 (stormy winter)

Portlethen Village – Males 126 – Females 165 – Total 291
Findon Village – " 120 " 133 " 253
Downies Village – " 89 " 91 " 180   TOTAL IN F.VILLAGES 724 (increase 20)

14th December 1861 – Prince Albert, The Prince Consort, died at Windsor at 10 o'clock and 50 mins., age 42 years, married 21 years.   War threatened by America.

7th December 1862 – Wm.Duthie, Fintray, entered as Precentor at £10.0.0

25th March 1866 – Read address by Gen.Assembly on the distress of the Cotton Manufacturing districts of Lancashire Intimated – Thursday 29th as a day of Solemn Humiliation to be observed throughout the Church, on account of the grievous plague among cattle, which no precautions or efforts of human skill have been able greatly to mitigate.The calamity among our bovine race is said to be Rinderpest It should be called the 'Finger of God'

16th February 1868 – Monday 3rd March fixed for the election of a new Trustee in the room of the late Alex. Carr

29th March 1868 – Intimated – First of the candidates for the Assistantship to preach this day week.

28th June 1868 – By Order of Privy Council,prayers to be put up for preservation of the life of His Royal Highness The Duke of Edinburgh by assassin abroad – and for success and safety of Her Majesty's Forces in Abyssinia for the rescue of captives imprisoned in that country by King Theodore

12 July 1868 – The Presbytery of Aberdeen, received a Presentation from the Trustees of Portlethen Church in favour of the Rev.Wm.Bruce, to be Assistant and Successor to the Rev.Wm.Law

28th September 1868 – The Presbytery of Aberdeen met for the Ordination of Rev.Wm.Bruce, as Asst. and Successor to the Rev. William Law, who for upwards of 42 years has officiated at Portlethen, 28 years as an Ordained Minister of the Parish and 15 years before as a Preacher

9th December 1868 – Mr. Bruce came to reside in the Parish

....

MISCELLANY - BOATS LOST

Entries concerning Loss of Boats and Lives at Sea

3rd February 1843 –
1st January 1844 – Tremendous hurricane of wind-a vessel wrecked off Partanha',4 lives lost-roof of Chapel damaged This day all the fishing boats were overtaken by a sudden and unexpected gale about 9 O'clock a.m., attended during the day by snow, all of which were accounted for by 10 o'clock p.m., except 5 belonging to Findon, of which no account could be obtained. It was hoped that they had been picked up by one of Her Majesty's Cutters, passing to the Southward that day – Storm off land, attended by high wind and severe frost – First of the boats, one belonging to Portlethen only reached home about 4 p.m., having first landed near Bervie

2nd January 1844 – Accounts have just been received (this day) 5 p.m. that the 5 boat crews amissing yesterday and belonging to Findon were landed at Arbroath, having been picked up about 14 miles from land by the Thetis of Dundee, Captain Aitken, Commander, who treated them with great kindness – boat lines etc. all lost.

3rd January 1844 – Remaining fishermen came home this day – 9 boats belonging to Footdee and Torry (navigated by 53 men) were also lost. The men were saved by H.M.R.C. Greyhound, Captain Dooley, who landed them next day at Leith.

7th January 1844 – Thanksgiving offered up this day to Almighty God for his Providential Deliverance of the fishermen on Monday last – many present.

16th January 1844 – Wrote all the Heritors of the Parish, for Findon Fishers' loss
8th April 1847 – Thursday, a Portlethen fishing boat was lost 5 miles off Portlethen in a heavy gale of wind, which continued for about 40 hours – it contained 5 men – 3 brothers of the name of Leiper, (George, Robert, Alexander) and 2 of the name of Craig (Joseph and John) leaving 5 widows and 28 children all almost destitute, but one.

18th August 1848 – This morning 2 Portlethen fishermen, Jo. and Alexander Craig, brothers, were drowned off the Cove, being at the herring fishing at Stonehaven, during a tremendous hurricane – many boats and tackle lost – 1 belonging to Downies, all hands saved – many lost at Peterhead – lost on coast, 100 men and 160 boats.

20th November 1852 – Dutch vessel sunk in (Broad——) of Portlethen yesterday – all saved.
1st February 1857 – Collection intimated to be made this day week in aid of the Fishermen and Shipwrecked Mariners Fund recommended by the Sheriff C.G. Robertson of Kincardineshire

26th April 1862 – John Leiper w.f. Findon, whose boat was wrecked on Saturday last, about 5 miles off Portlethen at sea, and his brother James, drowned (crew consisting of 6) was buried.

MISCELLANY - POOR MONEY

28th January 1841 - Distributed 25/-
Mary LEIGHTON, Clashfarquhar - John KAIRD, Portlethen - Jane BLAIR, Hill of Findon
George MITCHELL, near Seatown of Findon - Widow CRAIG or NICOL, near Mains of Findon - each 5/-

10th July 1842 - There was collected, for John ROBERTSON's family (a fisherman in Portlethen whose wife died
lately) in destitute circumstances £3.0.7½

28th October 1845 - New Poor Law Act for Scotland came into operation

1st April 1848 - Money sent on 7th ult. by Session, distributed as follows -

John MILNE, Hill of Portlethen	10/-	Widow FARQUHAR, Hill of Portletlen	5/-
William MOIR, there	5/-	Al. KNOWLES, Clochandighter	10/-
John SEANDILINGS, there	5/-	John WALKER, Hillside	7/6
John MAIN w.f. Portlethen	5/-	Jane BURNET, there	10/-
Geo. LEIPER, Findon	5/-	Isobel MASSON,Hillhead of Portlethen	9/-
Jas. LEIPER, w.f. there	5/-	Wm. MAIN, w.f. Portlethen	7/6
Wm. LEIPER w.f. there	5/-	Margt. DONALD, Findon	10/7½
Ann LONGMUIR, Sheils	4/-	John McCOAL, Portlethen	5/-
Jane ----, there	4/-	Geo. MAIN, w.f. Downies	10/-
James ----, Roadside of Findon	10/-	Robert MAIN, w.f. there	7/6
Wm. BROWN, there	7/6	John LEIPER, w.f. 17 there	10/-

TOTAL £7.17.7½

MISCELLANY - ELDERS

Appointment of Elders of Portlethen Church

20th February 1842 - Edict served by order of Kirk Session for the election of John Baird, farmer, Afforthies - James Stewart, farmer, Clashfarquhar - James Shepherd, farmer, Barclayhill - Alexander Hatt, farmer at Haughton of Bieldside - to be Elders, on the 6th March ensuing, if no objections are stated against them by any of the Parishioners, by that time to the Moderator of the Session, of which intimation was made.

14th April 1850 - This day, Edict served for Election of D. Hutcheon, farmer, Bourtreybush and John Napier, shoemaker, Portlethen, to be Elders in the Parish - Election on 27th.

17th July 1856 - John Leiper and James Keith, Elders, residing in the Parish at first Session Meeting of Portlethen Parish Quoad Sacra. A list of certain persons were laid on the table to be proposed as Elders as soon as possible.

21st September 1856 - It having been found necessary and agreed upon in the Kirk Session of the Parish of Portlethen that there should be an addition of Elders to their numbers, fixed on John Carr, E. Cookston - George Anderson, Bourtreybush - William Rust, Bankhead - George Hunter, Hill of Findon - James Leiper, w.f. Findon - John Craig w.f. Portlethen.

List of Persons at whose premises Diets of Catechising were held

BAIRD John - Elder - Aquorthies
CARR Alexander - Mains of Findon
CRAIG James - Elder - Portlethen
CRAIG John - Elder - Portlethen
EWEN Mr. - Schoolhouse
HOWIE R. - Lands of Glashfarquhar
KEITH James - Elder - Cassieport
KNOWLES George - Seatown of Findon
LEIPER James - Elder - Findon
LEIPER John - Elder - Findon
MAIN James - 20 Downies

MAIN John - 11 Portlethen
NICOL Mr. - Lands of Badentoy
ROBBIE Js. - Checkbar
RUST William - Bankhead
SHEPHERD George - Elder - Cairnrobin
SHEPHERD James - Elder - Barclayhill
STEWART James - Elder - Clashfarquhar
TAYLOR Al. - Crofts of Balquhain
WOOD John - Village of Portlethen
WOOD John - Seatown of Portlethen